Excellent Effect

The Edna Mahan Story

By Mary Q. Hawkes

Perry M. Johnson, President
James A. Gondles, Jr., Executive Director
Karen L. Kushner, Director of Communications and Publications
Marianna Nunan, Managing Editor
Jody K. Spertzel, Associate Editor
Kevin Ogburn, Production Editor
Elizabeth Watts, Contributing Editor
Alonzo L. Winfield III, Cover Designer

ISBN 1-56991-007-3

Printed in the United States of America by Graphic Communications, Inc., Upper Marlboro, Md.

This congress is of the opinion that, both in the official administration of such a [prison] system, and in the voluntary co-operation of citizens, therein, the agency of women may be employed with excellent effect.

—*from the National Prison Congress Declaration of Principles, 1870*

*To Austin MacCormick, Mary Stevens Baird,
Edna Mahan, and Anita Stillman Quarles*

Contents

Foreword

This book is unique in several respects. First, it is the only biography of one of the most remarkable corrections superintendents in U.S. history. Edna Mahan served as superintendent of New Jersey's Reformatory for Women—Clinton Farms—for a record-breaking forty years. During this tenure she led the nation in experimenting with innovative (indeed radical) approaches to rehabilitation. Arriving in 1928, when Clinton Farms was only fifteen years old, Mahan never abandoned the founders' rehabilitative vision, even as the spirit of reform faded elsewhere.

In addition, this book tells the story of a unique institution and its inmates. Clinton Farms, as Mahan ran it, formed a significant chapter in the history of U.S. corrections. It also formed an important chapter in the history of women—both the officials who ran it and the inmates, on whose records Hawkes draws extensively.

Hawkes's relationship with her subject, too, is unique in that she brings to it the combined perspectives of practitioner, scholar, and participant observer. Hawkes knew Mahan as an employer, role model, and family friend. Hawkes's mother served on the reformatory's board for nearly three decades, and Hawkes herself began working at the institution in 1943, when she was just out of high school. Later she wrote her doctoral dissertation on Clinton Farms and its extraordinary superintendent. Although she never loses her critical distance, Hawkes has thus written a study that is to some extent a biography of herself and other women active in the American Correctional Association. Their story, too, is told here for the first time.

Implicit in what I've already said is yet another sense in which this book is unique: it is a contribution to the feminist literature on mentoring. For this aspect of her study, Hawkes draws on (among other sources) a recently discovered series of letters by Miriam Van Waters, superintendent of the Massachusetts women's reformatory, to whom Mahan turned for advice on everything from prison management to matrimony. Much as Hawkes's mother mentored Mahan, Van Waters and Mahan helped one another, and Mahan in turn mentored Hawkes. One of the ways in which women's reformatories attempted to rehabilitate, moreover, was through providing inmates with helpful role models. In writing this study, Hawkes passes this accumulating tradition of support onto future generations of students and corrections professionals.

I am personally grateful to Mary Hawkes for writing this book because it records the work of one of my own mentors, Eleanor Little, who died not long ago at the age of 100, and her life partner, May Caughey. Caughey was Clinton Farms' first superintendent, Little its first psychologist. Both set the stage for Mahan's work, providing her with a context and model for trying to help less fortunate women. Mary Hawkes herself perpetuates the tradition through her extensive work on behalf of prison reform.

Reading this biography, historians, corrections leaders, and students in criminal justice and women's studies courses will discover that many of today's apparent innovations, including gender-specific programs for women in conflict with the law, were in fact pioneered decades ago at Clinton Farms by Edna Mahan.

Nicole Hahn Rafter
Northeastern University

Preface

Edna Mahan's untimely death in 1968 was a shock to all and a terrible loss to the New Jersey Reformatory for Women (known as Clinton Farms for its location near the town of Clinton) and the wider correctional community. She had lived and been superintendent at Clinton Farms for forty years, and she had been active in the American Prison/Correctional Association throughout that time.

Her story—her commitment to, understanding of, and work with female offenders—as well as her efforts to advance women who work in corrections had to be told. In 1984 as I looked toward retirement from my academic career in the late 1980s I made a commitment to write her biography, for I had known her and Clinton Farms since I was five years old. In 1930 my mother, Anita Stillman Quarles, was appointed to the Board of Managers of the Reformatory for Women and remained on the board for twenty-eight years.

Edna Mahan became a friend to me very early in my life. When my mother had business with her at Clinton she often took me along. As a teenager I admired her and looked up to her as a role model. In the summer of 1943, before I went off to my freshman year at college, I worked at Clinton Farms as a "seasonal assistant" with four other college students (including Janet Ellis, daughter of Commissioner of Institutions and Agencies William J. Ellis).

In the summer of 1956 I returned to Clinton Farms to work again, and I took with me four of my students from Berea College, Kentucky, where I was teaching. During this summer Miss Mahan (which is how I always addressed her) suggested I consider coming to work full time as a classification officer, the position I was filling for the summer. She told me she needed well-qualified young women in administrative positions looking to the time senior staff retired. She talked with me of the challenges that lay ahead in working with the increasingly young and disturbed population coming to Clinton Farms.

In the next months I made the decision to take up the challenge. To continue my career in academia necessitated pursuing a doctorate, something I was not ready to do. A career in corrections was certainly a feasible one for me. Working with Edna Mahan was a strong attraction. I knew Clinton Farms well. I knew many inmates, and I knew many staff. In the summer of 1956 I worked closely with Lois Morris, supervisor of cottage life, and began what has become a long and endearing friendship with her.

As classification officer I was part of the administrative staff and a member of the classification committee. I had an office down the hall from Miss Mahan and interacted with her every day. As a member of the Clinton Farms community—I shared a house on the grounds with Lois Morris and Assistant Superintendent Josephine Hull—I enjoyed the camaraderie Miss Mahan instilled there whether it was the Fourth of July picnic with fireworks or patrolling the back roads of Hunterdon County looking for runaways.

After three years, however, I did not see a career for myself at Clinton Farms or in corrections itself. I was ready to pursue a doctorate and return to an academic career where I would be able to teach criminology and hopefully influence some students into the field. When it came time to pick a dissertation topic, my adviser and I, with Miss Mahan's encouragement, settled on an organizational analysis of Clinton Farms through its first fifty years, which it was approaching in 1963.

The first three months of research was largely spent in the Clinton Farms attic going through the orderly files that were carefully stored there. Edna Mahan gave me carte blanche to remove papers I needed and instructed staff to cooperate by providing any information I needed from current files.

I interviewed May Caughey, the first superintendent of Clinton Farms; Eleanor Little, the first psychologist; and other early staff, one of whom still worked at Clinton Farms and several who lived in the vicinity. I interviewed current staff and, of course, Miss Mahan several times. I talked informally with my mother at home.

My biggest support and help on the dissertation from its inception was my friend Lois Morris, who in 1960 had become Miss Mahan's assistant superintendent. She lived in the staff house assigned to the position and in 1962–63 invited me to live with her while I pursued my research.

The dissertation was completed in 1966 and serves as a well-documented case study of the development of the New Jersey Reformatory for Women during its first fifty years. In 1966 Miss Mahan had been superintendent of Clinton Farms for thirty-eight years. The administratively skillful, innovative, creative, and unassuming role she played throughout these years—keeping faith with the founders and carrying their ideals further than they could have hoped—runs through the study. The dissertation was never published.

After Miss Mahan's death, the task of clearing out her professional files fell to Lois Morris. Mary Stevens Baird, a long-time member of the Clinton Farms Board of Managers and subsequently a member of the New Jersey State Board of Control of Institutions and Agencies and personal friend of Edna Mahan's, took the papers. She and other board members hoped to find someone to publish them.

I retrieved the papers from Mary Baird in 1984 with her blessing to write the biography. I organized the papers before my retirement in 1988. In that year I visited

Mahan's places of birth, childhood, university, and work in California hoping to gain more information and insights on her early years.

In writing her biography I have relied heavily on her own papers. These include correspondence (mostly professional), reports, handwritten notes for speeches, notes from inmates and her Progress Notes about inmates, her few publications, minutes of staff orientation meetings, and her diaries.

Minutes of the monthly Board of Managers meetings provided a regular account of what happened in the institution and Miss Mahan's and the board's handling of these affairs. Edna Mahan's interactions with all levels—the commissioners, board, staff, volunteers, and inmates—are recorded in these minutes.

Questionnaires and interviews with many staff at all levels helped me gain insight into their perceptions of her. I have spoken or corresponded with several former inmates, all of whom are referred to by pseudonym. Some staff members' names have also been changed.

I have tried to interpret all of these through my own personal and professional years of knowing and working with Edna Mahan to show her accomplishments, her sensitivities to and unfailing trust in "her girls," her courage and sense of justice, her love of freedom and of life, and her insecurities.

Women's roles in prison work have always reflected ideas of the broader society. Edna Mahan's life and career spanned a period from the end of the women's suffrage movement in the twenties to the resurgence of the women's movement in the sixties. Significant changes in the treatment of female offenders and the roles women played in corrections occurred over this period. Her career and the history of Clinton Farms illustrate these changes.

Acknowledgments

My scholarly excursions into Clinton Farms began in 1962 with doctoral research. I am indebted to the American Association of University Women for awarding me the Charlotte Dickson Fisher Fellowship, 1962–63, and Geraldine L. Thompson, one of the founders of Clinton Farms and thereafter for the rest of her life its guardian angel, for financial support of this research. Albert Morris, my adviser at Boston University, guided the study with patience, understanding, and many ideas.

Irwin T. Sanders began encouraging my sociological eye in 1950 at the University of Kentucky. In 1960 he became chair of the Department of Sociology at Boston University and encouraged me to apply there for my doctoral studies. He and his wife, Margaret, a historian and lifelong feminist, have a keen interest in my Edna Mahan biography. I have spent many pleasant afternoons at their Wellesley home talking with Margaret about what it was like for a young woman growing up in America in the era of World War I and the suffrage movement.

The "early bird breakfast group" at the University Club of Boston each morning shared my moods of despair and elation at the progress on the manuscript. They offered much support and interest. John Arbuckle, Margie Lipman, and Jack Lyle many times gave me sound advice and technical support. I thank them all for their encouragement.

I am grateful to Rhode Island College for two faculty research awards and a sabbatical leave. In the fall of 1986 I sorted through and organized all the Edna Mahan papers. Sociology Department secretary Deborah Cabral and I worked many evenings to accomplish this, and Debby then put the contents of each folder on a computer-readable file. I am indebted to Debby for her able assistance. Debra Stanley, one of my students, patiently helped me learn WordPerfect as I struggled with the start of the manuscript.

In the spring of 1988 I received a sabbatical leave from Rhode Island College and a travel grant to research Edna Mahan's early life in California. David Greene, dean of the Faculty of Arts and Sciences, and Willard Enteman, provost, provided encouragement and support in the early phases of the research.

Doris T. White, a Mount Holyoke College classmate now living in Long Beach, California, drove me to Corcoran, California, where Edna Mahan grew up and helped me research her life there. We had a good time doing this, and I am grateful to her.

Martha Wheeler, president of the Women's Correctional Association (WCA) in 1960 and of the American Correctional Association (ACA) in 1973, and Janet York, formerly superintendent of the Reformatory for Women, Niantic, Connecticut, met with me to clarify issues concerning WCA and Edna Mahan's role in revitalizing it. They also gave me details of their work with her in ACA and other correctional arenas.

Many friends at Clinton Farms have contributed to *The Edna Mahan Story.* Mary Stevens Baird not only turned over the Edna Mahan papers to me, she felt I was the right person to write the biography. I am saddened she died in 1989 and will not see the end product.

Sara Holmes Boutelle, former board member, friend of Edna Mahan and biographer of the architect Julia Morgan, helped me get started on the biography with practical advice, contacts at the University of California-Berkeley, and enthusiasm for the project. Lloyd Wescott, board member, later president of the New Jersey Board of Institutions and Agencies, and neighbor and friend of Edna Mahan's, filled in some important gaps in information and lent his strong support for my undertaking her biography. Elizabeth Boise Schley, board member since 1937 and president for many years, provided many helpful insights.

Robert Walton, superintendent in 1985 and 1986 when I returned to Clinton Farms to find material in the Administration Building attic, allowed me to look at what I needed and to take the early board minutes.

Lucia Ballantine DeGrazia became a Friendly Visitor at Clinton Farms in the late 1940s and later was appointed to the board of the State Home for Boys at Jamesburg. She and Edna Mahan served on the board of the Osborne Association, and a personal friendship developed between them. Miss Mahan shared information and insights about her personal life with Lucia. These have been invaluable to me as I have tried to interpret the tensions in Edna Mahan's life. Lucia's support of my efforts to write about Edna Mahan have added a great deal to her biography.

I was fortunate to reconnect with Janet Ellis DeGrouchy while I was writing this biography. Commissioner Ellis's family spent a lot of time with Miss Mahan and Reading Gebhardt both at the institution and vacationing at Mohonk in New Paltz, New York. I am grateful to Janet for sharing her remembrances of Miss Mahan and the Gebhardts.

I have talked formally and informally with many present and former staff, including Lee Belmont Moore, Marilyn Davenport Zwarych, Dr. Julia Duane, Lillian Kornitzky, and Ethel Sherman. I am indebted to them.

Institutional Parole Officer Beatrice Black became a good friend of Edna Mahan's in her later years. Bee, with her sister Ethel, took care of Edna Mahan in her last weeks at the Morristown Memorial Hospital. Bee was supportive of the biography and added much to it. She died in the summer of 1993 before she had a chance to read the manuscript.

I owe much gratitude to Alice T., former Clinton Farms resident, who read, criticized, corrected, and added to *The Edna Mahan Story*. It is a more creditable document for her help.

Charles Houston, former superintendent of the New Jersey State Home for Boys, related his experiences of working with Edna Mahan in the Division of Correction and Parole. He provided insights in her relationships with her colleagues in the division and the leadership she gave to the other wardens and superintendents.

Irene Springer, neighbor and friend of Lois Morris, read the final draft of the manuscript. I appreciate her reactions to it.

In 1991 I visited the New Jersey State Archives in Trenton in hopes of finding some Clinton Farms material there. There were thirty-five file boxes of materials that had recently come to the archives. Chief of Archives Karl J. Niederer allowed me access to them and Joseph R. Klett, archivist, as well as other staff were cheerful and very helpful in bringing out the boxes and copying appropriate papers. Lois Morris helped me go through them and pull out pertinent papers for copying. I am grateful to all of them, for there was a great deal of valuable material.

Estelle Freedman, professor of history at Stanford University, is writing a biography of Miriam Van Waters, Edna Mahan's early mentor. Dr. Van Waters' papers are at the Schlesinger Library, Radcliffe College, Cambridge, Massachusetts. As Estelle went through Miriam Van Waters' papers she made notes of references to Edna Mahan and gave them to me. These have added a great deal to my biography of Edna Mahan. Estelle and I have enjoyed talking together about these two great women who were so important to each other at one period of their lives yet so different from each other.

As I was close to finishing this biography, Margaret Van Wagenen, former staff member at the Massachusetts Reformatory for Women, who worked with Miriam Van Waters, discovered boxes of Dr. Van Waters' correspondence in the attic of the small house she (Van Wagenen) had shared with Ann Gladding, a former staff member and close friend of Van Waters. Estelle Freedman came from California, put them all in order, pulled out everything having to do with Edna Mahan, and called me. Van Wagenen turned them over to me so I could go through them immediately. They were primarily from the twenties and thirties and provided wonderful insights that were missing from my text.

Three friends who are active practitoners and scholars in the corrections field, Jane Miller Ashton, Tamara Holden, and Joann Morton, have talked with me informally throughout my writing and helped me clarify many current issues.

Roger Clark, professor of sociology, Rhode Island College, book critic, scholar, colleague, and friend, has reviewed each draft with care, concern, questions, suggestions, and encouragement. Nicole Hahn Rafter, professor at the College of Criminal Justice, Northeastern University, and recognized scholar in criminology, the history of women's prisons, and women's studies, has lent her expertise and understanding of the subject to the completion of the biography. Over the years our friendship and esteem have grown through much debate and talk about all aspects of the treatment of female offenders and the early female reformers. She has critically read drafts and offered detailed suggestions for getting the manuscript launched. I am fortunate to have Roger and Nicky as my friends. They are as anxious as I am to see Edna Mahan in print and have given tremendous support and love to me as I have grappled with putting her on paper.

Anthony Travisono, former ACA executive director, Elizabeth Watts, former ACA publications editor, and other staff recognized the merit in my proposal to write Edna Mahan's biography and encouraged me to pursue it. Liz Watts has been patient and perceptive in her questions and help from the beginning of the writing. Her appreciation and understanding of Edna Mahan's philosophy of treatment of female offenders and her editorial skills have transformed Edna Mahan's story into a readable one.

Liz Watts left ACA soon after the completed manuscript was submitted. It has meant a great deal to me that ACA's current executive director, James Gondles, Jr., made arrangements for her to continue the editing.

The biography as I have presented it reflects Lois Morris's understanding of Miss Mahan from twenty-two years of working with her and a friendship that extended to all of Lois's family who visited her regularly over the years. Lois has been my greatest help and support in all ways. I would not have undertaken to write the biography without her.

This book is dedicated to Austin MacCormick and his cheering section, Mary Stevens Baird, Edna Mahan, and Anita S. Quarles. Austin told me when I served on the board of the Osborne Association in the 1970s whenever he gave a talk or led a session at the meetings of the American Prison Association, those three were always in the front row cheering him on. I know all four are cheering me on.

Chapter I

Edna Mahan in Context: Women in U.S. Corrections 1830-1970

Edna Mahan's role in penology, if it is to be understood, must be put in the context of the history of women's roles in prison work beginning in the early nineteenth century. Women's roles in prison work are a reflection of ideals in broader society.

The first two decades of the nineteenth century saw only a few women involved with prisons in the roles of the kept, the keepers, or the reformers. The family was the basic social institution in society. Women and girls were closely bound to the family and were expected to remain so throughout their lives.

Changes in society's structure began after the turn of the century, as Freedman (1984) explains:

> In the beginning of the nineteenth century, Americans engaged in the restructuring of their economic, political, and social institutions. Commerce and later industry gradually replaced agriculture as the base of the economy. National political parties superseded local deference politics. Public educational institutions supplemented familial and religious training. At the same time, new legal and penal systems, partly adapted from European models, reorganized criminal justice and punishment.

The development of large state penitentiaries for the punishment and reformation of criminals was part of this reorganization. Although a majority of inmates held in penitentiaries were men, women were also sent to them.

Very few women were convicted and sent to these penitentiaries in the early decades because they were bound to family control more than men and committed few serious crimes, such as murder, manslaughter, or burglary. The crimes they did commit were petty crimes and those against moral and sexual codes, which called for sentences in local or county jails and workhouses. It was felt that women who committed these offenses were depraved and fallen and could not be redeemed.

Be they jails, workhouses, or penitentiaries, the conditions for women were usually the same: a separate room where they lived congregately with little or no supervision, not even a matron in charge, and nothing to do. They fought among themselves. They were sexually abused by their male keepers and by male inmates. They were brutally punished. Because there were so few of them, they were considered nuisances and therefore neglected by responsible authorities.

By mid-century changes occurred in the numbers of women prosecuted and incarcerated :

> Whatever protection from temptation or prosecution women enjoyed soon proved to be temporary, for their criminal statistics began to reveal a startling trend. New York and Massachusetts records show that after 1840 women joined the ranks of the criminal class in America, though in smaller numbers and for different crimes than men. (Freedman 1984)

New York's female inmates in the first decades of the century were housed in local jails like Bellevue Penitentiary in New York City or, after 1825, regional prisons like Auburn State Prison, which served the western part of the state. Increasing numbers of female inmates and scandalous conditions in the women's section of Auburn—a third-floor attic above the penitentiary's kitchen—finally forced New York to construct regular quarters for its female felons. This was the Mount Pleasant Female Prison, to which Auburn and Bellevue inmates were transferred in 1839. The prison was located close to Sing Sing in Ossining, New York, and the chief matron worked under the authority of a male warden. Thus, Mount Pleasant became the first prison for women in the United States, although it was still under the management of Sing Sing, which housed male inmates (Rafter 1990). With the increase in the numbers of women in prisons and jails by the middle of the nineteenth century, male officials were forced to hire matrons to supervise them.

> Quite early,...far-sighted penologists began to formulate a theory about matrons that later played an important ideological role in women's prison reform. According to this theory, matrons were necessary because female prisoners by nature needed special treatment that only other women could provide.... [F]emale supervisors were not only necessary but also possibly reformative agents. Carefully selected matrons, went the new argument, could provide role models and thus effect positive changes in their charges. (Rafter 1990)

Rafter goes on to explain that even though the idea of the matron as a constructive role model was stated at mid-century, it was seldom put into practice before 1870.

There was usually only one matron to supervise all the women. She was responsible for them twenty-four hours a day, and often she lived in the prison with them:

> [T]hey appear often to have been older women, widowed, forced by economic hardship into such unpleasant work. In other instances, they were wives of wardens. In any case, as working-class women they were unlikely to provide the middle-class role models that progressive penologists recommended. Moreover, even if some early matrons had had energy for reform, they had no authority with which to realize such an ambition. Hired by the warden, they could also be fired by him if they strayed too far from prison tradition. (Rafter 1990)

Women as Prison Reformers

Along with change in societal institutions in the first decades of the nineteenth century came change among American women. Scott (1984) writes:

> New personality types and new forms of behavior were appearing among American women.... By the mid-1830s two significant kinds of change were going on: able women, shut out by social convention from leadership, and often even from participation, in major social structures, were beginning to build organizations and institutions that they themselves could control; women engaged in these organizational and institutional inventions were also establishing bonds with others similarly engaged, creating networks for communication and mutual support. These developments, originally the work of a handful of mavericks, in time contributed to the great nineteenth-century movement for the "elevation of woman" and changed important aspects of American society.

One of "the great nineteenth-century movement[s] for the 'elevation of woman' " was the women's reformatory movement. This had its germination in lay visitors—groups of women who came into prisons in the early part of the nineteenth century "to comfort and educate female inmates" (Rafter 1990). Elizabeth Fry, a Quaker, began this work in England around 1815. In Philadelphia, Quaker women who belonged to the Association of Women Friends visited at the Eastern State Penitentiary. Similar women's groups arose in other parts of the country, particularly the Northeast.

Led by Quakers, charity workers, and social feminists, women's prison reform grew into an independent movement by the late nineteenth century. From their experience visiting women in jails, operating homes for discharged female inmates, and participating in postwar charities and social feminist movements, female reformers developed a unique perspective on the fallen woman. They challenged the view of her total depravity and substituted an indictment of society and particularly of men for causing her fall:

> Underlying both women's entry into prison reform and their reinterpretation of the fallen woman was a firm belief that women constituted a separate sexual class.... [W]omen claimed that if given a chance to bring their feminine influence to bear, the fallen could be redeemed and made into true women. (Freedman 1984)

Female reformers recognized that "fallen women" could not be redeemed in institutions designed for men and called for separate prisons for women.

Prison Reform Groups

Women were not alone in calling for prison reform. Men had been engaged in prison reform in America since 1682 when William Penn founded Pennsylvania as a Quaker colony. The first prison reform group, the Philadelphia Society for Alleviating the Miseries of Public Prisons, was formed in 1787.

In the nineteenth century, organizations dedicated to prison reform, such as the Boston Discipline Society, founded in 1826, and the New York Prison Association (NYPA), founded in 1844, sprang up in major cities. NYPA repudiated "the punishment methods of most prisons...[and] expressed the desire to 'aid the sincerely penitent in their attempts at reformation' " (Sullivan 1990).

Enoch C. Wines became secretary of NYPA in 1862. According to Sullivan (1990), "The prison reform movement gathered steam under Enoch Wines and his colleagues and culminated in the National Prison Congress held in Cincinnati in 1870."

At the National Prison Congress a Declaration of Principles was adopted setting forth the ideals and methods for prison reform. The last of these principles addresses the use of women in prison work.

> Principle XXXVII: This congress is of the opinion that, both in the official administration of such a [prison] system, and in the voluntary co-operation of citizens, therein, the agency of women may be employed with excellent effect. (Wines 1871)

It was an afterthought. It is not included in the Principles of Penitentiary and Reformatory Discipline *Suggested* for Consideration by the National Congress. In the course of the congress proceedings, using women for work in prisons was discussed. The proceedings and discussions during the second evening of the congress, 13 October 1870, include the following:

> Mr. F. B. Sanborn, [of Massachusetts], said in a discussion of his paper, ["How Far Is the Irish Prison System Applicable to American Prisons?"]...he had omitted to speak of one point, and that was the management of female prisoners. He would, however, supply the omission before the paper was printed.... [At the end of Sanborn's presentation he said] he saw a lady, Mrs. Stewart, in the audience, whom he wanted to hear say something on the question of woman's work among prisoners.
>
> Mrs. E. D. Stewart, of Ohio, said that she wished to have some unequivocal expression from the congress in reference to engaging women in this reform work. She said that some ladies had been engaged in it and had done wonderful things, as all knew.... Mr. T. J. Bigham, of Pennsylvania, thought that from what we had seen of what women can effect, we could do more by the use of that element than by almost any thing else.... Mr. Wardwell, of Rhode Island, said he knew instances where men had learned to read the Bible through the teaching of women. He stood a living witness of sixty-four criminal men who had been influenced by women to become better, and some of them had died rejoicing in the prospect of glory. He felt he could lose his right arm, if need be, in defence of the work of women in prisons.... The Rev. Mr. Quinby introduced a resolution recognizing the value of women's work in penal and reformatory institutions, which was referred to the business committee, and by them incorporated, substantially, into the declaration of principles, which was subsequently adopted by the congress. (Wines 1871)

Stewart from Ohio spoke forcefully that the congress should express itself "in reference to engaging women in this reform work." The fact that twenty-one women are listed on the Roll of Members attests to their interest.

Fourteen of these women were wives of wardens or superintendents—one was the wife of the governor's deputy. Three of them served as matrons in their husband's institutions. Two of the women listed had titles of their own: one a chaplain at a state penitentiary and the other a matron at a house of shelter. The remaining five women are listed without husbands or titles.

The need for the establishment of separate prisons for women under the management of women was affirmed in the first congress through a resolution. This statement affirming the tenets of the female reformers set the stage officially for separating the care of female offenders from men. At the same time, it formalized the roles of women to care for these offenders. With the opening of two new and separate reformatory prisons for women in Indiana (1873) and Massachusetts (1877), the arena for women's work in prisons expanded.

As the women's reformatory movement came to fruition with the opening of seventeen reformatories between 1900 and 1933, women's participation at the annual congresses grew. The table on page 7 shows women's participation in the congresses by five-year periods from 1870 to 1930. In 1895, over a third of the delegates were women, and though there was a drop in 1900, for the next twenty-five years one-fifth to one-third of those listed were women.

At this time women were members of committees and affiliated associations in increasing numbers and by 1915 began to hold office (other than recorder or stenographer). By 1930 twenty-two women were members of committees and associations and nine were officeholders in the association.

The increase in participation by women in the National Prison Association was largely due to the women's reformatory movement. It was swept along by the Progressive movement of the first two decades of the twentieth century. One of the basic tenets of the women's reformatory movement was to do away with the model of the traditional custodial men's prison and establish separate prisons for women, *administered and staffed by women.*

Although the participation of women in prison work grew and the percentage of women attending the prison congresses also increased, women were still in the minority. Their spheres of interest were primarily with female offenders, and the female reformers' ideology called for reformation rather than punishment as the guiding principle of their work. Their roles at the prison congresses were marginal. It is not surprising that in 1912 an Association of Women Members of the National Prison Association was formed, thus "creating networks for communication and mutual support" (Scott 1984).

Associations for Women in Corrections

At the 1912 National Prison Congress, Maud Ballington Booth, cofounder of the Volunteers of America and a prison reformer who began her work in men's prisons in 1896, was elected chair of the newly created Association of Women Members. She said in her address at the opening meeting of the association:

> It was thought at the last Prison Congress, and perhaps at some former ones, that it would be very desirable if the ladies, representing this great field, could get together for mutual help and advice. We also asked that there should be given a time upon the program when women who were directly concerned and interested in the work for women prisoners should have an opportunity to emphasize this very important and very difficult part of the field.

Women's Participation in Prison Congresses 1870–1930

Year	Attendance No. of Women	Total No.	% Women	Membership Commitees/ Assoc.	No. of Office Holders
1870	21	237	9	0	0
1875			No Congress Held		
1880			No Congress Held		
1883	36	334	9	0	0
1885	14	220	6	0	0
1890		No Listing of Delegates Available			
1895	39	113	35	0	1*
1900	28	173	16	0	1*
1905	58	240	24	6	1*
1910	82	232	35	8	1*
1915	74	262	28	18	2
1920	104	455	23	24	3
1925	82	309	27	22	7
1930	160	502	32	22	9

*Official reporter/stenographer

Source: National Prison Congresses, *Congress Proceedings* of 1870, 1883, 1885, 1890, 1895, 1900, 1905, 1910, 1915, 1920, 1925, 1930.

Later in her address Booth affirms one of the basic beliefs of the women of the reformatory movement: "It has seemed to us that one of those things we must emphasize in our section of the Association is the great importance of women's oversight of women."

Toward the end of her presentation Booth speaks of the warden's wife, whose role in men's prisons was unofficial yet very important. She represented another role played by women in prison work:

> In passing, we want to say that we hope in our little Association that we shall have the aid of all our wardens' wives. The warden's wife is not an official of the prison, yet, how often, as I have gone into these places, I have found her influence. (Booth 1912)

Presentations by other women of the association emphasize the need for separate institutions of the reformatory type for women, administered and staffed by women.

In sum, female offenders, their offenses, and their reasons for offending are different from men. They must be handled separately, thus creating separate spheres for women who work in reformatories with them. For the next five years the Association of Women Members met at the annual congress. Its leaders were women who worked with women. Presentations were made by these same leaders be they professionals or volunteers of the reformatory movement. The topics of discussion revolved around the spheres of these leaders' work.

No congress was held in 1918 due to World War I. In 1919 the congress resumed but the Association of Women Members is not mentioned in the proceedings. There is no discussion in the 1917 proceedings about lack of interest in the association. The lapse of a year of meeting undoubtedly broke the momentum that had built for the association, and as the table on page 7 indicates, attendance by women dropped by 5 percent between 1915 and 1920.

Women's participation in the prison congresses grew during the 1920s. At the annual business meeting of the American Prison Association on 24 September 1929, the following resolution calling for a women's committee was adopted:

> Whereas, the importance of the work with women offenders should have the concentrated attention of interested women for at least a part of the time devoted to this conference,
>
> BE IT RESOLVED, that a committee be appointed to be called the Women's Committee, for the purpose of affording official recognition of this special group; and that this committee shall act as an official Hospitality Committee to draw new women members into contact with the organization, shall form a liaison between the Association and local hospitality committees, shall arrange with the secretary of the Association for place on the program for group discussions and shall otherwise promote the interest of women executives throughout the country in the work and organization of the American Prison Association. (APA 1930)

Once again the American Prison Association formalized the separate sphere of women who work with female offenders by "affording official recognition of this special group." The resolution proposing the committee clearly states it is for "women executives."

Membership lists of the committee indicate that the predominant memberships are female superintendents, former superintendents, and women, such as Grace Abbott, chief of the U.S. Children's Bureau, and Judge Florence E. Allen of the Ohio Supreme Court, in executive state and national government positions. The other group of women who comprised membership were the lay board members of the institutions, younger sisters of the early female reformers. Matrons, teachers, even assistant superintendents, as a rule, did not attend the congresses or become affiliated with the association.

The Women's Committee's first meeting was held at the 1929 congress in Toronto. Mary B. Harris, superintendent of the Federal Reformatory for Women at Alderson, West Virginia, was chair. The twelve members of the committee who are listed in the proceedings include Katherine B. Davis, first superintendent of the Reformatory for Women at Bedford Hills, New York; Mabel Walker Willerbrandt, assistant attorney general of the United States and instrumental in the opening of Alderson; and Jessie D. Hodder, superintendent of the Women's Reformatory at Sherborn, Massachusetts.

In 1930, another group of female prison administrators was formed. The Conference of Superintendents of Institutions for Girls and Women (CSIGW) was founded by Martha P. Falconer, one of the female reformers of the late nineteenth and early twentieth centuries, best known as founder and superintendent of Sleighton Farms for Girls in Pennsylvania; Caroline F. Penniman, superintendent, Long Lane Farm for Girls, Connecticut; and Ellen C. Potter, M.D., director of medicine, New Jersey Department of Institutions and Agencies. There does not exist a formal statement of purpose of the conference. It was devoted solely to the concerns of the work of female superintendents of correctional institutions for girls and women.

A statement attached to the program for the Eighth Annual Conference in 1937, Regulations Concerning Yearly Conference of Superintendents of Correctional Schools for Girls and Women, clearly spells out, "Attendance to be limited to Superintendents. A superintendent not attending may appoint a member of her staff, carefully chosen to represent her. In co-educational institutions, superintendents of girls are included." At the Thirteenth Annual Conference the issue of who may attend came up again and the above regulations were reiterated. "This was deemed necessary to insure the greatest possible freedom of expression by the superintendents in office." However, "a motion was passed that the Founders' Committee which consisted of the beloved Martha P. Falconer, deceased, Dr. Ellen C. Potter and Miss Penniman be extended the courtesy of an invitation each year and that they be urged to attend the meetings."

Meetings were held for two or three days each winter at the Hotel Pennsylvania in New York City. There is also mention some years of a midwestern conference held in Chicago, but no agendas or minutes have been found. Minutes from the years 1933, 1936, 1937, 1942, 1943, and 1946 show the attendance ranged from a low of fifteen in 1943 to a high of twenty-six in 1946. Although the greatest number came from the Northeast, they also came from Tennessee, Canada, Michigan, Indiana, and in 1946 from Tehachapi, California. There were more superintendents of juvenile institutions represented.

The programs always devoted time to issues of immediate concern to the superintendents in running their institutions. They were all asked to send in ahead of time topics for these discussions. Speakers from outside were invited each year to address the conferences. Topics ranged from "Emotional and Social Needs of Adolescents" by the director of a child guidance clinic in New York City to "Female Homosexuality in Correctional Institutions" by a female psychoanalyst from Austria who had been held in a concentration camp.

These conferences were more closely knit than were the American Prison Association's. They offered a forum for mutual concerns, stimulation of new ideas, and moral support for each other. The conferences continued to meet into the 1960s according to Janet York, superintendent of Connecticut's Reformatory for Women in the fifties and sixties, though their agendas increasingly became limited to juvenile institutions.

Meanwhile, the Women's Committee of the American Prison Association (renamed the Committee on Women's Institutions in 1936) presented congress programs until 1947, after which there is no mention of the committee in the proceedings. There are probably three primary reasons for this. The first is changes that occurred in society after World War II. Immediately following the war there was a small increase in the number of women committed to correctional institutions, but there was a drop in the commitments to state penal institutions during the fifties. At the same time, middle- and upper-class women, the backbones of women's movements, were at home involved with families and their children.

Another reason the committee failed to continue is that it was peripheral to the parent organization. The women who were the leaders in the Women's Committee also were members of the Board of Directors and other committees of the American Prison Association. They were given time on the program of the Women's Committee for two or three sessions and on some occasions arranged speakers for a luncheon or dinner meeting. But they were not able to concentrate solely on issues around female offenders or female correctional professionals.

Perhaps the main reason for the lack of interest in the committee's American Prison Association meetings was the existence of the yearly Conference of Superintendents of Institutions for Girls and Women.

In the fifties there was not much going on for female superintendents of adult institutions either in CSIGW or the American Prison Association, which changed its name to the American Correctional Association (ACA) in 1955. Martha Wheeler, superintendent at the Ohio Reformatory for Women in the late fifties and sixties and in 1973 the second woman to be elected president of the American Correctional Association, and Janet York became active in ACA in the mid-fifties. They said that at the time they both began their careers in corrections, "underlings" were not sent to the congresses. When they began to attend as superintendents, there was not much happening of particular concern for the female members. Actually, they met at one of the congresses, became friends, and roomed together so they would have each other's company.

The rekindling of the feminist movement began in the United States in the sixties, and in 1960 at the annual Congress of Correction in Denver the Committee on Women's Institutions was reborn as the Women's Correctional Association (WCA).

The beginnings and goals of WCA are recounted in the May 1989 newsletter of the Association on Programs for Female Offenders (APFO), which followed WCA:

> Although it was intended from the inception of WCA that membership be open to anyone with an interest in female offenders, the Association's founders were, for the most part, superintendents of correctional institutions for adult women. The founders of the Women's Correctional Association had the following goals in mind:
>
> • Provide a forum in which this special interest group could meet during ACA congresses;
> • Design ways to keep in touch between congresses;
> • Establish a mechanism for impacting congress programming.
>
> Throughout the 1960s the most constant membership, action nucleus, and leadership remained with the superintendents. At that time not many groups or agencies identified themselves as interested solely in female offenders. This situation began to change with the coming of the 1970s as new groups declared an interest in female offenders. Community residential programs, advocacy groups, and researchers all became involved with issues relating to female offenders.

WCA was active throughout the sixties. It held business meetings at every ACA congress and usually invited an outside speaker to address those who attended. They were represented on the ACA Board of Directors. Members took turns producing a monthly newsletter, which gave an account of happenings at the various institutions. In 1968–69 they cooperated in a research survey, Psychological and Psychiatric Services in Institutions (Other than Jails) Serving Female Offenders (Wilson 1969).

The membership remained primarily top administrative staff of women's institutions. However, major changes that took place in the correctional field in the late sixties and seventies forced a realignment of WCA. As a result of these changes, women began to infiltrate ACA and the correctional field. No longer did women have to remain working in the women's sphere where opportunities for advancement were limited.

WCA became the Association on Programs for Female Offenders, an affiliate of ACA, targeted to female offender issues. In 1978 a Task Force on Women as a subcommittee of the Affirmative Action Committee of ACA was mandated "to address itself to the unique position of women working in the field of corrections both in the United States and Canada, identify areas of concern as well as opportunity and develop support systems for women in the field" (Nicolai 1982).

Edna Mahan's career in corrections spanned the Women's Committee and WCA. She was a leader in both of these groups, for two major themes in her career were the advancement of women in the field of corrections as well as the concerns of female offenders.

Clinton Farms, the New Jersey Reformatory for Women, was the setting for her career. Looking at its founding, which was closely tied to the women's reformatory movement, and at its first fifteen years of operation prior to Mahan's arrival, provides some insight into this remarkable woman because her career and life were closely intertwined with the institution.

Chapter 2

The Women's Reformatory Movement and the Founding of Clinton Farms

Reforms in penal treatment, both in the United States and New Jersey, during the latter half of the nineteenth century and the first half of the twentieth, set the stage for the creation of the New Jersey Reformatory for Women: Clinton Farms. Reformative rather than punitive justice lay at the base of the ideology of the times.

The first institutions to espouse this ideology were juvenile reform schools established by private societies in the early nineteenth century. The first public reform schools for juveniles were opened in Massachusetts in the middle of the century. They became a model for the women's reformatories that opened at the beginning of the twentieth century.

The call for reformation of the criminal was clearly stated at the first National Prison Congress in 1870 in its Declaration of Principles:

> Principle II: The treatment of criminals by society is for the protection of society. But since such treatment is directed to the criminal rather than to the crime, its great object should be his moral regeneration. Hence the supreme aim of prison discipline is the reformation of criminals, not the infliction of vindictive suffering.

Basic to reformation was the indeterminate sentence, which was stated in Principle VIII: "Peremptory sentences ought to be replaced by those of indeterminate length. Sentences limited only by satisfactory proof of reformation should be substituted for those measured by mere lapse of time" (Wines 1871). The indeterminate sentence was a major tenet underlying the ideology of the women's reformatory movement.

The Women's Reformatory Movement and Early Reformatories

By the middle of the nineteenth century, female reformers changed their perspectives on "the female criminal as beyond redemption...the Dark Lady, a woman of uncommon strength, seductive power and evil inclination" to one who could be redeemed in the care of female reformers. As Rafter (1990) goes on to explain:

> Just as the reformatory movement began, this image of the criminal woman began to fade from discussions of female criminality. It did not disappear, but it was superseded by a new concept of the female offender as childlike, wayward, and redeemable, a fallen woman who was more sinned against than a sinner herself.... With reformers' help, this new female offender could regain her place on the pedestal of true womanhood.

The women of the reform movement recognized that female offenders could not be helped in prisons for men and called for separate prisons for women that were run by women. The call of the founders of the women's reformatory movement was recognized at the 1870 congress by both a principle and a resolution:

> Principle XIX. Prisons, as well as prisoners, should be classified or graded so that there shall be prisons for the untried, for the incorrigible and for other degrees of depraved character, as well as **separate establishments for women,** and for criminals of the younger class.
>
> Resolved, That this Congress is of the opinion that **separate prisons should be established for women,** and that neither in city, county nor state prisons should women be incarcerated with men; and further, that women should have charge of the female department in all cases where the sexes are imprisoned within the same enclosure [emphasis added]. (Wines 1871)

The first two women's institutions that opened after the 1870 congress were the Indiana Reformatory Prison for Women (1873) and the Massachusetts Reformatory Prison for Women (1877). Their designation as "reformatory prisons" suggests the hesitancy of state authorities—who were male—to allow them to blossom full-blown into the models envisaged by female reformers. Their operation and architecture resembled that of men's institutions.

The model conceived by the women of the reformatory movement was realized in 1901 with the opening of the New York Reformatory for Women at Bedford Hills. The institution was built on the cottage plan adopted from juvenile reform schools. The cottage plan was the architectural design for the women's reformatories that opened in the next three decades. The individual cottages were to be homelike and under the charge of matrons who were to serve as role models to facilitate the transformation of their charges. The institutions were located in the country because "rural life was moral life" (Rafter 1990).

Female reformers called for reformatories to be managed by specially trained, intelligent women. Freedman (1984) points out, however, that "[t]he record of female correctional personnel during the late nineteenth century...was decidedly mixed. It was not always possible to attract 'specially trained, intelligent women' " because salaries were low, women had to live at the institutions, and in the beginning male managers' authority was imposed on female superintendents. This gradually changed as female authority for managing prisons was accepted.

In 1880, Eliza Mosher, M.D., who had been the physician at Framingham, became superintendent there. She was followed in 1882 by Clara Barton, who took leave from the International Red Cross to serve at Framingham for nine months. By 1900 women such as Mosher and Barton, though not all of the same stature as they, "established and helped make prison administration a new female vocation" (Freedman 1984).

The female superintendents at the beginning of the twentieth century, in the middle of the Progressive era, differed from their older sisters of the nineteenth century who usually began their prison work as volunteers and, with few exceptions, had no college education. The twentieth century superintendents "were more likely to have set their sights on paid, professional careers at the start of their adult lives" (Rafter 1990). Most of them had attended and graduated from college, and several had advanced degrees: Katherine Bement Davis, Ph.D., first superintendent at Bedford Hills; Mary Belle Harris, Ph.D., third superintendent at Clinton Farms and first superintendent at the Federal Reformatory for Women, Alderson, West Virginia; and Florence Monahan, LL.B., who was superintendent at both Shakopee, Minnesota, and later at Tehachapi, California. These women were active in the field and members of the American Prison Association when Mahan began her career.

The efficacy of the women's reformatories and the women who managed them was pointed out in 1934 by Albert Morris, criminologist and contemporary observer of that time:

> The women's reformatories as a group, as distinguished from the women's prisons, have maintained and improved upon the early reformatory ideal somewhat more effectively than the men's institutions. In general their task is intelligently conceived as one of socializing their charges through broad educational programs designed to fit them for decent living in their communities after their release. Considerable effort is made to arouse and provide for the assumption of responsibility by prisoners within the institutions. Emphasis is placed on normal living as nearly as it may be achieved by those confined in a correctional institution. Frequently handicapped by inadequate appropriations the women's refor-

> matories nevertheless manage to express a degree of ingenuity and willingness to experiment in their treatment of crime that is sadly lacking in the reformatories for men.

Morris makes note of "the women's prisons." When the women's reformatories opened in the early decades of the twentieth century, women who committed more serious felony offenses were not deemed suitable for reformatories. They were usually sentenced to the state prison, kept on a separate women's wing, and received determinate sentences as did the men.

Women sent to reformatories for primarily morals offenses received indeterminate sentences, which gave more flexibility in the amount of time they could be held. The argument of female reformers for the indeterminate sentence was they needed enough time for permanent reformation to take hold, and this could vary for each offender. The intention was benevolent, but it created a double standard for the treatment of male and female offenders convicted of petty crimes.

The Founding of Clinton Farms

New Jersey followed other northeastern states after the Civil War in calling for reforms in the handling of both juvenile and adult offenders. In 1867 the State Home for Boys was opened in Jamesburg and in 1872 the State Home for Girls in Trenton. These reform schools "provided for a differentiated treatment of both sexes in institutions that gave some promise of effecting reformation instead of increasing the mental and moral degradation of the individual offender" (Barnes 1918).

Other reform steps that took place included the establishment of the State Charities Aid Association in 1886, "a permanent semi-official organization for criticizing the penal institutions of the state," the adoption of the parole law in 1889–91, and the creation of a commissioner of charities and correction in 1905 (Barnes 1918).

Advocates for penal reform in New Jersey, concerned about the inadequate and poor treatment of women held at the Trenton State Prison and cognizant of the call for separate reformatory institutions for female offenders that was endorsed by the 1870 Prison Congress, agitated for such an institution. They came "near to reaching their goal in 1886, when the Legislature approved a special committee to consider the advisability of creating a 'Female Prison and Reformatory' " (Ellis 1945). Barnes (1918) explains:

> From 1886 to 1896 the women's ward at the State Prison was under the efficient management of Mrs. John N. Patterson. Her competent administration together with an appropriation of fourteen thousand dollars in 1899 for the improvement

> of the women's wing of the prison, tended to lessen to some degree the pressure of public opinion for the provision of a reformatory for women.

In the first decade of the twentieth century pressure from the Federation of Women's Clubs and the State Charities Aid Association for a state reformatory for women commenced anew with even more vigor. In 1903, "at their insistence, Governor Franklin Murphy appointed a Commission to study the need for a Reformatory for Women. The chairman of this commission was Mrs. Caroline B. Alexander" (Ellis 1945). In a report to the senate and general assembly, they strongly recommended the establishment of a reformatory for women. There was no action at that time.

In 1904 the commission looked further into the care and treatment of female offenders in the state and presented a supplemental report to the senate and the general assembly that stated that they found no changes in the conditions from 1903. Again they recommended the establishment of a reformatory for women. The house passed a law in 1907 "providing for the erection of a reformatory for women," but it failed in the senate. Finally in 1910 public pressure became so great that the state legislature passed "An Act to Establish a State Reformatory for Women, to Provide for the Government Thereof, and the Commitment Thereto of Women Convicted of Crimes and Other Offenses" (Barnes 1918).

The act also called for the appointment of a board of managers to oversee the reformatory with the authority to parole, set policy, and appoint the superintendent. Caroline Stevens Alexander (later Wittpenn) and Geraldine Livingston Thompson, both of whom served on the commission of 1903-1904, were appointed to the Board of Managers, and Alexander was elected president. They remained actively concerned with the reformatory after its founding and were involved with other New Jersey institutions and agencies for the remainder of their lives.

They typified the female reformers of the late nineteenth century and early twentieth century. They were born of wealth and influence and family traditions of service. Both were benefactors to Clinton Farms not only in material ways but in their continued interest in and influence on the management of the institution.

The Act of 1910 provided the necessary legal structure for the establishment of a New Jersey reformatory for women. The Appropriations Committee of 1911 allowed only $20,000. This was considerably less than the $148,000 recommended by the commission of 1903. Nevertheless, it did allow for the purchase of a farm in Clinton, Hunterdon County, New Jersey, a rural farming community that was considered desirable for its moral value. A beginning was made.

Clinton Farms opened in January 1913, with four staff and three old farmhouses plus some barns and other smaller outbuildings that stood on the property. Because there was no money for new buildings, the largest of the two farmhouses was renovated to accommodate twenty-four inmates plus staff. Grilling was added to the windows and locks to the doors to provide security. The second farmhouse, the Homestead, housed the utility man and his wife until the third, a smaller building, could be renovated for them. The barns and other outbuildings were repaired so as to be usable.

The first superintendent, May Caughey, was hired and started work in November 1912 to prepare the institution and also to visit other women's institutions. Caughey, a graduate of the University of Michigan, had taught in Mexico and Wisconsin. She had also worked at the Philadelphia House of Refuge, which later was moved out of the city and became Sleighton Farms (for girls). She was recommended for the position by Martha Falconer, superintendent of Sleighton Farms, one of the early female reformers and a founder of the Conference of Superintendents of Correctional Institutions for Girls and Women.

Caughey's reports for the first year indicate a lack of formality of the program due largely to the fact that the facilities available for carrying out the various aspects of the program were extremely limited, and the staff was called upon to use a great deal of ingenuity. Eleanor Little, a psychologist friend of Caughey's working on her master's degree at Columbia began to come out to Clinton on the weekends to test the inmates and in 1914 was hired on a full-time basis. Formal classification procedures were nonexistent, though the establishment of Clinton Farms in itself was a form of classification for the State of New Jersey. Legal authority for parole was available through the institution's Board of Managers, but there were no formal procedures within the institution. There was no staff member designated as parole officer, and there was no planning for parole. Board and staff members took on these duties in an informal way as best they could.

"Workshop for Character Building"

In the first Annual Report of the New Jersey Reformatory for Women in 1913, Caroline Alexander (Wittpenn), president, wrote "the shortness of our experience and the smallness of our numbers do not prevent our working toward certain ideals which might be summarized in the hope that Clinton will become more and more a workshop for character building."

The mood of the times determined that Clinton Farms' major purpose and goal should be humane correction and reformation rather than custody and punishment. The purposes and goals of the institution as stated in the Report of the Women's Reformatory Commission of 1903, the act of 1910 that legally established the reformatory, and the annual report of 1913 testify to the primacy of the goals of humane correction and reformation. Punishment is mentioned in only one of these statements as is detention.

Four major influences largely account for the priority given to these goals: (1) specific happenings in the field of penology, (2) founders of the institution and the first inmates, (3) lack of resources, and (4) a little benign neglect from above.

The atmosphere of reform and progressive penology that was taking place in the United States was illustrated by the first National Prison Congress in 1870. Recommendations for the establishment of reformatories for women were included. These things were necessary before an institution such as Clinton Farms could come into being.

Two women stand out as having great influence at this time: Caroline Alexander Wittpenn and May Caughey. The humanitarian interests of Wittpenn directed her particular concern for the welfare of women. These interests explain her hard work for the establishment of a separate institution for female offenders in New Jersey. Once the reformatory was a reality, her interest and close concern with it continued until her death twenty years later.

Caughey, by virtue of her position as superintendent at Clinton Farms as well as her ability to take hold of the institution with skill and understanding, was largely responsible for the foundation and early direction of the institution. At Sleighton Farms she had worked with Martha Falconer to develop a self-government system that became basic to the operation of the reformatory.

The inmate population during this first year of operation was important because it accepted the official goals of the institution and helped the staff and the board to implement them. There were few discipline problems, and the need for custody was minimal. Because the inmates cooperated and helped at this time, they facilitated implementation of the goals of an open and trusting atmosphere for the institution.

Although the act of 1910 provided the legal means for a well-rounded program at Clinton Farms, the legislation responsible for appropriating the funds for the institution provided considerably less than recommended. As a consequence, the resources for operation of the institution in the first year were meager. The operational pattern of the institution had to be adapted to the resources available. These limited institutional necessities forced the institution to limit its custody goal and strengthen its humane correction goal.

The limited number of staff necessitated developing leadership among inmates who had training and ability and also developing honor methods among all the women. The lack of disciplinary cases among inmates facilitated this delegation of responsibility to inmates. Reports indicate that in its first year of operation, the board, the staff, and the inmates cooperated to get the institution started on a path that was soon to receive much favorable comment in the field of penology.

Also, because the reformatory was so small, the officials on the state level paid relatively little attention to it; therefore, it was able to operate independently in setting up its program. The total picture of Clinton Farms during this first year was one of informality, flexibility, and adaptability with little interference from the more formal authorities at Trenton. This lack of direction from Trenton gave the board and the staff the freedom to work out and initiate programs of their own that might have been curtailed otherwise.

Clinton Farms, 1914–1930

Growth and formalization of procedures and programs characterized Clinton Farms in the sixteen years after its founding. According to the 1913 Annual Report, thirty-one women were cared for at Clinton Farms during 1913. Four women were transferred from the state prison at Trenton in 1913: three for personal crimes and one for property felony, probably grand larceny. The other women were committed for morals and property offenses.

By 1931, according to that year's annual report, the average daily inmate population was 230. Most of the women were committed for morals offenses and property crimes, even though by 1 January 1930 all the women had been transferred from the state prison.

The physical plant expanded with six new cottages built between 1915 and 1930. In addition to the cottages, a chapel (donated by Wittpenn) was built in 1915, a laundry/sewing room and a separate storeroom were added in 1921, and an administration building in 1930.

The number of full-time staff grew from five at the end of 1913 (a female farmer had been added to the original four) to fifty positions in 1930. The titles included superintendent, executive secretary (which became assistant superintendent), matrons, teachers, parole officer, psychologist, storekeeper, sewing room officer, and occupational supervisors.

Worn out and at odds with Wittpenn over the management of the institution, Caughey resigned as superintendent in 1917. At about the same time, the New Jersey senate and general assembly passed a resolution empowering the governor to appoint a commission of five people to "investigate into the conditions of the penal, reformatory and correctional institutions of the state, and also into what is known as the 'State Use System' and the employment of prisoners on roads, prison farms or in other capacities" (Prison Inquiry Commission 1917).

This commission, which became known as the Morrow Commission due to the chairmanship of Dwight W. Morrow, created in 1918 the New Jersey State Department of Institutions and Agencies and brought under its control all "the State penal, correctional, hospital, relief and training institutions" (Ellis 1924). The resulting administrative structure—the Department of Institutions and Agencies headed by a commissioner appointed by the State Board of Control, the State Board of Control appointed by the governor with the advice and consent of the senate, and the local boards of managers—remained unchanged in relation to Clinton Farms until 1977.

One of the greatest strengths of this system was its virtual elimination of political patronage, the curse of so many correctional systems. For Clinton Farms it meant more control from the state level and a lessening of its autonomy. This was a mixed blessing. With more attention from above came more resources. However, this increase in attention was from a male-dominated central office that often imposed regulations that were not appropriate or sensitive to the management of an institution for female offenders.

Burdette C. Lewis became the first commissioner of the Department of Institutions and Agencies in 1918. He set about formalizing the administrative system for the state's correctional institutions and requiring all to comply. Directives came from him to the superintendent with specific requirements, such as "to adopt a system of classification;...to adopt rules and regulations for the guidance of your Board and the officers of the institution in handling charges committed to your care;...to establish a required system of records and reports" (Lewis 1919).

The extent to which these procedures were formalized at Clinton Farms is doubtful. It was a small institution without sufficient staff and with an honor system that attempted to keep rules and regulations imposed from above at a minimum. It required a strong and creative superintendent to balance the demands of the central office with the needs of the institution.

Some years of instability in the administration of Clinton Farms followed the resignation of Caughey. Four women were appointed to fill the superintendency from 1917 until Mahan's appointment in 1928. The first was Mary Belle Harris, who left after a short time to undertake a position under Martha Falconer with the War Department's commission on training camp activities. Grace Robson, who had been the nurse since the opening of the reformatory, became superintendent in 1919 and remained until 1924 when she left to assume the superintendency of a juvenile girl's institution in the South. The superintendent who followed her, Cornelia Lounsbury, was a poor administrator and was asked to resign in early 1928. Ellen Potter, M.D., director of medicine of the Department of Institutions and Agencies, was appointed acting superintendent until Mahan arrived in August.

In 1925 Burdette Lewis was succeeded as commissioner by William J. Ellis, who had been with the department for several years as a psychologist and director of the Division of Classification and Parole. Commissioner Ellis served until his death in 1945. He was an outstanding person who undoubtedly did more to strengthen and shape the department than any other person. He gave tremendous support to Edna Mahan throughout her early years at Clinton Farms.

Chapter 3

Edna Mahan's Early Life

Yreka and Corcoran: 1900–1918

Edna Mahan's early life in California is largely a mystery. She almost never talked about it to her friends in later years, and she saved little memorabilia. In trying to put together the pieces of her life, her birth and years in Yreka are almost a total blank. She saved among her personal papers a few souvenirs from her high school days in Corcoran and more from her university days at Berkeley.

An affidavit of birth on file in the Siskiyou County, California, courthouse states she was born in Yreka 14 July 1900. Siskiyou County and Yreka are at the northernmost tip of California not far from the Oregon border. According to the *Yreka Journal* 1900–01, copper, gold, and quartz were mined there. Mahan's mother's family and her father may have been lured there by the gold rush.

Her father, James Franklin Mahan, born in Omaha, Nebraska, was fifty-nine years old and a miner when Edna was born. He left his wife and daughter sometime in Edna's early life. Edna never talked about him. In the spring of 1931 she wrote about her father's death in a letter to Miriam Van Waters, her close friend and mentor. Van Waters replied, "No matter how little you knew him—the sense of loss and yearning must come. He was a lovely person to have made you, Edna." She felt his absence in her life. In later years she said in speeches and staff orientations at Clinton Farms, "I have never seen a woman in here who had a good relationship with her father."

Her mother, Ruth Isabelle Ackley Mahan, was thirty years old when she gave birth to Edna. Isabelle Ackley was born in nearby Etna, California, of a pioneer family who had sailed around Cape Horn from Maine. After James Mahan left his family, Isabelle married a Mr. Chavis. No record could be found of when this occurred.

Although Edna Mahan was an only child, she had cousins in California with whom she kept in touch all her life. A letter from one of the cousins after Edna Mahan's death gives the depth of feeling the maternal family had for her:

> Our hearts are very sad. Her childhood comes back to me, and what a sweet wonderful girl she has always been. Her mother and my mother worshipped her. I just have to tell you I loved her more than she realized. I always hoped to come back and know her better in these later years.

Sometime between 1900 and 1913 the Mahans moved to Corcoran in Kings County, California. Located in the San Joaquin Valley between Fresno and Bakersfield, Corcoran was incorporated in 1905. Records in the Kings County Library indicate that people moved into the valley in the late nineteenth and early twentieth centuries for farming. Perhaps with the end of the gold rush and the promise of new opportunities in agriculture, the Mahans, with a young daughter to raise, moved south to take advantage of the new developments there. James Mahan found work on the Hall ranch, which raised wheat.

The earliest record of Edna Mahan's in Corcoran is a yellowed and tattered composition book with "This is a Character Book Belonging to Edna Mahan" inscribed on the inside front cover. Her friends wrote in it their "Greatest ambition, Favorite flower, expression etc." Lucile Macy, a classmate, is the earliest listed on 16 January 1913. Several of her other grammar school friends are included, more than one of whom noted that their greatest ambition was to finish eighth grade.

Beyond the "Character Book," she saved nothing from her grammar school days in Corcoran. She started at Corcoran Union High School on 14 September 1914. She did leave a few more clues to her life at that time. Among her papers were her report cards from her freshman and junior years in high school, signed by her mother, Mrs. J. F. Mahan. She was vice-president of her class in her freshman year and president in her senior year.

All the other memorabilia saved are from her graduation. Her high school diploma was awarded 24 May 1918. The invitation to the commencement exercises, in which she enclosed her engraved calling card, indicate the exercises were on a Friday evening. The *Corcoran Journal* the next week carried an article "Eight Receive High School Diplomas."

An attractively designed and presented booklet, "Graduation Notes," provides more information and insight on her friends and their activities. The "Class Will" was written by classmate Elliott MacDonald and includes the following:

> I, Edna Mahan, do give and bequeath the sole right of winking at Clarence Wilson in English to Juanita MacDonald and may she obtain as much pleasure from the pursuit of this pastime as I have. To Mary Betty I leave my wonderful musical ability, especially with the phonograph, and would like to offer one suggestion. That is that she change records at least once a week for therein lay my one great mistake in music.

Mahan wrote "Who's Who and What's What in Corcoran Hi." This covers the faculty: "Perhaps the faculty had better be mentioned for although they are not of much importance they sometimes tell us what's what"; members of each class: "the real substance, the flesh and bones of the school"; and townspeople: "our good friends who have helped us with their liberal generosity on every occasion." "Who's Who and What's What" portrays life in a small rural high school and gives vignettes of the cast of characters.

Life for a young woman growing up in Corcoran, California, during the years of World War I appears to be little different from that in other parts of rural America. The town and the school were small, so all the students knew each other and their teachers from their first school days. The girls were interested in the boys, the basketball and baseball teams, and working for the war effort. The girls and boys enjoyed friendships with each other and parties given in one another's homes. Mahan wrote to and received letters from her California friends throughout her life. She kept copies of some of these letters, which shed some insight on her life. An example is a letter she wrote to Hillis Hubbard 15 July 1946:

> Dear Hillis Hubbard:
>
> In the April 8th issue of LIFE there was an article about a young woman who got married on horseback at the ranch of a friend, Hillis Hubbard. Long, long ago when I was freckle-faced and wore pig tails I went to school in Corcoran with Hillis Hubbard. You must be that same Hillis who wore cowboy boots and ten gallon hats and loved horses and pretty girls!
>
> This is not a fan letter but a friendly "hello" from the past. Through the years you have evidently pursued your boyhood interest while I became delinquent and fled to the East. And so it goes....
>
> Anyway, I couldn't resist sending greetings and good wishes.
>
> Cordially,
>
> N.J. STATE REFORMATORY FOR WOMEN
> Edna Mahan, Superintendent

A friend writing a letter of condolence in 1953 to Edna after her mother's death gives some insight into Isabelle Mahan Chavis and Mr. Chavis:

> Your mother was very good to me when I was such a rather unwanted little kid....
>
> Is Mr. Chavis still alive? Wonder if you ever remember of a trip he took up to S.F. and when he came back, he had a beautiful silk handkerchief for each of us. It was one of the type the Chinese used to do, the very fancy embroidery in colored silk. Well I still have mine and of course never used it. Would perhaps fall apart after these many years.

The Hall ranch where Mahan lived was a few miles outside of town, but this did not isolate her from her schoolmates. Having her own pony for transportation in 1915 gave her the freedom and independence a car provides today. Indeed, it probably also laid the ground for two characteristics used often to describe her: daring and adventurous. Writing a report titled "Consciousness in Animals" for a college class, she recalls this adventure:

> Some years ago I had a Shetland Pony. One night as I was driving him home from school we came upon a dead horse by the side of the road. He was so frightened that, try as I would, I could not make him pass. Finally I let him turn around and we went home another way.

Mahan was a good horsewoman all her life. She loved spirited animals. The years on the ranch in Corcoran surely instilled this love.

Other than her enjoyment of many friends and the fact she was class president, there is little from her Corcoran years that give any indication she would devote the majority of her life working with the most unfortunate women in society. Her college years at Berkeley gave her the academic grounding and practical experience working with "atypical children."

Berkeley 1918–1922

When Mahan entered the University of California at Berkeley in 1918, the roles of educated women were changing rapidly. The country was at war. By 1920 women outnumbered men in the graduating class for the first time. In addition, the women's suffrage movement reached its goal in 1920. The ferment over issues concerning roles of women in society was reflected on the campus with special attention given to organizations, activities, and housing for female students. The college yearbook, *Blue and Gold*; the campus newspaper, *The Daily Californian*; and a privately published book by two female students on their four years at Berkeley, 1923–27, give a picture of some of these concerns.

According to the 1921–22 *Blue and Gold*, Mahan served as a senior adviser to a freshman to help acquaint her with the campus; she was a member of Women's Council 1921–22 as a representative of her house Al Khalail; and in the spring of 1922, her graduation year, she participated in the annual "Parthenia," a Greek drama written, produced, and performed by female students.

Women's Council was a branch of student government whose membership constituted one representative from each activity and organization of university women. *The Daily Californian*, 17 August 1921, noted, "The strength of Women's Council lies in forming campus sentiment. Their duty this semester is to act as an open forum for discussion of matters of campus interest."

Among Mahan's memorabilia of her Berkeley days is a short clipping presumably from the *Corcoran Journal*, fall 1921: "Mrs. Mahan announces that she received word from her daughter Miss Edna, who is attending the University of California, at Berkeley, that she has been initiated into the Al Khalail Sorority there."

Al Khalail provided Mahan in her senior year a social setting among female students and imbued her with issues concerning women. Florence Jury and Jacomena Maybeck (1979) describe the founding and life in Al Khalail, a house club. (House clubs were often referred to as sororities although they had no national affiliations).

According to Jury and Maybeck, housing for female students on the Berkeley campus became an issue of concern at the turn of the century. Sororities were for women who could afford to join them. Boarding houses apparently were used by most female students who were not commuters. The boarding houses, however, did not foster a feeling of belonging to each other or the university.

> These clubs had an interesting genesis. Early in the century, a number of women connected with the University felt there was a deplorable lack of good housing for women students. Mrs. Phoebe Hearst, that wise and dedicated woman, sent the women's physician, Dr. Mary Ritter, to visit the campus of Eastern Colleges to learn what living conditions women had there. When Dr. Ritter returned, she and Mrs. Hearst and several other women students decided that houses which would provide pleasant surroundings at low cost were the answer. Several women came together to form the nucleus of the house which eventually became Al Khalail. It is interesting to note that the landlord of the brown shingle they wanted to rent would not sign a lease with the women. It was necessary for Dr. Ritter's husband to do so....
>
> I had been impressed from the first time (at Al Khalail) at the feeling there seemed to be that the girls all sort of belonged to each other. In a way that did not prevail in a boarding house. We sat at a long table and were served by college men. After dinner someone played the piano and we all danced.... The cost was the same as at St. Margaret's (boarding house)—forty dollars a month for room and board with a five dollar monthly social fee....
>
> On alternate Monday nights, we had 'faculty' dinners at the house. Usually three couples, and sometimes an unmarried woman professor. Then it was necessary to balance the table with an unmarried male. Less easy in that case. However, Dr. Lehman [English professor] was for a period without his wife who had gone to Hollywood. So often he came, and it was awesome and delightful to sit near him and listen. (Jury & Maybeck 1979)

Mahan saved a couple of memorabilia from Al Khalail: directions for initiation into the club and an invitation to an "Al Khalail at Home." She kept some letters she received from members later in her life that referred to the club. This living experience in her senior year at Berkeley may have enhanced her lifelong interest and involvement with the advancement of women.

In the spring of 1922 Edna took part as a dancer in the annual "Parthenia: The Vision of Marpessa," an all-woman production. According to *Blue and Gold*, "Based upon an old Greek myth the 1922 Parthenia, a masque of womanhood, expresses, as it has year after year, the spirit of youth and beauty...and portrays the transition from girlhood to womanhood...and brings its message of true ideals."

A review of "The Vision of Marpessa" by Charles Keeler, noted Berkeley poet, appeared in the 7 April 1922 *Daily Californian*:

> The importance of the Parthenia in the art life of the University cannot be overestimated. A production of such magnitude: conceived, written, composed and staged by [female] students is an achievement of real significance in the cultural advancement of California....
>
> It is out of such performances as this, and the Bohemian Club Grove Plays, that the future of California will grow. This land of beauty, looking through the Golden Gate to the Orient, is destined to create a new art akin to that of Greece, and the Parthenia as an annual institution, is making an important contribution toward its fulfillment. Why should the men students not do something equally serious and fine or better still, the men and women together.

Months before the performance, *The Daily Californian* started reporting on the plans for it. At least once a week there was a notice of tryouts for major parts, then for the chorus and dancers, and reports on the progress of rehearsals. Around the date of the performance there were also apt to be a few letters by male students of a derisive nature suggesting too much attention is given to the women over this production each year. Keeler's final sentence is undoubtedly in reference to this derision.

Although Mahan herself left no diary of this time in her life, the fact that so many of her activities revolved around women's organizations and activities is significant in understanding the later course of her life. If her consciousness concerning women's issues was not aroused in Corcoran, it had a firm grounding in her years at Berkeley.

Why Am I at College?

Among Edna Mahan's Berkeley papers are a number of academic assignments from her psychology and education classes. There is also a handwritten theme she wrote 1 March 1922 during her final semester at Berkeley for English 51B with the popular professor, Dr. Lehman. It is titled "Immature Impressions" and provides one of the rare written insights into her insecurities, her concerns for a career so she will be able to take care of herself, and her questions about her philosophy of life. The students were evidently asked to react to an article about university education by someone named Newman.

The first page of the paper is almost entirely devoted to how much she hates to write. "My paper is overdue.... No inspiration to write comes.... It is always very nearly like pulling teeth to extract a theme from my mind.... I never have been and never will be able to write credibly." (Those who worked closely with Mahan later in her life heard her complain bitterly when she had to get something more than board minutes or routine reports written. Her papers contain pages and pages of handwritten notes for speeches to staff orientation, to judges, to parole officers, to community groups—she was an inspirational speaker—but she left very little in the way of published articles or other written material.)

She then goes on to express in the theme how much she wanted to take one good English course before she graduated and how good Dr. Lehman's lectures were. On page two she begins her reaction to the Newman article and asks, "Why am I at college?"

> To be educated.... I wanted to acquire a college education in order to be better prepared for my life work.... In this generation, the world over, people are coming to realize the importance of a girl's knowing how to earn her own living even though she may never be called upon to exercise the knowledge. But there is one thing that I am sure of, and that is that I shall be called upon to earn my own living. For being devoid of the requisite feminine charm, I shall see to it that no one says to me, "I am obliged to take under my wing a most unattractive old thing." An old maid school teacher or whatever, I felt that a college education would help me in the days to come in whatever I chose to do.
>
> And college has done a great many things for me.... In a sense it has been my intellectual awakening.... I know now that I shall never be satisfied with the things that I would have been satisfied with before—and I shall never be quite satisfied with myself either.
>
> I have learned one important thing and that is that no exceptions are made when you get out in the world.... You are one of many. You must always conform to the rule without asking why or making excuses for not being able to.
>
> Like most people who come to college I have had my religious ideas turned topsy-turvy. I have come to the point I do not know what I believe.... This might have come if I had not come to college, but I doubt it. A little science makes you an atheist, a lot of science makes you a profound Deist. I need a lot of science then.
>
> Newman's argument against mass-production in universities and against forcing upon the student so much that he rejects all seems to me to be particularly ap-

> plicable to this institution. I have often and especially this year felt that I am learning only a little about a number of unrelated and impractical subjects, and I have asked myself, what is the use of it all.... What shall I be able to do when I am through? I do not know.... When people ask us what we expect to do, we want to choke them, and if we answer at all, we probably say, "Oh, teach school if I can't do anything else, I suppose." We who go into it with this attitude will most certainly not improve the teaching profession....
>
> I have had no definite aim, therefore, I do not feel that I have been fitted for a life work. However, I do not think that my time has been wasted. While at times I feel dissatisfied with my college career at the same time I say to myself, "'Tis better to have come and gone than never to have come at all."

The teaching assistant who read the paper, graded it C- and commented, "This paper seems to me to have no point. You must have something to write about before you can write. R. W. W." These comments indicate a lack of sensitivity to the feelings of a young woman who came from a small California town to Berkeley and is soon to embark into the real world of work and probably marriage.

Her feelings, her questions and her insecurities about life, careers, and religion are the same that most young middle-class American women express as they face graduation from college whether it be in 1922 after World War I, in 1946 after World War II, or in times of peace. Is there really a God? Will I marry? If I don't marry, I am seen as a failure. How do I find a career that my family and peers approve of and is meaningful to me? What am I prepared to do?

In Mahan's essay perhaps the most striking insights she provides in helping to understand the evolution of her later life come from describing herself as "devoid of the requisite feminine charm" and "a most unattractive old thing." Pictures of her as a girl, as a college student, and a young career woman show her as an attractive woman. As she matured she became more strikingly handsome.

Men were certainly attracted to her. The men she worked with all her years at Clinton Farms respected her and enjoyed working with her. She was the woman who became part of a working team with some of the male leaders of the American Prison (Correctional) Association.

She expressed her fear that a man might be obliged to take care of her if she can't earn her own living. Is she thinking of her mother, left by her father and married to a stepfather she, Edna, doesn't like? Later in her life there is a hesitation or fear of becoming too close to anyone on a personal level. Though she married twice, she divorced twice and could not be dependent on a husband.

Startling to read in the theme is the phrase, "You must always conform to the rule without asking why." If there was anyone who didn't follow the rules, it was Edna Mahan. On more reflection, however, it becomes apparent that one of her most outstanding traits was her ability to be creative, innovative, and a leader while following the rules. She had an uncanny political sense of what to push, when to push, and how far to push to accomplish the things she wanted to accomplish. She would not compromise her principles, but she did know when to compromise actions.

The other academic papers she left were all from courses that were related to a career working with "atypical" children. Though she prepared herself for teaching these children at the elementary level, she did not pursue it. Her academic preparation qualified her well for what turned out to be her lifetime concern: delinquent girls and women.

According to the *San Francisco Examiner*, 18 May 1922, she was one of 1,983 students awarded degrees 17 May in "the largest class graduated by any of the world's great colleges and universities." It was interesting to read on the same front page about a man who would become a leader in corrections in California, a governor of the U.S. Virgin Islands, and a good friend of Mahan's, Walter Gordon. "Policeman Walter Gordon, erstwhile football star at the University, yesterday was awarded a jurisprudence degree automatically admitting him to the bar in California."

Early Career in Los Angeles and Boston: 1922–1928

The six years following Edna Mahan's graduation from Berkeley provided graduate training and work experience in Los Angeles and Boston that prepared her for her career as superintendent of the New Jersey Reformatory for Women. She did not become the "old maid school teacher" she thought she might when writing her English theme. She launched her career in social work in Los Angeles, met and worked with some of the leaders in criminology and criminal justice in Boston, and fell in love.

In the fall of 1922 Mahan began postgraduate work at the California Bureau of Juvenile Research at the Whittier State School, Whittier, California. She earned two certificates from there. One, dated 19 February 1923, was a "Credential in Special Subjects" that "granted the holder 'A Special Certificate' of the Elementary Grade...for the teaching of atypical children." The second, awarded by the California Bureau of Juvenile Research, 26 February 1923, was a certificate stating "that Edna Mahan...has satisfactorily completed the requirements for the twelve-week practice course in Social Case Investigation."

A booklet made by her friends that she saved from this period, "State of Call-It-For-You Bureau of Juvenile Preserves, *Social Case Mystery Goat Book* of Edna Mahan by Edythe K. Bryant (Instructor of her Social Case Investigation course), Date January 26, 1923" provides her friends' characterization of Mahan. The booklet includes pictures and words cut from magazines describing her.

They depict a young woman on the brink of her career who is seen by her peers to be endowed with intelligence, good health, and a desire to keep fit; is concerned about equal rights; loves sports and dancing; is a great social asset, is well-liked; and stays on top of things because she has confidence under difficulties. Every one of these characteristics was true of her for the next forty-five years, especially "confidence under difficulties." Clinton Farms board members and staff who worked with her spoke of her courage, willingness to take risks, and competency to handle any and all situations.

The last page of her *Social Case Mystery Goat Book*, "The Universal Desire" brings out her confusions about men and marriage and questions about death and the existence of the soul.

From this period of her life she also saved three personal letters written to her in August 1922 at Whittier State School by three Berkeley friends. The three women were staying at Coronado Beach, California, and "Ed," as they call her, had evidently been with them. They write of "some good looking 'Gents' in white trousers out on the porch. Can't you picture yourself gliding over the ball room floor with someone like that?" "Wish you were here to chauffeur us out to La Jolla again." All three write of their daily activities—swimming, strolling around, playing cards—and missing her. She was a young woman with friends who admired her and enjoyed having her with them.

She launched her career in social work with Travelers' Aid in Los Angeles, February 1923. She saved two newspaper clippings from Los Angeles papers showing her with a client, one a "lost babe," the other "a runaway girl." One of the clippings is dated 22 May 1923. There are no details of her work there.

While Mahan was at Travelers's Aid she met Dr. Miriam Van Waters, who was on the Travelers' Aid Society Committee. Van Waters was a referee of the Juvenile Court, County of Los Angeles, and superintendent of Los Angeles County Juvenile Hall. She soon brought Edna Mahan into the Los Angeles County Probation Department and became the most important influence in her work with female offenders as Mahan began her career.

Van Waters had a Ph.D. in psychology. In the first half of the twentieth century her research, publications, and work with juvenile and female offenders made her one of the most influential women in the country concerning these issues. She wrote many publications beginning with *Youth in Conflict* in 1925, which had a nationwide effect on the understanding and treatment of juvenile delinquency.

The handling of juveniles through the juvenile court system, which had originated in Chicago in 1899 and spread throughout the country, received a great deal of attention during this period. The doctrine of *parens patriae* underlay the juvenile court (e.g., dependent, neglected, and delinquent children were to receive parental care from the court). The court prescribed and oversaw treatment for each child on an individual basis.

Van Waters's work with the juvenile court and juvenile probation in Los Angeles and the publication of *Youth in Conflict* led to her appointment in 1924 to the Harvard Law School Crime Survey in Boston under Felix Frankfurter. She was in charge of all the juvenile aspects of the survey. In 1929 Herbert Hoover appointed her to serve as a consultant to the Wickersham Commission to look into federal prisons and federal handling of juvenile delinquents. In 1931 she was appointed superintendent of the Massachusetts Reformatory for Women, Framingham, where she remained until she retired in 1957. She made a lifelong effort to recruit well-educated young women into the field and served as mentor to several who became outstanding in it.

She brought Edna Mahan into the Los Angeles County Probation Department in 1923 and to Juvenile Hall in 1924. For the next fifteen years she served as a strong and loving mentor to Edna Mahan. They remained friends and worked for causes of mutual interest the remainder of Edna's life, but as Edna grew in her work in New Jersey and gained her own reputation as an enlightened leader in her field, their paths separated.

Miriam guided Edna Mahan's first years of work with delinquent girls and women, for she saw in Edna the compassion, sense of justice, confidence, and strength necessary for the undertaking. Letters from Miriam to Edna spell out both the love Miriam gave to Edna and the advice and direction she gave as she taught the sensitivities and skills of a good administrator. In a letter dated 2 July 1926, when Edna was at Juvenile Hall, where there were many problems, Miriam wrote, "Don't worry. Remember you are not alone—many people love you. You have such courage and such courtesy in such trying times. This experience will bring you maturity, without bitterness. You are so close to real things. Be careful of details—little touches that bring comfort and gaiety to the children." In the same letter Miriam expresses some concern about Edna's health and then tells her, "Be careful to drink milk three times a day—please—and take the shots. In all humility—I ask, even order you. You are my child. Yet not a child—nearly grown up."

When Van Waters became swamped with duties and demands on her time, she trained Mahan as superintendent of El Retiro, a small school for juvenile girls who were wards of the juvenile court. It was linked, financially and administratively, with Juvenile Hall. After Mahan's first few months there, Van Waters referred to her as "my fine, young new worker. Her name is Edna Mahan. I have really no fear for her. She is dandy, and already my loyal supporter" (Rowles 1962).

Van Waters wrote a letter of reference on 10 December 1924 for Mahan to become a member of the American Association of Social Workers:

> I have known Miss Mahan since February, 1923. Her work in the Probation Office was full of promise. We persuaded her to enter Juvenile Hall for more definite training in the field of administration and child care. For over a year her

> work has been of a high grade of excellence. She has indeed an unusual fitness for social work.

When Van Waters was asked by Felix Frankfurter of Harvard Law School to direct the juvenile delinquency section of the Harvard Law School Crime Survey in Boston, she took this on without resigning from her Los Angeles County Probation responsibilities. She left others in charge of those responsibilities and shuttled back and forth across the country.

She soon sent for her loyal supporter from California, Edna Mahan, to help with parts of the Boston survey. According to her diary, Edna started in Boston on 1 March 1927. Both her diary notes and reports she compiled and saved in her files indicate her part of the survey was with the courts themselves and their probation services. These reports consist of statistical data on the numbers of male and female delinquents, ages, offenses, etc., for each of the courts as well as written descriptions of her observations in the courts, primarily of the judge's handling of each case and the part played by the probation officer. This type of research provided another firm foundation for the work that lay ahead of her at Clinton Farms.

The year and a half she spent in Cambridge, Massachusetts, where she shared a flat with Miriam when she was in town, put her in contact with some of the leaders or soon-to-be leaders in the criminal and juvenile justice fields. These included Felix Frankfurter, who headed up the survey for the Harvard Law School and was later appointed to the U.S. Supreme Court by President Franklin D. Roosevelt, and Sheldon and Eleanor Glueck, Harvard Law School's distinguished researchers in the crime and delinquency fields.

The Gluecks' research and publications at this time were concerned with the effectiveness of the reformatory system. Their first major study, *Five Hundred Delinquent Men*, published in 1930, dealt with postrelease records of men from the Massachusetts Reformatory, Concord. This was followed in 1934 with *Five Hundred Delinquent Women* from the Massachusetts Reformatory at Framingham. Their later work was devoted to an understanding of juvenile delinquency.

Mahan worked closely with Eleanor Glueck and remained friends with the Gluecks the rest of her life. Her work with the crime survey gave her exposure to some of the most ambitious and seminal research ever undertaken concerning crime and delinquency and their treatment. This gave her a grounding in understanding the complex theoretical issues surrounding these problems, which strengthened her later work in the field.

In Boston she also met Frank Loveland, whose career started in 1927 with the Harvard Law School Survey. In 1929 he was appointed by the Massachusetts Department of Correction to start a classification system of inmates, and he later moved to the U.S. Bureau of Prisons as assistant director for inmate programs. Edna Mahan's relationship with Frank Loveland began as co-workers on the survey, then progressed through a romance to a lifelong friendship. He served as an honorary pallbearer at her funeral in 1968.

Her 1928 diary, which is evidently the first year she began to keep one, notes briefly her appointments for each day and her social engagements. Beside the professional appointments such as "Dorchester Court" and "1:30 with Dr. Glueck" and the social ones—lunch, tea, and dinner engagements—she notes at the bottom of almost every page her interaction or lack of it that day with Frank or "F": "Met F. at Kendall. Supper together, show"; "Phone F. re supper. 'No!' " On Sunday, 15 April 1928, "Told him re Clinton possibility." The diary notes, while reflecting the enjoyment of doing things be it work or play, alone or with others during the Boston days, also reflect her desire for more of a commitment from him than he was able or willing to give her.

Edna spoke and wrote to Miriam Van Waters often about Frank. She wrote Edna 9 December 1927:

> I am glad you wrote me about Frank—I am sure whatever you did was ok. But remember that equality of men and women means that each should be free to express his or her desires without ill feeling and with good sportsmanship.... Frankness is the main thing.

A month earlier Miriam states in the middle of a letter with no specific reference, "The stupidest thing is to imagine that men have the only right to act." Miriam's letters for the next two years often have references to Frank as Edna struggles with her frustrations in her relationship with him.

In June 1928 Edna Mahan was offered the position as superintendent of the Reformatory for Women, Clinton, New Jersey. She accepted this offer, finished up her work on the survey, visited family and friends in California, and started work at Clinton Farms on 14 August 1928. Stormy days lay ahead of her in the next few months in her beginnings at Clinton Farms.

Chapter 4

Beginnings at Clinton Farms 1928–1930

At the time Edna Mahan arrived at Clinton Farms in August 1928, it was building, growing, conforming to state directives, and in a state of some disarray. Cornelia Lounsbury, who had been superintendent from 1924, was not the competent, flexible, creative administrator most of her predecessors had been. She had a difficult time working with the student government system and often asked the board for permission to handle troublesome inmates on her own outside the system. She even turned the handling of student government over to someone else.

By early 1928 it was apparent to the board that there was disorganization in all the departments. Staff and inmate morale was low, the budget overspent, the office work so far behind that records were not up-to-date, and other problems beset the institution. The board met in executive session with Commissioner Ellis on 17 April 1928, and all expressed their opinions on the state of the institution. Lounsbury was asked to resign. The resignation would take effect the first day of July with the understanding that she could leave the institution any time after 30 April.

Dr. Ellen Potter came to the institution in June as acting superintendent and did much to pinpoint the areas needing attention and to address them. The board minutes of 19 June 1928 contain two-and-a-half typewritten pages of the "Superintendent's Report" enumerating these. These same board minutes report on the appointment of a new superintendent.

Jane Coggeshall (board president) reported to the board she had received several letters from applicants for the superintendency of the institution and letters of recommendation concerning them. There were two applicants who seemed best fitted for the work: Miss Edna Mahan of California and Miss Corbett of Kentucky. Corbett, however, told Coggeshall she wasn't quite sure she could handle the delinquent women and doubted she could cope with the discipline. Mahan was selected as the one more competent to fill the position. A letter from Miriam Van Waters recommended Mahan very highly. The board voted unanimously to appoint Mahan at an annual salary of $3,500.

Geraldine Thompson, one of the founders and original board members of Clinton Farms and in 1918 also a member of the State Board of Control of Institutions and Agencies, was a friend of Van Waters. Thompson asked Van Waters if she could recommend a woman for the superintendency at Clinton, and Mahan was the obvious choice.

Letters from Miriam Van Waters to Edna Mahan detail the depth of involvement Van Waters had in Mahan's appointment and decision to go to Clinton Farms. Once Edna was there Miriam wrote often to advise her how to handle the many problems she was facing. Because Frank was very much in the picture during Edna's decision making about Clinton Farms and her first year there, Miriam's letters often made reference to him too. These give more insight into the ambivalence and frustration Edna felt about him.

On 9 May 1928, Miriam, who was en route to Los Angeles, wrote to Edna Mahan wanting to know how her interviews went and offering the following advice:

> There is one thing you must learn. How shall I put it? You are always charming. You have grace. That's a kind of spiritual quality you have. Translated into practical life—you always treat people as if you wished to serve them, be a host, as if they were guests. That's our California way. Well, that's all right most of the time. But there comes a time when you have got to have a cutting edge. When you've got to slap people in the face, and hold their eyes while you do it. I think you have every quality for a big administrator but that one. Unfortunately most good administrators have only that quality, and the gift of energy and order.
>
> You could be quite wonderful if you would practice. No one seems to realize how much of life is technique. I want to teach you those little things.
>
> You are more interested right now—in big ones, I guess. Darling, there's technique in love too—that's the sad part. I see you grow, you keep on growing, and you might as well enjoy your suffering. After all you're the gainer—whoever feels the most is the gainer.
>
> For the rest—be unfailingly kind, and as merry as you know how to be. He can't withstand that long.
>
> Please tell me and ask me anything you want—be sure—just anything.

It was Miriam Van Waters who strongly advised Edna Mahan to take the position at Clinton. She saw not only Edna's abilities for the superintendency, but the opportunity it offered for her own theories to be put into practice.

On 3 May Mahan had traveled to New York to meet Geraldine Thompson and talk about Clinton Farms. She then went for a three-day visit with Van Waters at

Miriam's parent's home in upstate New York. Miriam and Edna talked about the position at Clinton Farms.

Mahan returned to New York City on 7 May, and according to her diary, met with E. P. Earle, president of the New Jersey State Board of Control of Institutions and Agencies, on 8 May. The next day she went to Trenton to meet with Commissioner Ellis and on 10 May went to Clinton Farms to meet with Board President Coggeshall.

In the next weeks letters were sent back and forth between Commissioner Ellis and Mahan. He was anxious to know her reaction to Clinton Farms and her visit with Coggeshall. She was positive in her response to him.

Acting Superintendent Potter telegraphed 4 June asking if Mahan could spend the weekend of 9–11 June at Clinton Farms meeting with her. Van Waters must have been told of the invitation to Mahan to return to Clinton as the following telegram of 5 June indicates: "If they offer position it is my advice you accept. Clinton is the outstanding progressive institution in America." On the same date she wrote her:

> My advice is to go to Clinton. This is the biggest opportunity offered to either of us. You can make it the leading reformatory of America. It will plant in that soil all that we have attempted, or dreamed of in California. It is work you can do—easily. I'll come and help all I can every time you ask me.

Mahan did visit Clinton that weekend. The board met 19 June 1928 and unanimously voted that Mahan be appointed. Coggeshall and Potter both wrote her on 20 June inviting her to become superintendent of Clinton Farms. Potter said in her letter, "The Board is convinced that you have the qualities which will make this institution one of the outstanding reformatory agencies in the United States."

A handwritten letter came from Miriam Van Waters in Los Angeles dated 22 June 1928:

> Dearest Edna:
>
> Yes you were right to go to Clinton. I am thrilled about it. When? Will you come here first? Better have a little rest before taking it on.
>
> I long to see you too....
>
> With the deepest satisfaction in you—
> Miriam

Mahan spent the remainder of June and the first week of July finishing up her work with the Harvard Law School study. On 6 July she left Boston for a month's vacation in California with a few days in Chicago both coming and going. On her first stop in Chicago on 7 July she visited Hull House. (She does not record in her diary anything of her visit to Hull House. Jane Addams was still alive and at Hull House in 1928. Van Waters may have arranged for Mahan to meet with Addams and the other prominent women who made up the social group at Hull House. Her diary notes for the next weeks tell of visits to Juvenile Hall, lunches and dinners with friends, and two trips to Corcoran to see her mother and friends there and ride and swim. She went to San Francisco 29 July to see more friends and visit at Berkeley.

She left San Francisco 31 July and was back in Cambridge Sunday, 5 August. The next seven days were full of social engagements with friends and a little time spent on her juvenile court cases.

On 13 August she left Cambridge and started at Clinton Farms the next day. Miriam Van Waters, who was extremely happy about Edna's appointment, wrote a friend she felt as if a California redwood would start growing in New Jersey.

Her first day at Clinton Farms was spent with Dr. Potter, Assistant Superintendent Mary B. Fitts, and an afternoon reception with staff. The first few weeks she was busy getting to know staff and inmates. It did not take long, however, for the disarray of the institution, divided loyalties among the staff, and an overbearing board president to make her administration difficult and near impossible. Edna Mahan's first two-and-a-half months at the New Jersey Reformatory for Women were frantic, frustrating, lonely, and challenging.

"Hell, Just Hell!"

Edna Mahan kept a diary of her routine professional appointments, social engagements, business telephone calls, etc., from 1928 until she died in 1968, except from February 1929 to January 1932. Among these notations there are only a few comments revealing her feelings. Her first two-and-a-half months at Clinton Farms are an exception. During this period she not only kept track of all her appointments, professional and personal, but she revealed with intensity her feelings about them.

At her first meeting with the Board of Managers in early September 1928, she writes "*Board*—One hell of a day—Sat on for opposing money reward for return of escapes. No success on idea of moving colored babies. Long drawn out meeting until 5:30." A few days later, "Budget Hearing (in Trenton). Trying day. Felt distinctly annoyed & discouraged at Mrs. C's [Coggeshall] attitude. [Commissioner] Ellis was fine. On way home (& last nite late) decided to go on record, definitely at next Bd. re things that must be changed in order to stay." She evidently conveyed her frustrations to her friends in Boston, because Eleanor Glueck writes in a letter to Mahan 7 October 1928, "If you stay at Clinton Farms, let us know how the Board Meeting comes out."

Her only comments on the board meeting of 9 October are "Board—disgusted—more than ever. Told J. C. [board member Juliana Conover] supt. not needed here."

"Hell, just hell!" is what Edna Mahan wrote in large letters across her diary pages for 25 and 26 November. On 25 November is the notation "7 [runaways] from Stowe" and on 26 November, "JH & I brought 'em back from Flemington jail." Other notations include: "Tired and disgusted. Not a real Sunday and no rest so far this week."

These diary notations during her first few months at Clinton Farms not only display her frustration with the Board of Managers, they also reflect the disarray at the institution that Potter outlined in the June board minutes and had started to address. Many of these matters dealt with staff: asking for resignations and hiring new people. The medical care, provided by a local physician, was poor. The babies were neglected. Many talks were held with matrons and inmates and in meetings at cottages trying to get the student government effectively operational again.

There are recurring references to Coggeshall: "Such blind interferences—they assume the proportions of mountains." At the same time Juliana Conover, vice-president of the board, spent much time at Clinton with Mahan, had her for supper often at her home in Princeton, and was tremendously supportive. In early October a notation, "J. C. for nite—up late—talking to J. C. Great comfort. She said she could say things to me & they would go no further—re Mrs. C. etc."

Commissioner Ellis backed her all along the way. In late September Mahan notes in her diary, "To Trenton. Saw Ellis. He does not think I did wrong re R.H. [nurse, not an R.N., Mahan had let go]. Said he would have to talk to Mrs. C. Told me several times not to be discouraged. Was quite frank in saying she could not do such a thing & that at least 3 of the Bd. members would resent her action."

Mahan communicated her problems to Van Waters and looked forward to letters, calls, and visits from her. Van Waters' letters came often. Some were short and supportive. A few were detailed in their advice to her. On 28 August 1928 Miriam wrote a long letter of support and very detailed advice:

> I like to have you write me—just as is—with all the stark realities and questions that are uppermost. To me, at least, there is a free outlet and you can let the sluices run over the dam.... Like God at the end of the Seventh Day you look at your world. The Devil has been busy too.
>
> Commissioner Ellis is your best bet.
>
> Advice is no good, but I think I would tackle the Board first. Explain to Ellis an institution is a business as well as a piece of social work. It can be run only by an executive responsible to a *whole* board. No individual board member should ask you questions, or ask inmates or staff questions. They must act as a unit, holding you responsible for your reports and receiving them only as a body—never as individuals.
>
> ...I am convinced of one thing—from the start—you should be clear, explicit and definite in your criticism of what exists. Later will be too late. If you muddle

> along enduring this and that, they get used to you and even say, you accepted every thing without complaint, why complain now?
>
> Executive function etc:
>
> 1 head—no psychologists interfering with the actual running of the place. Let her make her recommendation to you.
>
> The handling of women by women, or if a man in uniform must take fingerprints, let it be in your office or hospital with trained nurse present.
>
> Dear Heart—you must not worry about your youth or you will lose it! The staff, of course will be prejudiced against any new person, but what they respect...is training and being on the job. It isn't your business to make them like you. They will fear you a little. Waste no energy on thinking about *how* you effect them.... Grumbling and going as far as they dare is the policy of all institutional employees. Don't argue, don't explain too much—just give your policy, your orders. Take your matron meetings...with all the ease and verve in the world.... Soon they get used to the fact that you are accurate, and clear, and sharp on the details—also quick on the trigger.
>
> Your Board will toe in as soon as you make them—when they are all together. Explain that it is not fair to other individuals to have anyone act without the rest.
>
> Get some fun out of it if you can. Of course Clinton was in *need* or you wouldn't be there.
>
> I am glad Frank showed sympathy and friendship. That ought to help. He would be a queer sort if he didn't. Gradually you will feel easier about it all. You have been a brick....
>
> Someday you will come back here [California]. You will, I believe, win freedom first—for the good of your soul—in creating a worth while institution for people to live in. You are the kind that must express—through a hard job—the vital energy in you. After that is achieved, I feel that personal happiness will come to you....
>
> As for now—put on a little rouge, hold up your head, wear your best frock every day, smoke a little in the dark, and remember—I love you.
>
> Yours eternally, Miriam.

Van Waters mentions "the handling of women by women." Edna felt as strongly as Miriam did about this. Throughout her career there are references in letters, staff meetings, and talks to outside groups of the need for women's institutions to be administered and staffed by women.

Van Waters inquires about things at Clinton Farms in a newsy letter dated 2 November 1928 and goes on to mention a conversation she had with Felix Frankfurter. "Felix talked of you quite at length. He thinks you are the salt of the younger generation going into this sort of thing, and talks as if he had something to do with it. 'Some job!' he says!"

Van Waters came to visit in early October and brought her parents with her. She wrote a friend that under Edna Mahan the spirit at Clinton Farms was free and happy because the inmates there have more freedom than the inmates at El Retiro.

During this period her diary notes reflect her lonesomeness for friends left behind in Cambridge, her joy when she heard from them or they came to visit, and her comfort in the new friends she was making at Clinton Farms. There were other friends she spent a day with in New York or they came to Clinton for the weekend. A Sunday in mid-October: "With Marie over hills & talk. To N.Y. with her. Supper Marta's, met her sister. Home late." Through her years as superintendent, her friends were a great support for her. She lived alone most of those years and developed many friendships. However, she never allowed herself to become too close or dependent on any of her friends.

She spent the first week in December back in Boston finishing up some work there and seeing friends. The diary pages for that week are full of professional appointments during the day, lunch, tea, and supper with various friends followed by bridge or a night out dancing. She apparently took the Owl, midnight train, from Boston to New York on Sunday, 9 December. Her last notations for that day, "To S.G.'s [Sheldon and Eleanor Glueck's] for tea with Frank [Loveland]. Back to see M.V.W. Frank to work on statistics. Came at 9. To tell Nanny goodbye. Back for things and to the train. *The end*." There is a finality to the Boston phase of her life in this and a settling into her life and career at Clinton Farms.

Frank Loveland

When Edna Mahan returned to Clinton from Boston the second week of December, she had the board and other matters at the institution well enough in hand to commit herself to remaining there. Although she had left Boston behind and settled in at Clinton Farms, it was not the end of her relationship with Frank Loveland. In her first frustrating months at Clinton Farms, she kept in touch with Frank by letter, phone, or wire. Her diary notes reflect her longing to see him or at least hear from him, her sadness when she did not hear from him, her joy when she did, and her reflections on his reluctance to commit himself in any way. On 9 October: "Wish I would hear from Frank—but I can't write!" Two days later she writes, "Such a glorious day! The reason—Frank rang up before 8!" On 23 October: "Disappointed again—no letter. It just seems as if—everything together—that there is no use. How I would hate to back out tho!"

She heard from Frank only once between her return from Boston and Christmas—a letter came on 15 December. She had returned to Clinton Farms with a bad cold, which kept her in bed for several days, and then she was caught up in preparations for her first Christmas at Clinton Farms.

Edna Mahan loved Christmas and the activities of the season. Christmas pageants as a yearly event were first held at Clinton Farms in 1928 and continued after her death in 1968. Board members brought presents for all the inmates and babies, and local groups brought additional presents, particularly for the babies and children. The January 1929 board minutes note, "On Christmas morning after breakfast, Christmas gifts were distributed by one of the teachers, dressed as Santa Claus, and Miss Mahan who went from one cottage to another."

A friend from New York came out to stay with her, and another friend from New Jersey joined them. They went to chapel and ate Christmas dinner with the staff. It was surely not her easiest or happiest Christmas at Clinton Farms, but it set the pattern for all her Christmases that followed. She always spent Christmas at the institution and usually visited each cottage.

On 26 December she notes in her diary that she worked in the office all day, her friend having left early to return to New York. At the bottom of the page she writes, "Blue." This is because she has not heard from Frank for over a week. On 27 December she notes in her diary, as she did the day before, she is blue, and this time adds, "No word from Frank." He wired her the morning of 29 December, "re coming here" and phoned that evening to confirm his time of arrival in New York on 30 December. She went into New York to meet him, and they returned to Clinton Farms for dinner, chapel, and an evening talk in front of the fire.

The next day, New Year's Eve, she showed him around Clinton Farms, and then the men's reformatory at Rahway and to Princeton for lunch. They were back in New York at 6:00 p.m. "Had choc malts in Grand Central & Frank bought me pecans & sent me home. He went to his parents. Depressed on the way home." At the bottom of the diary page she notes, "He brought me a lovely desk pen set."

She starts her 1929 diary on Harvard Law School stationery. On 1 January: "Wrote to Frank after others went to bed to thank him for my pen. It is a lovely thing. I shouldn't have written what I did but that doesn't matter." The next day she came home from work and read an old friend's Christmas card, "She is married—and she believes her husband—after two months close observation—will always interest her. Lucky girl! (I dreamt all nite of F)."

Edna doesn't hear anything from Frank until 22 January. "Letter from Frank. I feel better—but I am still unable to understand. His delay makes me feel that he is trying to make me realize that it is useless for me to care. He thinks I should know it w/o his making it any plainer." Her last diary notation until 1 January 1932 is on 3 February 1929: "Haven't written F. and of course he won't write until I do."

Letters from Miriam to Edna between 1929 and 1931 shed some further light on the end of the relationship with Frank. On 6 March 1929, Miriam writes at the end of a letter, "I know how grievous it is for you to carry the load (in re F.). All I can say is I know, and I love you." Frank is not mentioned again in letters until Miriam writes 7 February 1931 from Baltimore, where she is staying and Edna is planning on joining her for a weekend. Miriam comments in the letter, "I am glad you are to see Frank."

Van Waters writes a letter a week later, which does not mention Frank's name but is forthright in its statement of love and support for Edna at the end of her romantic relationship with Frank.

> Edna—Dearest—
>
> Just a word to greet you at Clinton and to bring my love....
>
> In clearing out my desk—for the day—I came across the little envelope with your temporary address—and tore it all to shreds—as my contribution to an ending. Of course, ends are not important or final unless we consent. Somehow I feel you *have* consented. An old person's advice is never sound—(I am old only in the sense I may have experienced more defeat)—but in any case, avoid the sense of futility or regret, my darling.
>
> Be like our Orfa. In her heart she never says—I don't give a damn—but she has something better—a healthy simple acceptance of life as it is.
>
> Life is alright too. Your experience is pretty tough—but it is realism, and I am sure—a step toward growth. Perhaps—the very most needed thing to make you ready for more mature and satisfying living. Don't be impatient....
>
> It is a blessing to me that I raised you—Darling—and go on making Clinton a happy place.
>
> So very much love to you—
> Miriam

There is no indication in the letter what brought about the end of the relationship. They had known each other for four years, and their admiration for each other was great. Only two months later another man comes into Mahan's life, and he lives in New Jersey. Perhaps Edna met with Frank to tell him she was seeing someone else. Miriam's letter suggests Edna was hoping for some commitment from Frank, but he was hesitant to commit himself at this point in his life and his career.

In 1930 Frank Loveland began his career with the U.S. Bureau of Prisons. At this time, women who married were expected to follow their husbands in their careers and to make a home for them and their children. A woman who chose a career was not expected to marry. Frank Loveland had a great deal of admiration and respect for Edna Mahan. He saw the importance of her career to her and to the correctional field. His career path did not lie in New Jersey, and he wanted a traditional marriage and family.

Their friendship continued until she died, and at her funeral he told one of her friends he had always loved her. Mahan married and divorced twice and remained at Clinton Farms.

Accomplishments 1928–1930

Edna Mahan clearly established herself as an able administrator during her first year at Clinton Farms. She took over an institution that badly needed firm and enlightened leadership without the "blind interferences" of board members. She needed support from the board and from Commissioner Ellis. At twenty-eight she was the youngest female superintendent in the country. She had good experience in California and with the Harvard Law School study, and she came with the strong support of Miriam Van Waters. Although she fretted terribly through her first two-and-a-half months, she worked to educate the board and, with them and the backing of Commissioner Ellis, set the tone at Clinton Farms for the next forty years.

Mahan's philosophy for working with female offenders was based on the belief in human dignity, in trust, and in the worth of all individuals, and that change can most easily be effected in an open atmosphere. The founders of Clinton Farms held these same beliefs, but were more restrictive than Mahan felt was necessary. When she arrived at the reformatory in 1928 there was so much to be done, she could not address everything at once. During 1929, her first full year as superintendent, her accomplishments were manifold.

"Colored" Babies

One of the things that bothered Edna Mahan most when she arrived at Clinton Farms was the arrangements for the "colored" babies. They slept on a leaking porch at Stowe, the cottage for "colored" inmates, and were largely ignored by the local physician who was supposed to attend them. At her first board meeting in September 1928 she proposed moving them to the Wittpenn nursery where the white babies were cared for, but she was turned down.

At this time society was strongly against racial integration. In women's reformatories it was felt that "unhealthy" relationships developed between black and white inmates. Because of this in May 1926 the Board of Managers affirmed at its board meeting "that as complete segregation as possible of the white and 'colored' was the correct attitude and that policy should be continued at Clinton Farms." It is not surprising the board turned Mahan down on moving the babies. But she was concerned with the inadequate care of the babies, not their race or the fear of unhealthy relationships.

By the October board meeting, Mahan suggested moving the "colored" babies from the porch at Stowe to the unused section of Wittpenn as a solution to the crowding at Stowe. She was empowered by the board to do this, and on 12 November 1928 the babies were moved. A registered nurse had been hired for Wittpenn, and the "colored" mothers took turns taking care of the babies during the day and sleeping with them at night.

The intensity of community feeling against this integration was expressed three-and-a-half years later, 5 May 1931, by members of the Maplewood Women's Club who came to visit the institution. Some of them spoke to the nurse in charge, in the hearing of the mothers, saying the "colored" babies should be removed. This was very upsetting to the mothers.

Mahan reported to the board that when the visitors met with her at the end of their tour she called the psychologist, Elizabeth Connors, in because the women were strong in their criticism of the institution. According to the May board minutes, "They feel our point of view is entirely wrong; that punishment is the only basis for the treatment of offenders and that we should be called to account for permitting murderers to associate with innocent young girls!" These women must have felt uneasy walking around a reformatory where there was so much freedom and lack of restraints.

"You Can Build Restraints in People Rather Than in the Physical Plant"

Most of the reformatories for women built at the beginning of the twentieth century locked cottage doors and had bars or grates on most of the windows. Some, but not all, had walls or fences surrounding them. Grates were put on the windows of Fielder Cottage at Clinton Farms when it first opened. Subsequent cottages that were built had window grating except Wittpenn, which was the maternity and nursery cottage.

There was a lack of consensus among female superintendents as to how safe it was to put girls and women in rooms with unguarded windows and unlocked doors. Even those who favored the open institution were not able to realize it, because the men who ran the prison systems did not allow it. Mahan, however, felt strongly "that physical barriers to a normal atmosphere frustrate the emotional adjustment necessary for rehabilitation" (Mahan 1950).

In 1928 when she started at Clinton Farms, Conover cottage was in the process of being built, and Mahan recommended to the board that no bars be put on the windows. The board approved this at its 9 October 1928 meeting. Within the year she ordered the bars taken off all the cottages. The Clinton community was alarmed when she had the bars removed, and her staff predicted there would be mass runaways. This did not happen. She had the support of her board and Commissioner Ellis.

Runaways

Although there were no mass runaways, individuals did continue to escape. Mahan's attitude toward punishment for those who were returned again illustrates her belief in human dignity and the worth of all individuals.

When she came to Clinton Farms, she found some punishments used to discourage runaways degrading. These included cutting the hair of returned runaways very short and dressing them in garments covered with red patches. These she abolished with little resistance from the board. She was not immediately successful in abolishing reward money paid for returning women who escaped.

At the 11 September 1928 board meeting the practice of paying a reward to anyone apprehending and returning escapes was discussed.

> Letters were read from Rahway and Annandale as to amounts and manner in which rewards were paid for apprehension of escapes—Rahway pays $50.00 for a returned escape and Annandale pays $25.00. The Board decided to continue the practice of paying the $25.00 reward for the apprehension of an inmate as heretofore. The Superintendent stated she did not approve of the practice as she does not like to encourage the attitude of a price on one's head. The Board members preferred to carry out the precedent.

There is no further mention of this issue until the board minutes of 8 January 1929 report on a communication from Commissioner Ellis to Mahan:

> In regard to rewards paid for the return of escaped inmates
>
> At a recent meeting of the State Board of Control the Board discussed the question of the payment of rewards by the institutions for the return of escaped inmates, and the Board passed the following resolution which I am sending to you for your information:
>
> RESOLVED, that it is contrary to the policy of the State Board of Control to pay a reward for the recapture of an escape from an institution, and
>
> BE IT FURTHER RESOLVED, that a copy of this resolution be sent to the President of the Board of Managers of each institution and to the Chief Executive Officer.

Undoubtedly Miriam Van Waters, Geraldine Thompson (who was a member of the State Board of Control), and Commissioner Ellis all had a hand in helping Edna Mahan bring this about. In early October 1928, Van Waters visited Thompson, and they visited Clinton Farms for the day. This issue was surely a topic they discussed. Thompson would be at her best teaming up with the commissioner, and probably Caroline Wittpenn, too, to get the State Board of Control to pass this resolution. This way Mahan's disapproval of the practice was filtered beyond Clinton Farms to all the other state institutions.

Staff Changes

In June 1928 when Dr. Potter took over as acting superintendent of Clinton Farms, she detailed for the board "the acute problem of dealing with the staff due to lack of morale, and the fact that lines of authority throughout the institution were all mixed up." At the July board meeting Potter stated:

> The morale of the staff is not as good as could be desired. There is all together too much bickering and attitudes are critical rather than cooperative and constructive. One gets the impression that there are more people interested in "getting something" on somebody else than in helping fellow officers to make good. There are, of course, conspicuous exceptions to this small town attitude.

Mahan had to make immediate staff changes when she arrived, and she worked with the Board of Managers during her first years to raise the calibre of the staff. The first position she addressed was the assistant superintendent. Mary B. Fitts was apparently critical and uncooperative, as Potter wrote a postscript on a 22 June 1928 letter to Mahan, "I have not yet come down to brass tacks with Miss Fitts." By the September board meeting, however, Mahan presented Fitts' resignation to the board. She left 13 September. She was not replaced until July 1929, when Elizabeth B. MacKenzie, assistant superintendent at the New Jersey State Home for Girls and a former employee of Van Waters', was transferred to Clinton.

There were many staff hirings, firings, and problems reported each month in the board minutes. To reduce the problems, regular meetings of cottage staff were held. Not only did Mahan need to retain and encourage those who were competent, qualified, and loyal, she needed to find new staff who could be counted on. She also looked for new positions that would enable the work of the institution to be carried out more effectively and efficiently.

Two important new positions added in early 1930 were a full-time resident physician and a full-time resident psychologist. The need for a resident physician became crucial because the supervising nurse at the hospital was delivering many of the babies because the attending local physician often could not be reached. The search for a resident physician began in September 1929, and Dr. Hannah J. Beatty from Los Angeles, recommended by Van Waters, came on duty 1 February 1930. She remained at Clinton Farms until 1953, when she was retired because of illness.

Clinton Farms was served by a part-time psychologist from the Bureau of Mental Hygiene in Trenton beginning in 1920. The psychological work that was done was mainly diagnostic. Mahan recognized the need for a full-time resident psychologist who would do the diagnostic testing and also counsel inmates, advise staff, confer with judges, and collaborate on research projects. Elizabeth P. Connors, who had been coming to Clinton from Trenton on a half-time basis, was assigned full-time in January 1930. She remained at the institution until she retired in 1955.

Beatty and Connors were women with high qualifications in their fields who never married. They were highly competent in their work and held the same human values as Mahan. They added stability to the staff and provided great support for the young superintendent.

In 1929, Commissioner Ellis wrote Mahan for information concerning the history and development of the institution from 1922 to 1929. In answer to the question of "[a]dditions to personnel and raising of personnel standards" she wrote:

> There have been no radical changes in personnel requirements but persistent effort is being made to raise the general level of the background and training of the institutional workers.... It is hoped we will not have to depend upon employment agencies for obtaining institutional workers. If contacts can be made with some university or school of social work we could probably attract people better equipped for this type of work than those referred by the ordinary agency.

Throughout her years as superintendent, Mahan worked hard to raise salaries and improve working conditions for staff. Once employed, she kept an open door for them and supported and mentored them. She wanted to develop and hold good staff. Those who did not work out were asked to resign if they did not leave of their own accord.

Transfer of Women from Trenton State Prison

The act of 1910 that established the women's reformatory called for the transfer from the state prison of female inmates. A few inmates were transferred before Edna Mahan's superintendency. Although the prison was anxious to get rid of the women and the commissioner and state Board of Control urged the moving of the women, the Clinton superintendents were unwilling to take them until they had a secure place to house them.

In October 1929 the Board of Managers went on record as approving the transfer of thirty-two women from the state prison to Clinton Farms. Mahan brought these women up from Trenton herself two or three at a time whenever she returned from business at the central office.

The prison officials wanted to assign an officer to accompany her, which she spurned. One time when she had a couple of inmates the prison authorities thought were quite dangerous, the warden insisted on sending an escort. She set out followed by her escort. She sneaked down a side street, eluded him, and came to Clinton on back roads arriving before the escort. The inmates thought it was great. The escort arrived swearing. Mahan told him it was his fault if he couldn't keep up with her.

On another occasion when Mahan arrived at Clinton with an inmate who had been in the prison for several years, she dropped the woman in front of the cottage to which she was assigned and told her to go in alone and tell them who she was, they were expecting her. The woman sat back in disbelief that she was to be trusted to this extent after spending time behind bars in prison.

The transfer of the prison women was completed 27 December 1929, and the women adjusted well. E. P. Earle, president of the state Board of Control, wrote Jane Coggeshall 1 February 1930 expressing the Board of Control's appreciation and commending the board and staff "for the cooperative spirit manifested and the efficient manner in which this was met, and I want to particularly commend Miss Mahan for her part in the transfer."

Many other things were accomplished in the first two years of her superintendency. In response to a request made 19 July 1929 by Commissioner Ellis for developments at Clinton Farms, Mahan wrote:

> The disciplinary units in the various cottages which were formerly used as the principle form of discipline, are now being used only for the segregation of returned runaways....
>
> Thru the cooperation of the Central Department and the Trenton State Hospital we are now receiving routine psychiatric examinations. Formerly only cases requiring special attention were referred to the psychiatrist. Also through the cooperation of the Central Office and the Trenton State Hospital we are now receiving the services of an Ophthalmologist as a routine matter. Formerly women requiring eye examinations or treatment were transported from the institution to an Ophthalmologist in Plainfield, N.J.

The changes brought about in the institution in Mahan's first year were most appreciated by the women residents, who wrote her a letter on her first anniversary, 14 August 1929:

> Dear Miss Mahan:
>
> A year ago today the older girls in the institution attended a reception to greet you as their new superintendent. Those same girls review today the many changes and new privileges granted during the past year and they feel a deep appreciation that you have been with them, and take this opportunity to thank you for your personal interest in their welfare and to congratulate you on your success during your first year at Clinton Farms.
>
> To show that they are sincere in this appreciation, the older girls and Student Officers of the Farms hereby pledge you their loyal support by conducting them-

> selves in such a manner during the rest of their terms here, that all new girls will be so impressed that when they take the places vacated by the older girls, they, too, will be loyal supporters of all the ideals which you cherish for Clinton Farms and the girls who are committed here in your care.
>
> Sincerely,
> Older Girls and Student Officers

Commissioner Ellis expressed his own high praise of her to Helen M. Wilde from the Parole Division in Trenton, who wrote to Mahan 21 January 1929:

> Dear Edna,
>
> Your message has been delivered personally to the nicest Big Boss [Commissioner Ellis] in the state. He appeared very appreciative etc. and with a vast smile, chuckled—"She's some girl and some supt.—there's none better." Your stock is certainly away up. You'll undoubtedly have a friend in court in any emergency. It must be a relief for the Big Boss not to have to worry about your health resort any more—
>
> Helen

With her "girls" behind her, Ellis's backing, and the effective use of her Board of Managers, Mahan began what was to become a forty-year career of courageous and enlightened leadership at Clinton Farms and in the wider correctional community.

Chapter 5

Student Government

The concept of student government figures prominently in any discussion of Edna Mahan and Clinton Farms for three reasons: (1) it formed the core of the program at Clinton Farms for more than sixty years, (2) Mahan used it successfully and carried it further than any other administrator on the adult level, and (3) it has been a controversial subject in the correctional field.

Experiments in the self-government of inmates have been conducted for over 160 years. Self-government in correctional institutions refers to inmate governance of the institution to some degree. How it is structured and the amount of responsibility given to inmates varies.

Student government was used with juveniles as early as 1824 at the New York House of Refuge and in 1828 at the Boston House of Reformation. "They developed crude but real systems of promotion and self-government among their little charges. The children were promoted to the highest grades through their good behavior and were permitted to hold office and vote" (Barnes & Teeters 1951).

Self-government was introduced among adult offenders at Auburn Prison in New York in 1913 by Thomas Mott Osborne. In 1914 Osborne was named warden at Sing Sing prison, where he introduced the Mutual Welfare League, a self-government system:

> The prisoners were allowed to elect a congress of delegates that became the institution's prisoner government. Osborne routinely delegated prison policy decisions to this prisoner council. Most disciplinary infractions were handled by a prisoner court rather than by the administration. (Bowker 1982)

In 1916, political interference stopped this self-government system. Osborne's strong and persuasive personality played an important part in his success in establishing self-government. It also made him a very controversial figure, and this hindered him in some of his pursuits (Tannenbaum 1930).

One other experiment in self-government deserving mention was instituted in Massachusetts at the Norfolk Penal Colony by Howard B. Gill, superintendent from 1928 to 1934:

> ...various committees were inaugurated, each dealing with some phase of life close to the inmates and each representing the inmates and administration. Committees dealt with maintenance, education and library, entertainment, sports, food, prison publication, store, avocational, and the like. Joint responsibility was the keynote of the Norfolk plan. (Barnes & Teeters 1951)

Although Gill's progressive ideas were put into action successfully at Norfolk and permeated beyond Norfolk, his methods were criticized, and he was eventually forced out. Like Osborne, Gill's leadership and personality were important in the development of the Norfolk Colony.

Student Government at Clinton Farms

Student government was put into operation in the early days at the New Jersey Reformatory for Women. In a 1963 interview, May Caughey, the first superintendent of Clinton Farms, and Eleanor Little, the first psychologist, emphasized that when the reformatory opened there were no rules. Rules were added as the inmates made them necessary. The idea of student government came to Clinton Farms from Sleighton Farms with Caughey.

However, Caughey said it was the inmates themselves who first initiated the idea. It started in the dining room. Some of the inmates who were used to good table manners were upset at having to sit at a table with those who used poor manners. Those inmates exhibiting good manners put together a set of rules for good behavior and posted them without Caughey's knowledge. This was accepted by the other inmates, and it sowed the first seed of student government.

Although a student government honor system had been planned for the reformatory from the beginning, the extent to which it developed was not planned but was forced on the administration due to inadequate facilities and staff. The 1915 annual report describes the situation:

> We have always believed in honor methods in running a reformatory but we never thought to be able to safely give the liberty and privileges which we have at Clinton Farms. This has been forced on us for several reasons. Our buildings, with the exception of Stowe Cottage, have dormitories. In both Fielder and Homestead we have only four rooms where we can lock a woman by herself. Then our farm work has made it necessary for us to divide our women into small groups and let them go freely from one building to another, simply under the

> general supervision of the Farm Manager, who can not be with every group at once. We also have no regular laundry, cooking or sewing teacher. Each officer who oversees these departments has also other work to do, so that one of the women is placed in control of each and is directly responsible for the work and behavior of the girls in her charge to the officer in charge of her department. All of this has forced honor methods on us to a large extent.

Many years later in the 1950s at a staff orientation Edna Mahan explained the reasons for the success of student government at women's institutions:

> Women's institutions in general have been more humane, more individualized and more successful than prisons for men. In part this is due to the smaller size, but more important is the public's attitude toward women offenders and the women's attitude toward themselves. The press and the public are relatively unalarmed about the usual offenses women commit. Most women want to conform, they want to be respected, they want to fulfill their desires as homemakers. In prison, if they are treated with respect, they become self-respecting.

The philosophy behind a student government honor system is that reformation can take place more readily in an atmosphere of freedom and trust where individuals must assume responsibility for their own progress. Lack of bars and fences alone cannot change offenders. Lack of them, however, provides a feeling of respect and trust, which makes it easier for inmates to accept positive aspects of the reformative process.

Similarly, a self-government system per se will not change inmates. But a self-government system may help inmates develop a sense of responsibility for themselves and the community through its awards and privileges. Privileges included such things as being allowed to go unescorted on the reformatory grounds, movies, special parties and entertainment, and day parole. Not every inmate and not all staff functioned well under student government, and some expressed their dislike of it.

However, as the system was structured at Clinton Farms, it was not just staff who decided who received what privileges and when, it was also cottage-mates. These same cottage-mates were on hand to help and advise an inmate at any point during her stay at Clinton Farms. Mahan describes student government in her 1933-34 annual report:

> Student Government has always been a controlling factor in the organization of the institution. The women are given an opportunity to lead relatively normal lives, without undue restraint, in healthful surroundings. They are encouraged to assume responsibility, to develop initiative, to adopt better standards and to become self-supporting. An effort is made to have the institution life approximate

> normal community life. The wholesome relationship between staff and women and the women's participation in the affairs of the institution make it comparatively easy to maintain group morale.

The basic structure of student government at Clinton Farms throughout its years of existence consisted of the Student Officer Group, the Honor Group, the Probation Group, and the Demoted Group. In addition, each cottage had an improvement committee made up of the student officers in each cottage plus some elected members of the honor group.

Student officers were elected in each cottage by the Honor Group with cottage staff approval. The position of student officer required leadership and trust. Student officers helped cottage staff in many ways. At the same time they served as advisers to the rest of the cottage population. For the responsibilities they assumed, they were awarded a few extra privileges, such as staying up later than the other inmates. In some cases they were given a small remuneration.

An inmate who had been a resident of Clinton Farms for three months and maintained a good record was eligible for the Honor Group. Each cottage held honor meetings when the head cottage supervisor requested one of the superintendent. All inmates eligible for the Honor Group were considered at this time. Other honor inmates, student officers, and cottage officers spoke on behalf of the inmate or told her where she needed to improve. It was felt that this experience contributed to character formation in a reality-testing situation. If the inmate was judged ready for the responsibilities of the Honor Group, her cottage-mates elected her. She read and signed her honor pledge:

> I pledge my loyalty to Clinton Farms. I promise to be worthy of the honor and responsibility given to me by electing me to the Honor Group. I will perform my duties to the best of my ability. I will do all I can to uphold the ideals for which Student Government at Clinton Farms stands.

All new inmates were automatically members of the Probation Group, where they remained for at least three months unless they got into some kind of trouble and were demoted. The probation period provided a time for each inmate to get acquainted with Clinton Farms. At the same time it gave the institution a chance to know each inmate and to judge what might be expected of her. Inmate privileges during this period were limited. Inmates on probation had to be escorted by an honor inmate or student officer wherever they went.

Any inmate at Clinton Farms who was guilty of a serious offense was placed in the Demoted Group. Runaways or attempted runaways automatically earned this status as did anyone who precipitated a fight. The superintendent, assistant superintendent, or the classification committee made the final decision on demotions, usually after hearing recommendations of the cottage improvement committee.

There was no set length of time for an inmate to remain in demotion. The seriousness of the offense and the inmate's conduct determined this. Once in demotion, inmates had to work their way into probation status and perform satisfactorily to be elected to the Honor Group.

About You and Clinton Farms, a handbook written by inmates for new admissions in 1950 and revised in 1961, describes the cottage improvement committees:

> This committee,...acts as an advisory group in the settlement of difficulties arising between any members of the cottage group. The committee acts with the [cottage] officers when minor infractions of the cottage rules occur. Any penalties they invoke require the sanction of the superintendent. Appearing before such a group acts as a check-up not only on your conduct but also on your manners and language. This committee also interviews all new girls in the cottage to acquaint them with the cottage rules and to urge them to seek help and advice from committee members when they need it.

Workings of Student Government

Mahan's own writings best describe the way student government worked. In 1950 she wrote a paper, "To What Extent Can Open Institutions Take the Place of the Traditional Prison?" which was presented at the Twelfth International Penal and Penitentiary Congress in the Hague. She wrote:

> The institution has always had some form of student or cooperative government. The aim is to develop individual leadership and group responsibility. The women participate in the planning. As they become aware of the needs of others, they gain personal insight and a realization of the need for self discipline. At cottage meetings they have the opportunity to air their grievances. Girls' committees elected in each cottage meet frequently with cottage supervisors and are concerned about the general welfare of the cottage; the behavior of individuals; they plan recreational activities; they represent the public opinion of the cottage. The girls may suggest disciplinary action for individuals but they may not administer it. They are almost without exception more severe than the staff! The whole system operates on a cottage rather than an institutional level. This seems to be desirable and effective and develops more leadership ability than a general organization could do. (Mahan 1950)

Emphasis in this statement is on the constructive aspects of student government, those that attempt to avoid problems. Mahan always emphasized to cottage staff positive approaches, such as rewards to bring about conforming behavior, instead of disciplinary actions.

Student officers were crucial to the smooth functioning of student government in each cottage. Outside observers, as well as some cottage staff, questioned why inmates in each cottage elected them rather than cottage staff appointing them. Mahan pointed out that if student officers were chosen by staff, they were seen by their cottage mates as "trusties" to staff rather than representatives of the cottage-mates.

A weakness in this process occurred at times when a group of cottage-mates got together and elected a friend who would represent their interests against the interests of the cottage as a whole. Mahan and cottage staff cautioned inmates that the election of a student officer was not a popularity contest. When this happened the cottage was generally in for an unsettled period as the student officer assumed prerogatives for herself and her cottage "clique."

Strong and seasoned cottage staff could help the group weather the period until the next honor meeting when the honor group usually voted her out of office. There were times, however, when cottage-mates became so upset, staff asked Mahan to allow them to remove a student officer from the position and occasionally from the cottage. Although a cottage might be disrupted for a period of time, in the long run it was felt this process of electing student officers facilitated the aim "to develop individual leadership and group responsibility."

Discipline

From the opening of Clinton Farms through Edna Mahan's time, two basic methods were used to deal with discipline. The first was the loss of privileges through the student government system, and the second was restraint, mainly through locking inmates in rooms. Serious offenses were dealt with in both ways; less serious offenses were usually handled through loss of privileges only. While Mahan was superintendent, the institution did not have the position of "disciplinarian." The Board of Managers, the superintendent, the assistant superintendent, and the classification committee handled discipline cases.

In the early years of the institution, inmates were brought before the board for various kinds of trouble and the board's counsel and decision for punishment. By the time Mahan came to Clinton Farms the board was not usually directly involved in discipline except for policy changes regarding discipline.

In a 1944 article, "Reflections on Institutional Discipline," Mahan wrote the following about the philosophy of discipline on which Clinton Farms operated:

> Those who get shut up in institutions for breaking laws are disciplined not only to encourage good conduct while they are in, but to give them the habit of conforming with the hope that they will continue when they go out.
>
> If the discipline has to be imposed rigidly, the result is reluctant conformity. The only way discipline has any moral value or develops the character of the individual is in proportion to the desire you awake in him to discipline himself.
>
> The ideal situation is where enough of the group disapprove certain types of wrong doing and hold the others in check. Good behavior is made attractive as possible by reserving for the "honor" group the privileges that can be granted.
>
> The most effective means of discipline for misbehavior then becomes the withdrawal of these privileges. Usually only temporary deprivation of privileges is necessary. *Everybody deserves another chance.*

As incidents that demanded disciplinary action occurred, the superintendent or assistant superintendent called together classification committee members who were readily available to deal with the situations. In this way responsibility was taken off any one person.

Restraint as a method of discipline included locking inmates in a room and handcuffing. Handcuffs were used during the first fifteen years of the institution to deal with very troublesome cases. When Mahan was appointed superintendent she did away with this practice as she did away with bars on windows except the windows in discipline rooms. The superintendent, the assistant superintendent, the administrator on call at night, and the classification committee were the only staff who could order an inmate locked up. Runaways were, however, automatically locked in a room when they were returned.

In her 1950 paper, "To What Extent Can Open Institutions Take the Place of the Traditional Prison?" Mahan wrote:

> When there is no unusual crowding in the institution and when there are enough well trained cottage supervisors the escape problem is not serious.... The public does not usually become alarmed or demand that the institution's policies be changed or a wall built unless runaways are too frequent or a notorious offender escapes. The institutional authorities are just as concerned as the public about escapes and attempt to find out where the system is falling down. A few runaways may be healthy if they indicate that the program is not too repressive!

Staff and Student Government

Although the student government honor system had been the basic philosophy guiding the operation of Clinton Farms from the beginning and superintendents who followed May Caughey used it successfully, Cornelia Lounsbury, who became superintendent in 1924, had a difficult time working with student government. One of Mahan's big challenges when she succeeded Lounsbury in 1928 was to make the system fully operational again. The staff were crucial to this.

Mahan wrote, "Each staff member must teach and guide; each should try to be like a *wise* parent. Half the battle is won if the staff members have earned the reputation for fairness, honesty and truthfulness and are accepted as friends by the girls" (Mahan 1944). Cottage staff who were with the inmates more than any others were particularly important.

The cottage staff at Clinton Farms were, for the most part, local women. The reformatory was located in a rural county of New Jersey, and the town itself did not have public transportation available. Most of the women who worked there came from the county, had raised their families successfully, and wanted the income. Some were widows. In some cases, husbands and wives both worked at the institution and raised their families there.

One hundred years after "matrons" were urged to become positive role models to "effect positive changes in their charges" (Rafter 1990) cottage officers who were "mature," "well adjusted," and "wise parents" were the role models.

In handwritten notes for a speech on "reeducation for normal living," Mahan listed the following as qualifications for cottage staff: "understanding women, tolerant of human weaknesses and individual problems, good health and energy, sense of humor, to be objective, to have a philosophy of life, to know what is important & what not, emotionally well adjusted."

At a staff meeting 15 May 1945, Mahan spoke on "our responsibility as staff members":

> Let us never forget that we are LEADERS. In our dealings with one another and with the girls we must so conduct ourselves that they will wish to follow, imitate and respect us. We cannot demand respect; we get it only if we deserve it. Unless we are ourselves honest, truthful, sincere, industrious and loyal we can never develop these qualities in them. By example, we are preparing them for decent living here and now and later in their communities. The Founders of this institution bequeathed to us a humane and progressive philosophy. We are not here to judge and punish. Our duty is to guide and teach and by the kind of people we are to inspire them to want better standards than many of them have known before. If they leave here to remember us as good friends we can have no greater reward for our efforts.

Some staff members had difficulty working within the framework of the student government system, which offered so much flexibility. Often staff members requested a compilation of all the rules, so they would know exactly where they stood in all situations. They felt it was difficult to operate when they did not know exactly which punishment followed what behavior. Mahan recognized this, and she wrote in notes for a speech, "It is harder for staff with student government because you relinquish direct methods of restraint for indirect influences."

Some new staff never adjusted to student government and did not stay at the institution. Others who remained and fought the system were eventually forced to leave or did so on their own. Some never understood the real meaning and operation of student government. Over the years, however, the majority of staff worked successfully with the system.

Interpreting student government to the staff was a continuing task. Orientation for new staff was held periodically at the institution, and staff meetings, particularly for cottage staff, were held regularly. These formal means of interpreting student government to staff were reinforced on a personal level in contacts between Mahan and individual staff members. These personal contacts with Mahan, both reprimands and praise, were important to the staff's understanding and incorporation of her philosophy in their daily work with inmates.

Many of the staff noted, "She had a way of making one have confidence in oneself. You did what Edna Mahan asked you to do. You were not afraid because Miss Mahan instilled in you that you could do it. You didn't refuse her!"

A blind social worker recalled, "Edna Mahan had unbelievable trust. People related to that. She let me take the A.A. girls on a picnic to Tank Hill."

"Miss Mahan was a 'teacher' by example and by word. I felt she was easy to talk to and confide in. The interest, drive and energy that she devoted to Clinton Farms was contagious. She was compassionate, patient, fair and a wise individual. All of my experiences with Miss Mahan were learning experiences."

"When I was still fairly new at Clinton Farms, and young, and a little cocky, I did something or said something I shouldn't have at an honor meeting at Williamson. Afterward Edna Mahan pulled me into one of the offices and laid me out. Then she put her arms around me and gave me a hug and said, 'Now we're friends.' "

"Miss Mahan was very outgoing. She communicated well with young people—not just inmates, young staff."

The student government honor system required that effective staff-inmate relationships operate in an open manner. Mahan served as the role model and support to staff. Staff members who accepted this and operated within this framework day to day found their work easier.

Inmates and Student Government

In 1919 the inmates sent the board members "Christmas Greetings from Clinton Farms—The Reasons Why Clinton Farms Is a Success." One inmate wrote, "Because we like the potters clay are molded in stronger and finer forms. Also character has a greater chance to develop here." Another inmate stated her reasons:

> Because it has helped many girls to live good respectable lives. If the girls who are here had not been sent here, they could have been sent to prison where they would not have the privileges they do have here. It has helped me in many ways. The board members do everything in their power to make the girls as comfortable and happy as they can, and we girls thank them. Student government has also helped us girls.

The above represents only two of seventy-seven reasons sent to the board, and there were approximately ninety inmates in the institution at that time. Some of the inmates did not respond or their responses were not appropriate for the message.

There is no clearly defined indication of what inmates got out of student government. The official aims were directed toward giving each inmate a sense of responsibility for herself and the community in a setting that was as much like the outside as possible. This was assumed as enabling the reformation process to function at an optimum level.

Some inmates over the years did not like the student government honor system. In October 1931, Mahan evidently asked inmates how they felt about student government at Clinton Farms. One inmate who advocated abolishing it wrote:

> I do not believe in student government in penal or reform institutions. As a rule the class of people in them are not capable of understanding what student government means, and instead of being a help to those under them, they are domineering and inclined to have a big head. It also causes much hard feelings between inmates and many arguments. Every inmate is here for some crime, and, therefore, they should all be treated equally and all have the same rights and privileges. I think that student government should be abolished in Clinton Farms.

One inmate who had an extremely difficult time adjusting in the 1930s wrote to her mother, "I don't like it here. I'd rather be in the penitentiary." Mahan wrote of the same inmate two years later, "She wants me to know that she is not the only girl who would rather serve time in a jail or penitentiary."

On the positive side, an inmate indicated her support of student government in a statement to Mahan dated 16 October 1931:

> My dear Miss Mahan,
>
> I think student government as a whole is one of the most important factors in the life of any public institution. It places the institution on a co-operative base,

> and at the same time, restores responsibility as well as self respect to any individual connected with the same.
>
> It is the means by which 75% of the girls' interests are aroused to the fact that although misfortune has been the cause of placing them in a rather difficult position, that there are ways by which they can not only restore confidence in themselves as well as others but regain their self-respect. It also proves that with the desire to better themselves and help others at the same time, will lead them to better and finer things and will help them to return to their normal life with a different attitude in general as regards to life.
>
> The student government is run on a square and equal policy and it is up to the individual to make good.
>
> I think that in order to have a successful student government, that a white dress [student officer] should be given to those that have made good or rather tried hard, and they in turn should do all in their power to encourage the efforts of others in the same direction, and also do what they can to encourage the moral side as well as the mental side of the girls.

The inmate monthly newspaper, *Ad Lib*, which started publication in 1959, carried editorials commenting on the student government honor system. These were written by the editors, inmates who mainly conformed to the system, so their comments were not necessarily representative of the attitudes of the total population. The June 1961 issue contains an editorial "Are We Doing Too Much Time?" which relates the indeterminate sentence to the minimum security institution:

> Most of the inmates of Clinton Farms are serving indeterminate sentences which are also referred to as indefinite time.... A girl who comes here on an indeterminate sentence is told, "Your time is up to you. How well you utilize it is the deciding factor in the question of parole".... With the indeterminate sentence structure such as we have at Clinton, go the privileges of the minimum security institution. These include freedom to come and go alone to work assignments (after election to the Honor Group), and many enjoyable activities such as movies once a week, dances, ball games, outdoor recreation of various sorts, a swimming pool and many types of entertainment.
>
> In a maximum security institution...we would not have the many privileges we have now. Locked up and shut off from the outside world, many of us would come to resent the hardships of enforced imprisonment. We would sit counting the years, the months, the days, rather than filling our time with wholesome activity as we do now.
>
> The question, therefore, should not be: are we doing too much time? It should be: Are we using our time to better ourselves? Are we taking advantage of the opportunities afforded us by the minimum security arrangement?

One editorial for *Ad Lib* was written by a nonconformist member of the population while she was locked in Center Annex (the disciplinary wing). This inmate was typical of those who ran away, got into fights, cursed officers and other inmates, and generally was unable to adjust either inside or outside the institution. The editorial, "A Word to the Wise," written in May 1964, does not speak to the point of student government. It does tell of the help given her by the staff and of the justice of being sent to the Annex when conformity to behavioral expectations is not met. And it warns, "stay out of trouble so that you will not have to see the inside of Center Annex."

There is a recognition in these statements, limited as they are, that the atmosphere of freedom provided for an ease of serving time, which reduced the inmate's bitterness and resentment and allowed her to make more constructive use of her time in the institution.

Most important is the relationship of the student government honor system to the success of inmates when they leave the institution. As Commissioner Sanford Bates wrote, "After all the real test of our success is the behavior of the inmates after they leave the institution.... Our records indicate that a lesser number by far are recommitted by the courts to Clinton for new crimes than to any other of our institutions." Bates wrote this in a letter to a reporter of the *Newark Sunday Call*, 4 April 1946. He also notes in the letter "our records indicate that for the last ten years, from 1936 to 1945 included, only 10 women were recommitted by the court to Clinton for a new crime." In answer to "How does this compare with other institutions?" Bates replied, "It is a considerably better showing."

Knowledge of Inmates: "A Good Superintendent Knows Her Girls Intimately"

Experiments in self-government in men's institutions were initiated by reform wardens and were short-lived because political pressures forced them from their positions. At least two superintendents prior to Mahan used the system successfully at Clinton Farms and used the system when they moved to other institutions. The most notable was Mary B. Harris, who became the first superintendent of the first Federal Reformatory for Women at Alderson, West Virginia, in 1927. The leadership of these wardens and superintendents was vital to the initiation and successful operation of the student government system.

At the New Jersey Reformatory for Women the Board of Managers was always supportive of the student government system and would have fought any outside interference with it. The commitment, devotion, and skill of Edna Mahan's leadership made it possible for student government to operate successfully at Clinton Farms longer than at other adult institutions.

Her work with the staff was a necessary element of this success. Her firm, sensitive, and wise reaching out to her "girls" was her strongest attribute:

> A good superintendent knows her girls intimately. She does not make rules she cannot enforce; she remembers that prohibitions invite violations; she removes as many causes of friction between the girls and the staff as possible.... Try anything. After repeated failures with certain problem cases there may be something that will work. (Mahan 1944)

Among Mahan's papers were found very few letters written to her by inmates after they left Clinton Farms. There were surely many, but these were filed in the inmates' individual files. One letter among her papers was signed "Virginia" and was received by Mahan 2 July 1946:

> Dear Miss Mahan,
>
> I may never see you again, but through life I shall always remember you.
>
> If you recall, when I first came to the institution, I was lost, stubborn, stupid—yes, stupid. I thought my problem was the biggest in the world; my selfishness was right. I was self-satisfied....
>
> My interviews with you really started the change. At first they were for reprimanding, and when it was over, your words kept me thinking and learning.... In secret I tried to copy all the virtues you possess and in later years when I shall finally have accomplished them all, I still will be thanking just you.
>
> I want you to know and I really mean it, that my change of character is largely due to you. Not only I realize this. Many of your girls admire your understanding and your talent in correcting our faults. Those who haven't just didn't learn as yet and your patience with them will be rewarded.... Not all of us can half repay you for helping us to find the good in ourselves and bringing it out to form a profession, or a virtue, or any such blessing.
>
> In all my life I have never thought or would have believed anyone would take such humane interest in the less fortunate. There are many facts I would like to express that Clinton Farms has taught me to believe in, but all I can say is, I think you are a marvelous person, you really are.
>
> A heartful of "Thanks" is all I can give you, for you have everything, and a promise to keep growing, keep learning and succeeding....

Another inmate wrote in a letter to a friend in November 1944, "If it were not for Miss M. I don't know what would happen to me. When I am really discouraged like today I have to think of her and her understanding and concern of us girls. Then I know, nothing can hurt me."

Edna Mahan interviewed every inmate who came to Clinton Farms, usually on the day she arrived. After she returned from a vacation, even though the assistant superintendent had interviewed each new inmate, Mahan spent a Saturday or Sunday meeting the new admissions who had come while she was away.

She took a brief case history and always the inmate's story of the offense. She explained the inmate's sentence. She asked the inmate what her plans were for when she left Clinton Farms. And she wrote her own initial impressions of the inmate.

Almost without exception she saw every inmate who sent her a note requesting to speak with her. Cottage officers often called to talk about one of the inmates and request Mahan see the inmate.

Mahan saw inmates alone, with the cottage officer, with the assistant superintendent, or whatever was appropriate for the situation. Some of the meetings were brief; some lasted as long as two hours. She saw inmates during working hours, after working hours, and on Saturdays, Sundays, and holidays. She left folders and folders full of her handwritten notes of each interview.

A sampling of these notes provide insight into her work with inmates.

> [*Gloria W.* state inmate with long sentence] in to say definitely will not petition [Board of Pardons] now & may not in Spring. "Miss M (w. tears in eyes) do you think there's any chance for me down there?" *How I wish I could answer that!*
>
> [*Emma R.*] refused to go to work until she saw me. Nervous wreck @ not knowing date she is free (6/26). Thot I was adding time for destroying state property! (Wanted *Vogue* to buy an outfit for going out!) Wanted to go to library now to get one. (I had tried to get her one in town & couldn't.) Told her to go to work p.d.q.! (If she isn't possessed of the devil I don't know who is. She can think up more things to get upset about w/o reason than anyone I know!)
>
> [*Ruth M.*] We started out on mascara again unfortunately! Just can't bear to have people see her w/o etc. Disgusted: 1. no mail 2. behind in school work. Finally said *had* to get diploma—sister has one! My long talk re live only once—too many chances here—girls are cruel—see her weaknesses & try to make her make more of a fool of herself. Most people give you up as hopeless—we can't because I know you have it in you. No matter what a mess you made, you can still amount to something. "That's what I've been waiting to hear!" Very responsible—sort of inspired look came—when I phoned to see by chance did she have a letter—there was one—said she: "This is fate"—Let's think so & make this day a turning point. Shook on it!
>
> [*Eliza S.*] Just to tell her I was sorry re baby, to see how she is & to let her choose Wittpenn or Stowe. Prefers to stay where she is. O.K.

At a staff orientation meeting in the late fifties Mahan recalled a different kind of encounter with an inmate in her office:

> In my early days here we got a very disturbed girl from the State Home for Girls, and I had done something or hadn't done something she expected. She just walked over here, past the front desk and the switchboard operator, she walked into my office, stood there and looked at me and said: "God damn you any way!" Well, I was slightly surprised—I sat at my desk and I didn't ask where did she go, I didn't run out. I don't mean that I was so wise in those days, but I didn't know what to do, so I did nothing. Three days later she wrote a note and asked to see me, and she was so unhappy because I didn't take after her and do something drastic....
>
> All of this means that they have to find ways to show their defiance, and if you don't rise to the bait, I think you help them—to put it simply.

Edna Mahan always had an open-door policy for inmates and staff. This was crucial to the successful functioning of the institution because every correctional institution operates in an authoritarian setting. The open-door policy allowed for open lines of communication among all members of the Clinton Farms community. Those in authority were in a position to know all the critical things that occur.

Chester Barnard (1940) wrote in *Functions of the Executive*, "authority depends upon a cooperative personal attitude on the one hand, and the system of communication on the other." The student government honor system provided the conditions for this to operate at an optimal level. Mahan's humane, skillful, and wise leadership carried student government further than any other correctional administrator had.

Many references have been made attesting to the success of student government at Clinton Farms under Mahan's leadership. In 1929, Garrett and MacCormick wrote in *Handbook of American Prisons and Reformatories*:

> The Cooperative Government is the backbone of this institution. It is apparently an effective measure of control and gives a large amount of training in social responsibility to the women. One of its most interesting features is that the commissioners elected by each cottage to act as head girl of a cottage or department is subject to recall. The sincerity and wisdom with which the system is directed by the officials is one of the major reasons for its success. Its value as a constructive social force can hardly be overestimated.

The 1933 edition of the handbook states:

> As is found in most of the better institutions for women, the inmates to a very large degree participate in the planning and responsibility of institutional activities through their cooperative organization. Beyond doubt, this cooperation is responsible, together with the wise leadership of the superintendent, in keeping the reformatory free of traditional rules and regulations. In addition, it provides

> definite opportunity for the inmates to develop initiative and affords real training in preparing them for community life upon discharge. (Cox, Bixby & Root 1933)

In 1963 in the program for the fiftieth anniversary of Clinton Farms, Austin MacCormick, executive director of the Osborne Association wrote "In Appreciation" of Mahan:

> What Clinton Farms is today, the outstanding correctional institution for women in the United States, is largely what she has made it. Sensible, capable, warm-hearted, inspired and inspiring in an unassuming sort of way, she has extended a firm but gentle hand to many hundreds of women and given them not merely professional guidance but personal friendship.

For the forty years Edna Mahan served as superintendent of Clinton Farms it remained an open institution with a student government honor system. During most of these years crowding was severe. Except for her first few years at the institution, staffing was inadequate. In her last ten years the inmate population changed to a majority of younger inmates, many of whom were aggressive and assaultive. In addition there were a significant number of narcotic users committed.

Three commissioners, Ellis, Bates, and Tramburg, supported her philosophy and advised her in making adjustments at the institution to carry it on. In the final analysis, however, the longevity and success of the student government honor system at Clinton Farms was due to Mahan's belief in it and commitment to it as well as her leadership skills and personal charisma, which affected almost all who came in contact with her.

Chapter 6

The Thirties

In Edna Mahan's first decade at Clinton Farms, she set the stage for her career in penology both within the institution and in the wider correctional community. The minutes of the Board of Managers meetings for this decade reflect a bright, creative, and strong superintendent working with a dedicated board to keep faith with the founders in running an open and progressive institution. The minutes document her direction and involvement of the board, staff, and inmates in carrying out the aims of the founders, implementing progressive innovations, and educating the public. Commissioner Ellis was always behind her.

The thirties was the decade of the Depression, which affected all socioeconomic levels of society. Few families were left untouched by unemployment and lack of income. Family tensions heightened. Although there was an increase in crime among men, there was a decrease among women, at least in the early years of the Depression.

At Clinton Farms there was a slight increase in the population between 1930 and 1935, but a much larger increase between 1935 and 1940 when economic conditions improved and unemployment decreased. The Depression also meant at Clinton Farms the curtailment of building, letting go of staff, not filling vacant positions, and more reliance on inmate student officers and volunteers. Many recent college graduates worked for room and board until a salaried position opened up at the reformatory or elsewhere.

Marriage—"The Universal Desire. Stop, Look, Listen! Why Not?"

Although Mahan's professional life was increasingly successful during the thirties, and she was beginning to make a name for herself and Clinton Farms in the correctional world, her personal life was less serene, at least at the beginning of the decade.

By 1930 Edna Mahan was launched on what was becoming a successful career. Like most American women, however, she also desired marriage and a meaningful relationship with a husband as an emotional dimension to her life. Any prospect of marriage to Frank Loveland came to an end in February 1931.

There is no record as to when she met Richard Steinmetz. Indeed, very little is known about her relationship with Steinmetz. He was a psychologist who worked at the state prison at Trenton, so she may have known him from the time she moved to New Jersey. The first mention of him from Miriam Van Waters is in a letter dated 22 May 1931, "As to your lad, and your question—my comments await your more complete recital—they would be of two kinds professional and all-for-you."

Edna wrote her "more complete recital" in two letters to Van Waters, who was in Washington with the Wickersham Commission (a national commission on law observance and enforcement). Miriam answered 26 May 1931:

> Edna—Dear—
>
> Your two letters in one arrived a few moments ago.... Of course, Dear Heart, you are not "crazy"—and if the world has suddenly grown a happier radiant place—that is as it should be. I for one have expected this state of affairs with confidence for you and have often said so. I am *so glad*, Edna. If he is a nice person, you should marry him. How you will hate this—"if"!
>
> Don't you think your ghostly Mother (I suppose you don't go to church often enough to know what that is—but *I* am—your ghostly or spiritual mother) ought to look him over with cold appraising eyes? Well—I am coming up to do it sometime soon—10 days—2 weeks—or less.
>
> In the meantime, do use discipline. First, because of the need of cherishing and safeguarding what you have—in its own right and essence. Your saying that you do not wish to express enthusiasm for fear you will lose some of it—is sound sense—and has to go deep enough to include a kind of self mastery. If Nietzsche is right about thought—being a tightrope dancer—(to think effectively one does not labor and plod—or plunge)—it is doubly true of love. Let yourself—love—as much as you can—but remembering there is plenty of time—and love has to grow underground for considerable depth before it can flower. Keep yourself well in hand.... I wouldn't go wandering by the light of the moon till 3 A.M. anymore....
>
> Undoubtedly you are loved for yourself—which is a combination of all you are—and seem. So you have to go on being a good and wise and an authoritative superintendent—until you are carried off into matrimony. I thoroughly approve.
>
> Bless you. Take care of yourself....
>
> Love to you—Your Mother

There are no letters indicating Miriam ever went to New Jersey to meet Steinmetz before he and Edna were married sometime in June. They went to Nantucket and Cape Cod for a honeymoon. Miriam writes Edna 9 July 1931 saying she has received her note telling her she had a bad cold and she didn't like Nantucket or Cape Cod. She also writes, "It was dear of the Commissioner to tell your staff and give you such a fine send off. Nothing could have been nicer."

On 21 July Miriam answered a letter she had received from Edna that indicates that Edna has questions about the marriage. Miriam writes:

> Geraldine [Thompson] wrote most appreciatively of you, your appearance, poise, apparent "quiet enjoyment"—et cetera. So my precious child—no one knew you had lost your peace of mind. (Though I knew it.)
>
> Of course no one person, no man—can give you "all you need"—but that is not the point. By taking "life"—on terms of marriage which the community recognizes—and which gives you security and discipline(!)—you grow up—and that "all you need"—comes gradually—from work, from thinking, from books, beauty of nature, exercise, friendship, and the satisfaction of building a human relationship—which as far as possible "gives *him* all he needs—"

As a postscript Miriam adds, "I thought you were going to keep your 'precious name.' Shall I give up calling you EM?"

Miriam answered another of Edna's letters on 3 August. Edna must have written a letter of despair because Miriam assures Edna she "can go on." She inquires about Edna's health and asks if she shouldn't see a doctor. Miriam says she will be coming to Cambridge to finish up the Harvard Law School study and expects Mahan to come for two weeks in October to help her. Miriam's adopted daughter, Sarah, Edna Mahan's godchild, and Elizabeth Bode, another Californian taken on by Van Waters to take care of Sarah and help Van Waters, will be there.

Miriam then goes on to write:

> Have you read Marie Stopes *Married Love*? I did long ago when it was banned by the gov't. Now you can buy it everywhere. It is very good and sound and true.
>
> Do write me when you wish to—and how you wish to. Stone House [Van Waters' home in Los Angeles] outdoor fireplace blazes nightly with my mail, and I hate to tell you—often with pages and pages of the day's attempted manuscripts....
>
> Yes—Frank's letter hurts—yet he tried to write a nice unselfish sort of letter.
>
> Poor child: but don't imagine getting old settles anything: you have to do it now, partly by settling things, partly by letting things settle themselves.

> How absurd all advice is. My only advice to you is to remember—I love you—and probably understand—dumb as I am. Ever your Mother.

A letter from Miriam to her parents 17 September 1931 tells of Sarah Van Waters' and Bode's visit to Clinton Farms and Steinmetz's blow up:

> Miss Bode and Sarah had a nice time at Clinton Farms but saw enough to realize poor Edna is having a difficult time with her Richard. I only tell you because it is coming to a crisis. Geraldine [Thompson] says—she thinks it will not hurt her job—because he was told by the commissioner when he married—that Edna had obligations—first to her institution. She has lived up to everything; he has not. He stormed violently at the presence of one of Edna's board members who came to spend the night. Sarah heard it all.
>
> They packed up and left so hastily that Sarah arrived without a hat—and minus her two pairs of good shoes—no brush, comb or tooth brush. I presume Edna will send them. Edna spent the night at the home of the commissioner and his wife in Trenton. Richard had brought three guns into her institution—without her consent—from the prison!
>
> Mrs. Thompson is on the job—so I know Edna will keep her job—and—not be too miserable. They can't get a divorce in N.J. on "these grounds"—but I presume a separation is in order....(Schlesinger, Van Waters, File 62)

Edna Mahan told a friend years later she was very frightened of Steinmetz. Steinmetz was hospitalized for several months, possibly for mental problems. Van Waters writes 12 October "Perhaps soon you will have more definite news from the hospital—but the time is long for you...."

On 13 November Miriam inquires again about Steinmetz and offers her advice:

> Tell me the latest news from the hosp. in re—Richard?—and are you going to see him? I think of you—hour by hour. Always my slant is to go meet trouble far more than half way—and so my feeling is—you ought to go see him! But I may know nothing about it. My point is that realism is better than imagination. You could probably end a lot of fevered imagination in him if he saw you. He may think you are afraid to go: that would be bad for him.

Miriam writes and advises Edna again on 25 January 1932. "As to your own burden, all I can say is to work for your own peace and stability of mind. Try to free yourself from fear and anxiety by the practical method of realizing—nothing can touch you inside—that you do not welcome."

The above letter from Miriam may relate to issues around Edna's divorce, which she was able to obtain. Miriam Van Waters became superintendent at the Massachusetts Reformatory for Women in March 1932 and sent some of her staff to Mahan at Clinton Farms to learn about Clinton's program.

On 24 January 1933 Edna Mahan sailed from New York for a two-week Caribbean cruise aboard an Italian liner. Irving Berlin and his wife were also passengers. A diary she kept relates a good time sightseeing, shopping, playing bridge, and dancing with other passengers. She was unaccompanied on the cruise. She may have wanted to get away because her divorce was becoming final.

By 1934 there are indications of a special interest in Reading Gebhardt. Gebhardt's family had a long history in Clinton. His father served in the New Jersey state legislature, and his mother was appointed to the Clinton Board of Managers in 1926. His sister taught Sunday school there. Reading Gebhardt was a lawyer, a bachelor, and a gentleman. By this time Edna Mahan had many friends in the Clinton community and its environs, and Reading Gebhardt was one of the eligible young men. A mutual friend advised Edna Mahan to marry him.

They were married in 1935. He moved into Homestead, one of the original buildings on the Clinton Farms grounds, which had been remodeled in the 1920s as the superintendent's home. It would seem to be an ideal arrangement because they provided each other companionship and love while they pursued their separate careers.

Janet Ellis DeGrouchy, Commissioner Ellis's daughter, recalled her family spent considerable time with the Gebhardts. They often went to Clinton Farms as a family on Saturday. Her father and Mahan played tennis on the Homestead court. Mahan also played tennis with DeGrouchy. They all vacationed together at Mohonk in New York state. Janet remembers Edna and Reading as a loving couple.

Babies

Although Edna Mahan never had any children of her own (she had a hysterectomy soon after her marriage to Gebhardt), she devoted tireless efforts to establish the best care and training for inmate mothers and their babies while they were in the reformatory as well as to work out the best community plans possible for both mothers and children. Coordination with other state agencies, primarily the State Board of Children's Guardians and the Division of Parole, was essential.

The custodial care of inmate mothers and their babies has always been a distinguishing factor between men's and women's correctional institutions. Many of the early women's reformatories that opened at the beginning of the twentieth century included nurseries. However, there has always been a debate as to the proper placement and care of babies born to inmates, and it continues today as is illustrated by an article in the *New York Times*, 23 September 1990, "Maternal Bonds Behind Prison Bars; A debate renewed; Should infants join their mothers in jail?"

Serapio Zalba (1964) in *Women Prisoners and Their Families* highlights the questions that are raised when mothers are imprisoned:

> When separation results from the mother's incarceration because she has been judged guilty of committing a felony, the consequences for the children take on dramatic and troubling dimensions.... Aside from such considerations as who—if anyone—is available to keep the family together and/or provide the children with material and emotional care, there are special and particular elements to take into account. Are the moral and social attitudes of the extended family members and of the community towards a person who has committed a crime harsher with regard to the woman offender? What will be the nature and frequency of continuing contact, if any, between the imprisoned mother and her children—**will** there be, **can** there be, **should** there be visits to the prison, an exchange of letters or presents, consideration of the mother's wishes or ideas in planning with respect to the children? What rights does she retain as a parent? What stigma, if any, do the mother or father or children attach to her imprisonment, and what is the effect upon the present and future functioning of the children?

The first babies were born at Clinton Farms in 1916, and in 1917 Paddock Cottage was opened as a reception cottage and hospital, which included a nursery for the babies. In 1921 when Wittpenn Cottage was opened, it housed mothers, babies, and children up to two years of age and occasionally a little older. There is little reported in the board minutes about any special programs for the babies or the mothers during the first years Wittpenn was in existence. When Potter took over the institution in June 1928 she hired a woman to develop a program for the children. However, at Mahan's first board meeting, 11 September 1928, Mrs. Kremer, board member on the Educational Committee, "stated she had visited the nursery school and that the children were now being cared for by an adult and one who is supposed to have been trained. She said it seemed to her, however, that Mrs. Burgess was not doing more than an untrained person would do, which was principally to help to feed the children and to direct their play, and doubted whether it was wise to have such a person in this position. Miss Mahan was instructed to observe this part of the work and to make a report at the next meeting."

Mahan did not report on the nursery school until the minutes of the board meeting of 12 February 1929:

> The progress of the nursery school is encouraging. The children are being trained to eat properly, to play with blocks and balls, to share playthings, and to form other desirable habits. Since we have received the little correct posture chairs and the tables, the older children are sitting down at tables in groups of four using peg boards and stringing wooden beads.

> Baby Hygiene classes have begun with Miss Jessie Chalmers, District Supervisor, Bureau of Child Hygiene, Phillipsburg, in charge. Miss Chalmers' class is composed of about sixteen of our more intelligent girls who can profit by such training.

The baby hygiene classes under Chalmers continued through the 1930s. The course was ten weeks and was given twice a year. The 13 February 1934 board minutes report, "Each year this course becomes more popular."

National interest in issues concerning inmate mothers and their babies in Mahan's first years at Clinton Farms is illustrated by conferences held in June 1929 and July 1930 on the "Care of Infant Children of the Inmates of Correctional Institutions." The conferences were held under the auspices of the National Committee on Prisons and Prison Labor's Sub-Committee on the Care of Infant Children of the Inmates of Correctional Institutions, chaired by Potter. Mahan, Jane Coggeshall, and Caroline Wittpenn all took part in the conferences and the recommendations that came out of them. These recommendations and all the committee's work were referred to the 1930 White House Conference on Child Health and Protection (Potter 1930).

Concern over the nursery school program resulted in a nursery school conference as reported in the 9 February 1932 board minutes:

> A Nursery School conference was held in the afternoon of January 21st attended by Dr. Ray, Miss Connors, Dr. Beatty, the Nurses in charge of Wittpenn Cottage, Mrs. Owen, Nursery School Teacher, Miss Tibbot, Supervising Nurse, Miss Greenhalgh, Director of Education, and Miss Mahan. The conference was profitable to all concerned in that many matters were brought out and amicably adjusted.

Another important innovation concerning the babies started by Edna Mahan early in her career at Clinton Farms was infant classification. This included planning for the babies when they left Clinton Farms. Some of the babies would go with their mothers. Some were referred to the State Board of Children's Guardians (SBCG). The 13 January 1931 board minutes state:

> The first classification of infants was held at the institution on December 19th, 1930. Two representatives of the State Board of Children's Guardians were present in addition to the regular Classification Committee and Mrs. Lindeman of the Board of Managers. Thirty-one cases of babies were considered and of the thirty-one, twenty-two were recommended for commitment to the State Board of Children's Guardians.

SBCG was a group the institution had to interact with on a regular basis. The institution's primary concern for long-range planning was always the mothers. SBCG's was always the children. This often resulted in misunderstandings and tension between the two. Mahan and her board worked diligently to have SBCG workers come to the institution for infant classifications and to keep in touch with the mothers and the children they would be supervising in the community.

Babies born at Clinton Farms and the occasional baby who accompanied its mother when she was committed were allowed to remain in the Wittpenn nursery until they were two years old. If the mother was not able to be paroled by this time, plans were made to place the child in the community. The most desirable plan was usually placement with a relative. Often, however, foster home placement was necessary, and this was arranged by SBCG. Community plans also had to be worked out for the older children of mothers at the time of their commitment. Again, if foster placement was necessary, SBCG was in charge. Over the years there are many references in board minutes to matters pertaining to SBCG. A recurring problem was SBCG workers' perception that the mothers and other Clinton Farms inmates were bad influences on the children.

Tension and misunderstanding concerning the children's visits with their mothers is illustrated in Mahan's letter of 30 June 1938 to Joseph Alloway, director of SBCG:

> What kind of an institution do some of your supervisors think this is? Do they think it has the physical aspects and the philosophy of some of the old prisons of fact and fiction? My question is provoked by the following excerpts from letters written recently by two of your supervisors:
>
> "Have you any particular reason for wanting the two little ones to visit their mother?...If we do send them up I must ask you to have them visited somewhere near the gate as possible so that the children will see just as little of the institution and other girls as possible as we do not want them to get upset." (Mary T. Walker's letter of May 16th, 1938 regarding my request that Anna T's children be brought to visit her.)
>
> "If you feel the trip to be necessary it might be better to arrange the mother's interview with the children in some place where they will not come in contact with other Clinton Farms residents." (Mrs. Lipton's letter dated June 21, 1938 regarding Emily B's request that her children be brought to visit her before they have tonsillectomies.)
>
> This whole situation almost moves me to write a long article of protest. I shall spare you that and end this letter by saying to you that I hope that your department and mine can come to a reasonable and enlightened understanding of our mutual problems.

Alloway replied to Mahan on 13 July 1938 thanking her for bringing these matters to his attention, assuring her that he does not share the opinions expressed by the workers, and saying, "I am asking...the Director of Social Service to confer with you for the purpose of working out a plan of cooperation that will effect the most desirable results."

With such attitudes toward the mothers as poor influences on their children, SBCG workers focused their efforts on long-range planning for the children that did not take into account the mothers. Indeed, the mothers sometimes found out from other family members or friends about plans for the children that were never discussed with them. Mahan spent hours with inmates upset after a visitor informed them of plans for their children they knew nothing about. A great deal of this time was devoted to tracking down SBCG workers to get the correct information and urging them to discuss planning with the mother.

It is well-documented that most inmate mothers have multiple health, economic, family, mental health, and social problems. Many, however, provided excellent care, concern, and love for their children before their commitments. Almost without exception they all maintain an interest in their children and wish to be reconnected with them when they leave the institution, although their planning for their children may be unrealistic. If SBCG workers spent time helping the mothers with planning, the plans were apt to become more realistic, and the mother more assured of the well-being of her children. It was around these issues that much of Mahan's and the Clinton Farms board's concerns with SBCG centered.

Besides the babies, there were many matters in the running of Clinton Farms that needed to be addressed. During the Depression cutbacks in resources made the challenges greater. Educational offerings and work assignments had to be upgraded to provide more realistic preparation for the inmates when they left.

Work and Education Programs

The work programs at Clinton Farms when Edna Mahan arrived revolved around domestic service and the farm. Domestic service was the main work available for the inmates who needed it when they left the institution. Farm work, although it did not provide training for inmates who needed to support themselves and their children when they left Clinton, was extensive because the operating budget was so small, and it was cut during the Depression.

The institution was dependent on the farm for almost all its food. Besides the truck farming (growing vegetables) there was a dairy herd, a piggery, and chickens. A cannery was opened each summer and operated into the fall. There was always one board member knowledgeable of agricultural matters who oversaw the farm work, and the State Department of Agriculture lent its expertise.

Board minutes during the thirties report such things as "Clinton Farms high in milk production," "egg surplus," and "loss of pigs." Mahan was, of course, responsible for hiring the staff to operate the farm and to see that production was high. Judge Daniel H. Beekman, the board member who headed the farm committee throughout the Depression, was very conscientious and gave a great deal of time to overseeing the farm operations.

Other work programs listed in the 1931 annual report were for the maintenance of the institution and revolved around domestic service. They included cottage kitchens and dining rooms, an institutional sewing room, a laundry, and a hospital.

The first training that qualified as industrial was the State Use Department of Institutions and Agencies (SUDIA) sewing room, which opened in 1932. The inmates were trained in the use of power sewing equipment and could qualify for work in the garment industry.

A small beauty parlor was opened in 1931, and one of the regular officers who was a trained beautician taught classes. Although there was very little equipment, the board minutes of 10 March 1931 report, "There is already a great deal of interest aroused, and we hope to develop the work further when we get a small appropriation for necessary supplies."

Beautician training was expensive. Mahan and the board fought to keep it and upgrade it, not only for its vocational training, but because of its value in increasing the self-esteem of the inmates. The board minutes of 10 March 1936 note, "When you get a woman to look into a mirror and see that her face is prettier, she's feeling better and takes a new interest in life." The beauty culture program was accredited by the state in 1942, and from that time on two classes of twelve inmates were trained each year and almost without exception all passed their exams for certification.

The beauty culture program came under the responsibility of the education department as did baby hygiene and domestic science. Beauty culture remained through the Depression because it was a part-time program taught by a Clinton Farms staff member from another department. The baby hygiene classes were taught and financed by an outside agency.

Domestic science lacked adequate facilities in 1930, but there was a teacher until 1933, when she left because of a lack of salary appropriations. On 9 June 1936 the board discussed domestic science again. "Although one of the first responsibilities of this institution is to train women for domestic service on parole, no proper facilities for such training have ever been provided." In September 1937 a new domestic science teacher was appointed, and in November a cooking school was opened in a renovated building.

The head teacher when Edna Mahan came to Clinton Farms proved to be a poor administrator and caused considerable dissension among the teachers working under her. The education committee of the board in 1932 began to monitor her work and her department very closely. The 9 August 1932 board minutes report that "[t]he Head Teacher, whose position was abolished for economical reasons...left on July 22nd." The education committee oversaw the work of the education department for the next year. Hildreth Cronshey took over the work of the education department in 1933. She had come to Clinton Farms in 1930 with the strong recommendation of the Reverend Thomas A. Conover (brother of Juliana Conover and relative of Caroline Wittpenn) and became his assistant. She was a capable and creative person and provided strong leadership of the education department for many years.

The education department in 1933 had only three teachers, including the nursery school teacher. The academic programs offered at this time concentrated on literacy and obtaining an eighth grade certificate. High school courses were offered with emphasis on business training. Few inmates qualified for this, and there was often discussion among the board as to the relatively high cost of this in relation to the few inmates served. Mahan wrote in 1933, "The commercial work is being done this year by one of the superior women who held reliable positions as bookkeeper and stenographer before commitment."

Besides classroom work, the teachers were responsible for helping each cottage plan recreation programs. They organized and officiated at institution recreation programs, such as track meets. Christmas and Easter pageants and other dramatic productions were under their direction.

As the population at Clinton Farms changed after the Depression and more funds became available, the educational programs were expanded. Farm work was eventually cut back and other work opportunities developed.

The Board of Managers

The importance of the Board of Managers and Edna Mahan's use of them in the management of the reformatory cannot be emphasized enough. The challenges of working with all the constituencies concerned with inmates, developing and improving programs, and keeping the day-to-day operations running smoothly with fewer staff were enormous. Mahan trained and used her board to help bring about desired and necessary changes.

The act of 1910 that established the State Reformatory for Women specified broad powers for the Board of Managers, which included the following:

> [P]ower...to manage and control the property and concern of said reformatory, and make all needful rules and regulations for the management thereof, and for the care, support, discipline, detention, discharge of the prisoners; to adopt and

> use any method of education and employment which in their judgment will best promote the interest of the prisoners and secure their reformation. . . .

By the time Edna Mahan arrived at Clinton Farms, the Board of Managers was organized on a committee structure: House, Hospital, Parole, Farm, Finance, Christmas, Education, Religious Education, Library, and Building and Grounds. Each of the seven board members served on at least one committee and was expected to give a committee report at each board meeting. Board members often spent a day at the institution looking over their particular area, talking with staff and inmates or outside professionals involved in some aspect of the reformatory. They took turns each month interviewing inmates eligible for parole consideration. Board members, who were appointed by the governor, were paid for their travel expenses only.

The fact that many of the board members served more than two decades at Clinton Farms or in several instances started at Clinton Farms and later were moved to the State Board of Control of Institutions and Agencies provided continuity and stability to the running of the institution. Those who moved on to the "Big Board," as the State Board of Control was called, added the dimension of power.

Caroline Wittpenn, one of the founders and the first president of the Board of Managers, was appointed to the State Board of Control when it was created in 1918. She remained on that board until her death in December 1932. While on the State Board of Control her interest in Clinton Farms continued. She visited often and was generous in the support and maintenance of the Chapel of the Good Shepherd, which she donated to the institution in 1915 in memory of her only son.

Geraldine Thompson, another founder and member of the first Clinton Farms Board of Managers, also was appointed to serve on the State Board of Control when it was created in 1918 and resigned thirty-nine years later in 1957. She remained actively involved with Clinton Farms throughout those years. From 1957 until her death in 1967, Mahan kept in close touch with her and always called Thompson her "guardian angel."

There were two other board members appointed in Mahan's time who were later promoted to the State Board of Control. One was Wittpenn's niece, Mary Stevens Baird, and the other was Lloyd Wescott, who owned a dairy farm across the highway from Clinton Farms.

Juliana Conover, who was a tremendous source of strength and support to Mahan in her first months at the reformatory, was appointed to the Clinton board in 1918 and resigned in 1940. Jane Coggeshall, appointed to the Board of Managers in 1926, was elected president of the board in November 1927. A long illness in 1937 and her family's decision to spend most of their time on their farm in Florida necessitated her resigning from the board in November 1937.

Two others appointed in the 1930s who had long tenure on the board were Anita S. Quarles, who was recommended by Wittpenn and served twenty-eight years, and Elizabeth B. Schley, who was appointed in 1937, became president of the board in 1958, and continues to serve in this capacity. Schley was a young bride when she was first appointed to the board. Her father-in-law was president of the State Board of Control, and her husband, Reeve Schley, Jr., eventually took over that position.

Most board members served more than ten years and were active because Mahan knew how to involve them. The occasional board member who was not active or with whom Mahan had difficulty was eased off the board.

Edna Mahan often used the board, individually and as a group, to educate and enlighten professionals, such as judges, the Board of Pardons, the parole board, and parole officers, to the Clinton Farms philosophy. These groups had power and a great deal of influence on the lives of the inmates. They were primarily men, with the exception of female parole officers whose department was run by men. Most of the offenders they worked with were men. Mahan and her board were persistent and relentless in their efforts to educate these groups to the needs of female offenders.

Board of Pardons

The Board of Pardons was the paroling authority for the inmates with determinate sentences who had been transferred from the Trenton State Prison and those who came directly to the Reformatory for Women beginning in 1930. Clinton inmates who were to be heard by the Board of Pardons were taken to Trenton three or four times a year to appear before the board. Recommendations for parole readiness by the Clinton classification committee and Board of Managers were sent in advance to the members of the Board of Pardons.

The concern of the Clinton Board was that the determinate sentence did not take into consideration the individual needs and adjustments of each inmate. It set up a dichotomy between the "reformatory" inmates and the "prison" inmates or as they were usually referred to "Clinton" versus "State" inmates. The frustrations of Mahan and the board around these issues and their efforts to educate the Board of Pardons are reported in the Board of Managers minutes throughout the next three decades.

The Clinton Farms board minutes of 9 June 1931 detail board members' concern that the state inmates may not be considered by the Board of Pardons for parole. They feared that this division of parole responsibility would create a feeling of discrimination as regards the prison inmates:

> When we set up the standard of individual needs and adjustment as the basis for parole consideration for those women who are committed to us directly, we must set up another standard for those prison commitments who will have to serve

> definite periods unless they are acted upon by the Board of Pardons prior to the expiration of that definite term.

Geraldine Thompson suggested "that the institution should prepare a brief and concise statement outlining the various phases of the problem to be presented to Commissioner Ellis and the State Board of Control." She noted there were two alternatives:

> [T]o attempt to change the law which would probably be very difficult; to try to educate the Board of Pardons to our point of view and to give them confidence in the wisdom and desirability of dealing with offenders on an individual basis so that they may know if we permit women to apply for consideration from them that they are deserving cases.
>
> This is a subject which we of the institution shall appreciate having the minds of the State Board Members and the Commissioner ponder over.

In the next year there are several references to the meetings of the Board of Pardons to consider the cases from Clinton, communications among board members and the Board of Pardons around specific cases, and frustration of the Clinton board with the Board of Pardons.

Thompson met with the Clinton board in August 1932 and said she was trying to arrange a meeting between some of the members of the Board of Pardons, Commissioner Ellis, and representatives of the institutions "with the hope of bringing about some correlation between the recommendations of the local Boards of Managers and Classification Committees and the action of the Board of Pardons."

The meeting did not take place, and the actions of the Board of Pardons in the parole of prison inmates over the next five years indicate its unwillingness to listen to the recommendations of the board and classification committee. The frustrations of the board and superintendent as reported in board minutes revolve around the few inmates the Board of Pardons approves for parole, the lack of attention given to personal appeals made by individual Clinton board members to individual members of the Board of Pardons on specific cases, and the unwillingness of the Board of Pardons to meet with the Board of Managers.

At the June 1933 board meeting it was reported that of eight inmates who were heard by the Board of Pardons in May, only one received favorable consideration.

The May and June 1935 board minutes report in some detail on Coggeshall's interest in the case of Sadie R. "The institution has attempted, without success to persuade the Board of Pardons that Sadie is eminently deserving of a trial on parole." In May Coggeshall interviewed two members of the Board of Pardons and the prosecutor from the committing county. However, Sadie's name was not on the list to be heard by the Board of Pardons in June. Coggeshall reported at the June meeting, "She is very much disturbed because she has not been able to make any headway in Sadie's behalf and she is determined not to give up. She has not yet decided what the most effective next move will be."

The 14 July 1936 board minutes report:

> The Board members were distressed to learn that not one of the eight women who appealed to the Board of Pardons at the last session was given consideration. Several of the cases were very deserving ones. Failure to recognize their efforts makes it difficult to maintain good morale among the other prison women. Out of the discussion of this whole situation came a suggestion to acquaint the members of the Board of Pardons with the work of this institution by inviting them here to hear our cases at their next meeting. It was suggested to issue an invitation to the members of the Board to come for luncheon with the Board of Managers on a day suggested by the Judges.

On 7 May 1937 the Board of Pardons met at Clinton Farms to interview inmates petitioning the board and had lunch with Mahan and three Clinton board members afterward. This was arranged through a meeting on 27 March between Mahan and board member Anita Quarles with Judge Hetfield, Board of Pardons, at his office in Plainfield. Quarles, a member of the city council of Plainfield, was a friend of Judge Hetfield's. It was Judge Hetfield's suggestion that "Mrs. Quarles address a letter to the Judge to be used as an invitation to the other members of the Board [of Pardons to meet at the institution]."

The board minutes of 13 July 1937 report the results of the action taken by the Board of Pardons in May. Mahan reports on the visit and the board's action to Coggeshall, who had been ill and unable to attend board meetings for a year, in a letter dated 21 July 1937, "The Board of Pardons actually did meet here. They behaved very well and evidently they liked Ethel's dinner so much that they approved her for parole and no one else."

It was not until 1946 that the Board of Pardons began to meet regularly at Clinton Farms to hear cases. Edna Mahan continued her efforts throughout her lifetime to diminish the dichotomy of "Clinton" and "State" inmates (any inmate or staff who referred to an inmate as "Clinton" or "State" was strongly admonished) and to educate the State Board of Pardons and its later incarnation, the State Board of Parole, to the Clinton Farms philosophy.

Parole Officers

Parole officers were another constituency outside the institution who had a great deal of influence and power over the inmates. Though they had little interaction with the inmates before they were paroled, they had considerable interaction with them once they were out in the community.

Edna Mahan believed that parole planning started the day the inmate arrived at Clinton Farms. In her first interview with each inmate, which was usually the day or day after the inmate was admitted, Mahan asked the inmate what her plans were when she left the institution. The parole officer was apprised of the plan, was responsible for approving the plan when the inmate was being considered for parole, and supervised the inmate once she was released on parole.

Inmates' lawyers, family members, and members of the state legislature often requested that the board give early consideration for parole to particular inmates. Almost without exception these requests were rejected on the grounds that the inmate needed more time in the institution for reform to take place.

A typical case discussed at the 17 October 1933 board meeting was Frances W.'s. Her lawyer, her father, her aunt, and an assemblyman had all contacted Mahan and the board asking for consideration of an early release for Frances. Frances had been committed to Clinton Farms in June 1933 for receiving stolen goods. After going over the circumstances of her case, the board concluded: "Since the girl has been here only four months and since there are no extenuating circumstances which would make it advisable to consider her case at this time, the board requested that those interested in her case be so advised."

In August 1935 Elsie H.'s lawyer wrote requesting the board consider Elsie for parole. Elsie, who had been committed in January for adultery, was a heroin addict. On admission she was in such poor health that she spent the first three months in the hospital. At the 13 August 1935 meeting the board noted: "Her physical condition is improving rapidly, and she is adjusting very well. However, because of her history of drug addiction over a long period and only recently terminated, everyone agreed that she should receive a reasonably long period in the institution." The secretary of the board was instructed to write to Elsie's lawyer to explain why his request for immediate parole could not be granted.

Helen M. Wilde, supervisor of work with women and girls of the division of classification and parole, worked closely with Mahan concerning parole issues and parole plans. However, individual parole officers did not regularly come to the institution to meet with the inmates concerning their parole plans and to become acquainted with them before they actually left the institution. The board and the superintendent encouraged more active involvement of the parole officers with the inmates while they were still in the institution. The board minutes of 9 February 1932 report, "Miss Helen M. Wilde...has arranged to have her women parole officers spend a day each month in the institution. We welcome this arrangement since the girls benefit by intimate contact with their parole officers before leaving the institution."

The 13 March 1934 board minutes include the following:

> Parole Meeting
>
> Miss Wilde, Mr. Lane, the women parole officers, the members of the State Home for Girls Classification Committee and Miss Calwalader of the State Health Department were guests of the institution for a luncheon meeting. Several parole matters were discussed, especially the problem presented by parolees who must be treated for venereal disease.

The effort to keep parole officers involved with their parolees prior to parole was ongoing. Some parole officers were conscientious; others seldom came no matter how much they were prodded. They were usually invited as a group to a luncheon meeting at the institution at least once a year. In 1947 an institutional parole officer position was established. This proved to be a more satisfactory way of maintaining a liaison between the institution and field parole officers.

In the late thirties, the board became concerned about the many paroled Clinton inmates who were placed in domestic service in New York City by the Salvation Army. The arrangement was through a connection Mahan had with a major in the army who visited Clinton Farms regularly and donated many items, particularly at Christmas. The inmates complained of long hours, impossible duties, and often cruel treatment. In 1939 the board questioned placing so many inmates there, for while the New Jersey Parole Department gave its blessings to this arrangement, it did not supervise the inmates.

The board's concern for these inmates and the creativity of Head Teacher Hildreth Cronshey led her to find out for herself what was expected of the inmates. Cronshey obtained a job at domestic service through the Salvation Army in New York. Her letter to Mahan in June 1940 after two days on the job is disheartening and revealing:

> Dear Edna,
>
> Tonight I feel very flip—and certainly a *flop*!...I never worked so hard in my life and though I originally thought of this to get a slant on what an employer expected of a girl I'm now very much on the girl's side, specially if she gets only five dollars a week for all this.
>
> You'd never believe it but I arrived here yesterday at 8:30 A.M., was put right to work giving breakfast to the 2 year old lad who won't eat for either "Mummy or Daddy"...Well from there I was put to work at everything—the whole works and at 9:15 last night I was apparently done. I *crawled* into bed and my one thought was that I didn't blame any girl for running away her first night if she

> was expected to do all that the *first* day.... Soon I'll be able to laugh it off I suppose but I certainly was "disgusted" at the pace I was driven—and this is supposed to be an above average place....
>
> I may turn out to be as unstable as some of our more noted ones but I think I'll stick it out—if no more than to see if things work out after a routine is established....
>
> As ever, Hilda

The practice of placing parolees in domestic service continued as a prominent arrangement as long as Edna Mahan was alive. In the 1930s domestic service was essentially the only option for these inmates. The institution's responsibility was to see that inmates received adequate training. It was the parole department's responsibility to supervise the placement.

With the board's expressed concern with the arrangement and Cronshey's first-hand experience, it is presumed fewer parolees were sent into New York. However, not until the board minutes of 8 February 1956 is it noted, "The Salvation Army is not permitted to supervise adults from out of state."

Judges

On more than one occasion the superintendent and board took issue with judges who recalled many of the inmates they sentenced to Clinton Farms or sentenced them inappropriately. The board minutes of 12 September 1933 discuss the fact that Judge Shay from Camden had committed six inmates to the prison for twelve to fifteen months for operating disorderly houses. The board voted to have Coggeshall and Mahan visit "Judge Shay in an effort to change his attitude toward this institution; ie., to show him why it is desirable to commit minor offenders to this institution for indeterminate periods."

The minutes of 11 December 1934 report on the case of Kathleen B., who was committed to the institution on 23 October 1934 by Judge Van Riper of Essex County. She ran away 19 November 1934 and was picked up by officers of the institution and returned within an hour. On 20 November, a recall was received by mail signed by Judge Van Riper. Though the superintendent communicated the runaway to the judge, he still wished to have the inmate brought before him on the order to recall the following morning.

> Feeling that this young lady, who had been unusually uncooperative since admission, should receive serious disciplinary action the superintendent initiated proceedings, through the local Prosecutor's Office, to have her indicted and recommitted on an escape charge. When the local authorities came to have Kath-

> leen sign the allegation for escape she refused to do so. The Justice of the Peace, the County Detective and a State Trooper thereupon removed her to the Hunterdon County jail. This stubbornness and further lack of cooperation on the part of the girl made it impossible to produce her in Judge Van Riper's court on November 21st. A wire was sent to Judge Van Riper that afternoon explaining why it was impossible to produce her in court the next day. Following this there was considerable correspondence between Judge Van Riper and the superintendent. The Judge was highly incensed and considered that the superintendent had deliberately taken steps to avoid honoring his writ. The matter was finally satisfactorily adjusted after Commissioner Ellis arranged for an interview between the Judge and Miss Mahan. The correspondence was read to the board members for their consideration. They voted to approve the action of the superintendent.

At the July 1939 board meeting it was "suggested that it would be a good idea to invite the Judges who commit women to this institution to visit in the Fall." At the 11 June 1940 board meeting, "It was again suggested that plans be considered in the fall for inviting the committing judges to visit the institution."

Although a few individual judges visited the institution regularly, once or twice a year, to meet with the inmates they had sentenced and the superintendent, committing judges as a group did not visit until 1954 when New Jersey Supreme Court Justice William J. Brennan, Jr., gave the county judges a two-day holiday to visit correctional institutions. They visited Clinton Farms on 9 April.

Smoking Policy

From her beginning at Clinton Farms, Mahan gave the Board of Managers strong guidance in dealing with outside constituencies, and the board gave her strong support as it tried to educate groups and individuals on the Clinton Farms philosophy. An issue of a different nature Mahan felt strongly about changing was the no-smoking policy at Clinton Farms. On this one not all board members supported her at first, and it was Commissioner Ellis who had to be persuaded that it was okay for women to smoke. Edna Mahan smoked all of her adult life, and her many efforts to stop were short-lived.

There had been considerable agitation and discussion on this issue by the board, and Mahan felt that the inmates should be allowed to smoke. By the 1930s smoking was widely accepted for women. It helped to relieve tension, and the connection between smoking and lung cancer was unknown. It was a constant source of infractions because the inmates managed to get hold of cigarettes or discarded butts.

The first mention of smoking in the board minutes appeared 17 February 1931:

> On several occasions previously the smoking question has been discussed informally by the Board members. It is no longer possible to ignore the fact that the problem exists and will have to be dealt with somehow. It was suggested that the commissioner should be asked to bring the matter before the State Board of Control for decision.

No action was taken at this time. The 1933 edition of the *Handbook of American Prisons and Reformatories* commented on the absence of smoking at the institution.

> The mandatory rule against smoking seems somewhat out of place here where natural living is so much encouraged. Such a rule doubtless had its merits before the practice of smoking became so prevalent among women. It would seem desirable to dispense with it now that the custom has become universal. This privilege, properly restricted, has been granted at the Delaware State Institution for Women. (Cox, Bixby & Root 1933)

In May 1936, when there had still been no change concerning the smoking regulation at Clinton, Coggeshall sent a letter to each board member asking them to sign it if they favored permitting inmates in the institution to smoke. The board was unanimous at this time in approving smoking for inmates. However, Commissioner Ellis was reluctant to establish the practice at the women's reformatory, and the board took no further action at that time.

On 9 November 1938, the board sent Commissioner Ellis a letter beseeching him for his and the State Board of Control's approval.

> From time to time the Superintendent of Clinton Farms has acquainted you with the problems created in the institution by not permitting the women to smoke. About two years ago the Board unanimously went on record recommending that smoking be permitted under supervision. Mrs. Coggeshall...sent you the original of the letter bearing each member's signature to the recommendation dated May 13th, 1936.
>
> At today's meeting the problem was again discussed and Dr. Schaefer's [psychiatrist] letter of August 30th, 1938, read, copy of which I understand you received. It was the consensus that some action confirming the Board's recommendation of two years ago be taken at once. Again the Board unanimously approved smoking under supervision. The Board is reluctant to institute this new policy without first obtaining the approval of yourself and the State Board of Control. Since in the judgment of the Superintendent, the Staff including the resident physician, psychologist, visiting psychiatrist and the Board such action is urgent, may we anticipate your usual splendid cooperation?

By the 13 December 1938 board meeting a letter had been received from Commissioner Ellis stating that the State Board of Control approved the recommendation to allow inmates to smoke "provided reasonable and comprehensive restrictions are employed." They were allowed to smoke beginning Christmas Day 1938.

Excerpts from a few letters inmates wrote after Christmas give some insight into the meaning of the smoking privilege to them. The January 1939 board minutes quote one inmate as saying:

> The atmosphere on the farms is different already. It certainly feels like heaven now. We don't have to get into any more trouble now and we won't have to pick up any more old butts off the ground.

In this situation Mahan initiated action about the smoking regulation eight years before actual change took place. Although it is not officially recorded in the minutes, one board member was opposed to smoking, and this caused the board to hesitate to recommend a change of policy. When this board member finally agreed that a change in policy was in order, the board sent a unanimous recommendation to the commissioner. Although it took another two years and considerable pressure to bring about a change in policy, the commissioner told Mahan that the thing that did more to influence his change of thinking was the fact that the reluctant board member had changed hers.

Professional Affiliations and Visitors

Although Edna Mahan's major focus during her years at Clinton Farms was on the inmates and the running of the institution, she maintained affiliations with professional groups on the local, national, and international levels. She was very active and a leader in some of these. She made many professional friends throughout the United States and Europe and encouraged all to visit Clinton Farms.

Mahan recognized the importance of professional associations for her own career. She encouraged board members and staff to affiliate with appropriate ones. She visited other institutions and greeted many professional visitors at Clinton Farms. In her first years at Clinton Farms, she, with a car full of board members, visited the Reformatory and Prison for Women at Bedford Hills, New York, and the Federal Reformatory for Women at Alderson, West Virginia.

Mahan was an active member of the National Conference of Social Work before she came to Clinton, and she attended their annual meetings whenever she could. She attended her first American Prison Association (APA) Congress in 1929. Board members often accompanied her to these meetings and reported on them to the other board members. She not only encouraged board participation, she also encouraged the staff, too. It was the Depression, however, and travel funds were not available. Board members paid their own way, and the superintendent did, too.

By the mid-thirties Mahan had become an active member of APA. In 1938 she was first appointed as a member of the board of directors and served until 1949. In 1937 she served for the first time as chair of the Committee on Women's Institutions. Commissioner Ellis was president of APA at the same time. The annual congress was to be held 10–15 October in Philadelphia.

There is much correspondence between Edward R. Cass, general secretary of APA, and Edna Mahan concerning the Committee on Women's Institutions program for the congress. She wrote him on 29 April 1937 asking, "Am I supposed to be doing something about the program for the Women's Committee for the conference next October in Philadelphia?" He replied 3 May:

> I am glad...you are thinking about your duties and responsibilities relative to the Committee on Women's Institutions.... This is an important group and I am sure you are planning to do all you possibly can to make it a worth while section of the Association.
>
> Although October is some time off I think that you should very soon canvass those who are likely to be interested in the Committee on Women's Institutions for the purpose of learning just what their ideas are about the functions and the program of the Committee. That would give them the opportunity to feel that they are a part of the group and have had something to do in the shaping of its plans. Although you reside in a Republican State I feel sure that you will agree with the democratic procedure in this instance.
>
> You have the rare opportunity this year of an evening dinner meeting, and I think that we must jointly plan carefully, and in a big way, to make the occasion one of the outstanding features of the Congress.... I congratulate you on the opportunity which you have to make the New Deal in the Women's Committee a big deal and wish you every success.

Mahan did canvass the members of the Women's Committee and received suggestions from them. On 11 July 1937 Helen H. Hazard, superintendent, Reformatory for Women, Dwight, Illinois, wrote, "What would you think of having Mrs. Roosevelt? [Eleanor Roosevelt was a vice-president of APA at the time.] She has interested herself in women's institutions and for many people at least she would be quite a drawing-card. As I understand it, she is also rather accessible."

Secretary Cass and President Ellis were both enthusiastic about inviting Roosevelt. It was Geraldine Thompson, a childhood friend of Eleanor Roosevelt's, who extended the invitation. When Roosevelt accepted, Mahan made the follow-up arrangements. The dinner meeting was changed to a luncheon meeting, that was held 13 October. Roosevelt spoke on "What the Community Expects of Institutions for

Delinquent Women and Girls." It was "one of the outstanding features of the Congress," and Mahan received considerable publicity for her part in the event, including her picture with Roosevelt in the Philadelphia *Evening Public Ledger*.

Her chairmanship of the Committee on Women's Institutions in 1937 and her part in planning the committee's luncheon meeting featuring Roosevelt was an auspicious beginning to her leadership role among women in the association. Her appointment to the Board of Directors in 1938 set the stage for her wider involvement in the affairs of the association.

It is not surprising to find many visitors anxious to see Clinton Farms and meet the young superintendent. Perhaps the most prominent visitor during the 1930s was the Honorable Alexander Patterson, His Majesty's Commissioner of Prisons for England and Wales, who visited in 1931 and again in 1939.

Florence Monahan, one of the leading female superintendents at the time, visited in March 1930 when she was superintendent of the Reformatory for Women in Shakopee, Minnesota, and again in 1937 when she was superintendent of the California Institution for Women. James Bennett, director of the Federal Bureau of Prisons, sent Emma Houchins, the superintendent of the women's department of the new federal prison in California, to visit and observe in 1938.

Three men with whom she would later have a great deal of interaction in APA and elsewhere visited. They were Richard McGee, Austin MacCormick, and Sanford Bates. At the time of their first visits they were all with the federal system.

On 3 June 1938, Nina Kinsella, executive assistant to the director, Bureau of Prisons, Washington, D.C., wrote Mahan that the bureau was considering building a new facility for women near Dallas. She had some questions about the advantages and disadvantages of the cottage plan, central dining rooms as opposed to separate dining rooms in each cottage, etc. Kinsella ends her letter by asking, "If at a later date a conference were called here in Washington of a few outstanding women in this field would it be possible for you to attend, provided we could arrange for your transportation?" No answer to the letter or any further reference to a conference could be found. The letter testifies to Mahan's reputation as one of the "outstanding women in this field" just ten years after she took over at Clinton Farms.

Not all visitors to the institution were professionals. Dale Harrison wrote "I have been to prison with a jazz band, and I have cried to the romping rhythm of 'A-Tisket, a-Tasket' " in 1938 in his column for a New York newspaper after accompanying Tommy Dorsey's band from the Terrace Room of the Hotel New Yorker to Clinton Farms. Ralph Hitz, the owner of the hotel, had a country estate a few miles from Clinton Farms and was a friend of Mahan's.

> It was Hitz's idea that the women might be made a bit happier and the tedium of their lives lightened if they could see some of the things Broadway pleasure

> seekers see.... As the rhythm rolled through the room the women clapped their hands, stomped their feet, swayed in their seats and sang. There never was a jam session quite as happy as this.

Ralph Hitz visited the institution often in the late thirties and early forties and always brought two or three guests with him. Mahan encouraged and enjoyed neighbors coming to see the work of the institution. It allayed anxieties they might have about being neighbors to a reformatory and its inmates. It sometimes brought entertainment to all the residents of Clinton Farms. It dispelled the guests' stereotyped ideas of reformatory inmates. Harrison testifies to the "crumbling" of his stereotypes.

> I have been schooled against waxing sentimental over criminals—especially women criminals.... Yet in a few brief moments at the Clinton Reformatory for Women all my hard boiled philosophy crumbled. I had seen the hearts of women thieves and women murderers lighted and made gay by music.

Old timers from Clinton Farms, inmates and staff, still reminisce about the night Tommy Dorsey's band came and played. However, not all the entertainers who came to Clinton Farms over the years had the celebrity status of Tommy Dorsey. Local community bands, choruses, dramatic groups, and Boy Scout Christmas carolers were all welcomed enthusiastically by Mahan, the staff and, most important, the inmates because they brought a change to the daily routine.

Staff

Good staff committed to the Clinton Farms philosophy were vital to the smooth running of the institution. New staff bring new ideas and fresh approaches, which Edna Mahan was quick to pick up on if they made sense. Continuity of committed and creative staff added to the stability of the institution.

During the Depression Mahan had to curtail positions, and she was not able to do much about salaries or working conditions. Regular meetings with cottage staff and an open door for all staff did a great deal to raise their morale.

Besides achieving full-time positions of psychologist and physician in 1930 and filling them with two highly competent women, Mahan was able to get rid of less qualified people from key positions who did not work well under her administration. When Dr. Beatty came to the hospital, she brought with her Ida Tibbot, R.N., who took over as head nurse and remained until 1953.

An important addition to the staff in 1935 was Mary Cox as assistant superintendent. Elizabeth MacKenzie had been loaned in October 1934 to the North Jersey

Training School at the request of the superintendent there, and the position of assistant superintendent was vacant at Clinton Farms. Cox was a superb addition to the administrative staff. She was a complement to Mahan in many ways. She remained in this position for twenty years and helped Mahan quietly but strongly during that time.

There were many staff who stayed with the institution twenty years or more. Having a job during the Depression was, of course, a primary incentive. However, in later years of Mahan's superintendency, staff commented on the wonderful atmosphere at Clinton Farms and how much they loved working there. Edna Mahan engendered these feelings.

Inmates

The inmates, the residents of Clinton Farms, were the purpose for the existence of the reformatory. The board and the staff were to bring about change in their behavior. Change in human behavior is a dynamic process, and the inmates' actions and reactions did much toward their own change, or lack of it. They also did much to shape Clinton Farms.

We already have seen the "older" inmates (which at a correctional institution are those over 30) commitment to Mahan at the end of her first year as superintendent. It was the older inmates who became leaders and assumed positions with more responsibility. For the most part these were inmates serving long determinate sentences.

Long-term inmates, many of whom had committed an assault or homicide offense against a family member or close friend, usually a husband or boyfriend, made up less than 15 percent of the population during Mahan's superintendency. The battered woman's defense was unknown. If they were found guilty they were given determinate (e.g., minimum/maximum or life sentences) to the New Jersey State Prison to be served at the Reformatory for Women.

Because of their long residence they had special needs that were primarily related to boredom due to the routine of institutional life. Mahan was sensitive to this and sought and encouraged avocational programs, such as garden club and art and ceramic classes, all sponsored by volunteers. These were open to all the population who were in the Honor Group. These programs appealed particularly to the more mature long-term inmates because they were small, relatively quiet, and often could be done in their leisure time in between regular meetings or classes.

Mahan also challenged these inmates to take on more responsible jobs. Many of the student officer group were long-termers. When there were staff shortages, these inmates were on night duty. They supervised some work assignments, such as the lawn group, and for several years they supervised a small unit of young, volatile inmates. Mahan often granted these inmates special privileges, such as allowing them to keep a pet dog, cat, or canary, after they had been at Clinton Farms several years and were well settled in. She was creative and innovative in helping them serve their time.

No matter what the offense or prior history, every inmate who came to Clinton Farms challenged Mahan to find the best that was in her and build on that so that the inmate used her time there to prepare for her return to society. Because of the seriousness of their offenses and consequent coping with the reality of the criminal act they committed, some of the long-term inmates presented the greatest challenges.

In the late 1930s one of these inmates, Alice T., was sentenced to life in the New Jersey State Prison for first degree murder. She served more than twenty years at Clinton Farms. During the first ten, Alice challenged Mahan as she fought the system and abused the trust Mahan put in her and struggled with the memory of the crime she had committed.

On Alice's admission, Mahan noted the following:

> [She] emphasizes tomboyishness [and] feels she must keep up her air of bravado.... She is keen active and energetic. She is probably the type of hyperactive person, who, if not kept busily occupied all the time can be so much dynamite. She is a daredevil who would try anything once. She is friendly and seems to care about the impression she makes.... I believe she can be appealed to in time after she settles down to a regular routine under close supervision and reasonable discipline.

Edna Mahan saw in Alice a great potential for leadership if her energies could be channeled in the right direction. The dialogues between the two during the next two decades show Mahan's firmness, patience, daring, and trust as Alice fought her authority, gained increasing insight and self-esteem, and became a trusted leader who admired Mahan above all others.

Mahan recorded her interactions with and dialogues about Alice in progress notes, which she kept routinely on every inmate. Alice often requested to see Mahan, or, during her first ten years particularly, Mahan would send for her at the request of a staff member who sensed Alice's depression or restlessness, which often preceded trouble.

In Alice's later years at Clinton Farms she wrote notes to Mahan about how she was doing, often made suggestions as to how to help another inmate, and when she was put in charge of a group of hard-to-manage young inmates, Alice reported regularly on each one's progress or lack of progress and the activities of the unit.

The progress notes give insight into Alice's coming to terms with the reality she had committed a very serious crime and with her struggles in adjusting to her confinement at Clinton Farms. They also show Mahan's sensitivity to Alice's feelings about her crime and her persistence in making Alice understand what was acceptable behavior at Clinton Farms and what she must do to earn the privileges she wanted.

Open Institutions Versus Need for Security

In most states where reformatories for women were opened in the first three decades of the twentieth century with ideals set forth by the female reformers, the incorporation of female felons from men's state prisons in the late 1920s and 1930s necessitated more concerns for security. The addition of the prison women combined with the effects of the Depression—shrinking resources, crowding, fewer staff, and inadequate programming—led to the "demise of the women's reformatory. The criminal justice system was returning to practices common before the reformatory movement began" (Rafter 1990).

In 1928 Clinton Farms' demise as a progressive reformatory was at hand. Edna Mahan's arrival at that time with her determination, energy, enlightened outlook, skillful use of the board, and strong backing of Commissioner Ellis reversed this demise.

By the early thirties Clinton Farms was gaining a reputation as a progressive institution under Mahan's leadership. The 1933 *Handbook of American Prisons and Reformatories* opens its "Comments" on Clinton Farms as follows:

> This is a most interesting institution. Both in policy and management it is very progressive. The absolute breaking away from old traditions is everywhere apparent and the almost complete discarding of formal rules, regulations and routine places the reformatory in the foremost group of modern institutions. Rehabilitation of the inmates is the "watchword" and all efforts are directed to this end. One of the most important features in connection with this institution is the fact that the inmates are never locked in. (Cox, Bixby & Root 1933)

The philosophy of an open institution was expressed by Commissioner Bates in his letter to a reporter from the *Newark Sunday Call*, 4 April 1946, "...we bring greater protection to the communities in the long run by building responsibility and self-reliance into the inmate than we would by building steel cells into the institution." Mahan's strong commitment to this philosophy was symbolized in her first year at Clinton Farms when she ordered the bars removed from all cottage windows. As late as 1959 she wrote in the American Correctional Association's *Manual of Correctional Standards* chapter on "Women's Institutions":

> The institution which has very few or no locked doors will find that a high morale and sense of responsibility in the inmate population is a more effective

> bar to runaways than mechanical devices. At least one superintendent [she probably refers to herself] feels strongly that there should be no segregation building for problem cases. The more normal situation is to distribute them in the various housing units where the well-adjusted individuals will help stabilize difficult and irresponsible ones.

The two commissioners she worked with the longest, Ellis from 1928 to 1945 and Bates from 1945 to 1956, supported and applauded her running Clinton Farms as an open institution. Her success reflected well on them and the state of New Jersey.

During Mahan's superintendency the first reference to a maximum security building is in a letter to Commissioner Ellis dated 12 February 1938. She wrote a detailed response to questions he had raised "...as to whether we should consider building a maximum security cottage at this institution at some future date." She reports:

> [T]he six inmate cottages are absolutely open—the doors are never locked and there is no protection on any of the windows. There is no employee on duty in the cottages at night except the matron and the staff members who sleep in the cottages. That is why we are asking for night supervisors. Whenever we have an inmate who does not respond to discipline or to detention under open conditions the only place we have to use for segregation purposes is the hospital...[where] there are only two disciplinary rooms as such.

She lists with details of their offenses "[t]he...women in the present population...considered to be in need of more secure custody than the open cottages provide and therefore have been held for various periods of detention in the hospital." She notes "During the past five years...94 women have run away or attempted to run away (all but 10 have been returned). She concludes:

> There will evidently always be a certain number who will not respond to the reasonable policy we are maintaining. In my judgment we do need such a building as you mentioned to house probably from 35 to 40 women to give them close supervision and secure custody in this open institution. This need was never before so apparent when we had a smaller population and could give close, individual supervision.

On 15 February 1938 Commissioner Ellis acknowledged her letter and "the need of a special detention building...and I will bear this in mind in case the opportunity is afforded to present a construction program during the present session of the Legislature." Mahan discussed the letters with the Board of Managers at its 8 March 1938 meeting, and it endorsed the request for the building.

In light of Mahan's strong belief in an open institution with no bars on windows and no locked doors, it seems surprising that she would express the need for a special detention building. A look at the population figures during the Depression provides insight into the situation.

Between 1930 and 1940 the inmate population increased by a little over 100 inmates: the average daily population 1930-31 was 230, 1935-36 it was 257, and 1940-41 it was 332. Clinton Farms needed more inmate housing, and Mahan and the board would take whatever the commissioner could get from the legislature. The building did not materialize during Commissioner Ellis's tenure, and, it is doubtful it would have been used as a maximum security cottage had it been built.

Runaways were, of course, major concerns of the commissioner and Mahan because they reflected poorly on the institution and threatened the open environment. In June 1938 the commissioner asked F. Spencer Smith, director, division of inspection, Department of Institutions and Agencies, to "check through with Miss Mahan the possibility of additional safeguards to the buildings, particularly more adequate night supervision and possibly more secure screening of the windows." Smith wrote Mahan on 15 June 1938:

> When I was telling Commissioner Ellis of the circumstances surrounding the two recent escapes I ventured an opinion that possibly more secure screening should be placed on some of your buildings....
>
> I am wondering if you agree at all with this suggestion. I realize fully that the whole set-up at Clinton is intended to be one of minimum custody, but it seems that if a few sections were to be screened with wide mesh wire, neither the appearance nor the philosophy of the institution would be affected appreciably.
>
> Whether or not you would be able to follow the Commissioner's thought of more adequate night supervision I do not know.

Mahan notes at the bottom of the letter in large red letters "No reply. Discussed 6/20/38. EM." No screening was added to any of the buildings at this time. There is no record of the commissioner's thought "of more adequate night supervision," but as Mahan stated in her letter of 12 February they were in need of additional staff for night supervision. Student officers were assigned to night duty.

The institution's budget requests for additional staff positions during the last half of the decade were not granted. The board minutes of 14 June 1938 state "that in several accounts the allowance for next year is less than for the present fiscal year."

When Mahan started her work at Clinton Farms she believed that all the inmates could be worked with in an open institution. In 1946 she expressed a modification in her belief at the Seventh Annual Conference of Correctional Institutions for Girls and Women. In a session on "Temper Tantrums and Controlling the Disturbed Girl," she pointed out that her institution was for adult women, and when she first went to the reformatory there were eight cells for solitary confinement, which she abolished. "However, after seventeen years I have gone back to believing in isolation for some cases."

The change came in the late thirties when the population increased but there was no increase in staff or housing. Close, individual supervision was diminished. The institution continued to operate without a secure unit until 1946.

By the close of the decade, the Depression was coming to an end. World War II had started in Europe, and the United States would soon be involved.

Chapter 7

The Forties: "Administrative Skill and Philosophic Insight"

Commissioner Ellis wrote in 1944, "Much of the credit for the successful operation of this institution [Clinton Farms] rightly belongs to the present superintendent, Edna Mahan, who has brought to her work a rare combination of administrative skill and philosophic insight" (Ellis 1945). These skills and insights had been developing from her early life. They were recognized by Miriam Van Waters, who shaped and supported her early career, and they were honed by Commissioner Ellis in her first fourteen-and-a-half years as superintendent. His encouragement of her determination to run an open institution built on the student government honor system allowed it to happen.

By the end of the Depression in the thirties and the build up toward World War II in the forties, Mahan had made her reputation in New Jersey and in the wider correctional community through her activities with the American Prison Association. In 1940 she was elected to the Board of Directors of the Osborne Association in New York. Founded by Thomas Mott Osborne, the association was devoted to prison reform. Membership on the Board of Directors was honorary and included Sanford Bates, James Bennett, William J. Ellis, and G. Howland Shaw. Austin MacCormick was executive director.

She shepherded Clinton Farms through the war years, initiated innovative programs, and desegregated the institution. During this period she confronted a scandal created by a long-time and trusted staff member who publicly challenged her integrity. At this same time she lost Commissioner Ellis.

Toward the end of the decade her friend and mentor, Miriam Van Waters, faced her own problems in Massachusetts. The decade began with continued challenges from long-term inmate Alice T.

The Walk across the Highway and the Runaway

In her first two years at Clinton Farms, Alice T. was continually in trouble with other inmates and committed serious breaches of Mahan's trust. She told Mahan many times she would prefer to be locked up in a prison.

The freedom of Clinton Farms allowed her to use her leadership abilities with other inmates in both conforming and nonconforming behavior. When Alice was depressed, Mahan talked with her of the need for self-discipline and inner strength to give her the ability to face life as she found it.

Less than a year after Alice had come to Clinton, Mahan heard rumors that she had walked across the highway to a tavern and bought cigarettes. When Mahan confronted her about this, she said she had found the money at the barn where she was working. The superintendent tried to make her see the seriousness of her act. She told her she would have to report it to Commissioner Ellis in case it got into the newspapers and caused a scandal.

Alice recalls reminding Mahan that if the Board of Control and Board of Managers had a heart, they would approve smoking. Most inmates smoked. She also reminded Mahan that she didn't run away, she just went to buy "necessities." Mahan had Alice locked up for punishment.

When Alice was released and sent back to a cottage, she continued her usual behavior and even boasted that she got what she wanted at Clinton Farms. When Mahan heard that, she quickly sent for Alice and had a long session with her and demoted her. Alice cried and said now she had lost everything. Mahan explained to her that she couldn't have everything and give nothing; she tried to hurt everyone who did anything for her. Two days later when it was reported that Alice was being defiant and unreasonable, Mahan sent for Alice and told her she was through talking with her until she made up her mind to follow the normal routine at Clinton Farms. She sent her again to the hospital to be locked up.

A few days later Mahan met with Alice and sent her to see the psychiatrist and then let her return to a cottage. In less than a week rumors were circulating that Alice was planning to run away with other inmates. Alice denied the rumor. Two weeks later when a staff member's car keys were reported missing and found in the possession of one of the other inmates rumored to be in the runaway plans, those inmates were locked up.

By the end of December 1939, Alice was living in Silzer Cottage and was reelected to the Honor Group. Mahan tried many ways to help her come to a better understanding of herself and her problems and to be more conforming in her behavior. She regularly gave Alice books to read she felt had some message that might help her. They often talked about the books in their many sessions together.

On 2 February 1940 after a difficult session with Alice, Mahan wrote in the progress notes, "Sometimes when I think I see an improvement in [Alice] or a little more maturity, I believe it is only her acceptance of the fact that she cannot get by with too much here. It is her acceptance and her resentment of that fact. She realizes that a halt will always be called before she gets too far."

On 8 February Mahan gave Alice permission to keep a stray dog she had been feeding. Jo-Jo, however, had distemper and died in a week. On 11 March Mahan wrote:

> To break the news to [Alice] that her dog was dead I brought her back from Trenton's dog town a little black and white haired terrier, tied a tag around its neck saying, "Hello, [Alice]. Call me Shady if you like. I have come to take Jo-Jo's place. Love me or my little heart will break." When [Alice] came in the dog ran to her. She was tickled to death with the dog and did not seem to mind so much about Jo-Jo.

For the next two months things went relatively smoothly for Alice at Clinton Farms. But by early May rumors were circulating again that Alice was planning to run away. When Mahan talked with her and told her she was worried about this, Alice assured her that she would never run away. The rumors persisted into June.

On 14 June 1940, Alice went to see Mahan with a bouquet of roses from the cottage. Mahan was a little suspicious and asked Alice if she had something on her conscience. Alice assured her everything was fine.

At 12:50 a.m. on 16 June 1940, Mahan received a call from the switchboard telling her that Alice was missing. Ten minutes later a second inmate was reported missing.

Mahan immediately got all Clinton Farms staff with cars out on the roads and called all nearby state and local police. She asked the superintendent of Annandale Reformatory for Men in the neighboring village to send as many officers out as possible and notified the authorities in Trenton, including Commissioner Ellis. Families of the runaways were contacted, and Mahan interviewed all inmates she thought might be able to shed some light on the situation.

The press quickly heard of the runaways and, because of Alice's notoriety, called constantly to get the story or any late information. One reporter arrived about 3:00 p.m., just as Mahan was about to go home for a little rest, and said he wanted to take pictures of Alice's cottage and room and his paper would fire him if he didn't get them. "We had a good heart-to-heart talk—I laid all the cards on the table—told him we didn't deserve much consideration, that [Alice] was good news and they wanted to make the most of it. Then I told him our side of the story." Mahan was amazed when he left agreeing only to take pictures from the air. He had flown out and landed at a little airport near the reformatory. He was soon "to be heard zooming around over the institution taking his pictures."

On 18 June at 9:20 a.m. the state police called to say that a girl resembling Alice was reported to have purchased coffee and sandwiches from a garage on the highway not far from Clinton Farms. The proprietor told the police "[h]e was suspicious when he saw her look through the daily newspaper he had on the counter and sort of start when she saw a picture of herself." Mahan immediately sent as many people as possible from the institution out to search that area. About 11:00 a.m. one of the troopers called to say the inmates had been picked up by an Annandale office worker who called the state police. On their return to Clinton Farms they were locked up in the hospital.

Many reporters called and began to arrive. By 2 p.m. when the commissioner arrived with one of his deputies from Trenton there were six reporters asking permission to interview the inmates. The commissioner told them they could not but "he would report what they said when he got back from the hospital where he would interview both of them." The commissioner, his deputy, and Mahan went to the hospital and talked to each one in turn.

Alice told them she didn't want to discuss it with anyone. She answered a few questions. She told Commissioner Ellis she did not like it there. She preferred to be in a prison. She said that "Miss Mahan was all right but the girls got her goat."

On 22 June 1940 Mahan took the runaways to the courthouse in Flemington where they were sentenced to three consecutive years on escape charges. They had a long wait because the judge wasn't there. Alice was dumbfounded when Mahan left them sitting alone behind the courthouse in a small park while she went into the courthouse to find out why the hearing was delayed. As the two inmates sat there and talked, they wondered if Mahan was testing their trust. After being sentenced, they drove back to Clinton Farms. Alice asked Mahan what her chances were for being allowed to work before the year was out. Mahan asked, "Which year?"

However, Alice was a very good worker, and the head farmer soon requested he be allowed to have Alice work directly under his supervision. She continued to work with him until he became too busy to supervise her directly.

The Settling Down Years: July 1940–July 1948

Alice started to work in the storeroom 31 July 1940. She was advanced to the Probation group at the same time. She continued living in the hospital. In January 1941 she began to press Mahan to advance her to Honor status. Although her work was going well in the storeroom, there were persistent reports of affairs with other inmates and plans for another escape.

On 21 March 1941 when she and Mahan were talking, Alice began to cry when she reminded Mahan that the next day was the third anniversary of her admission. Mahan noted, "When she got up to go she walked around the desk, so I got up and shook hands with her. (It was quite a touching moment. She is not frequently so humble and submissive.)"

Alice moved into Williamson Cottage on 8 March 1942, and on 2 May 1942 she was reelected to the Honor Group there. She continued to live there for the next two-and-a-half years and work in the storeroom. She and another long-termer coached softball teams in the spring and summer.

When Mahan was talking with her on 5 August 1943, Alice said "she often thought of how much she must have bothered [Mahan] at one time when she was such a problem! She talked about all there is to do recently, especially working on the ration cards, and she made a joke about having 50 years and still not having enough time to get things done."

Alice did not continue in the Honor Group or living in a cottage the next few years. Her records indicate she lived in the hospital from September 1945 until April 1946, July 1946 to March 1947, and October 1947 to March 1948. Apparently there were plans to escape on more than one occasion, money that she could not account for was found in her possession, and she continued her pattern of involvement with other women. She also continued to have periods of depression.

Alice recalls the following:

> Miss Mahan knew me like a book. On one of my yearly visits to see Miss Connors, the psychologist, she told me that a life sentence meant *life*! I thought for a moment and quite disturbed, left and headed for Miss Mahan's office. Without knocking, I entered the office. Fortunately, no one was with Miss Mahan, who looked up at me and said, "Yes?" I told Miss Mahan what Miss Connors had said. I told her, "If I have to remain here for a lifetime, I'll go hang myself in one of your chicken coops." Miss Mahan, very serious-looking, said, "How much rope do you think you'll need?" I left madder than a hornet.

In March 1948 she moved from the hospital to Stowe Cottage to live and on 12 July 1948 was reelected to the Honor Group there. Her years as an increasingly responsible leader at Clinton Farms began at this time.

War Years

Clinton Farms felt the effect of World War II in many ways. The institution received government contracts to make shirts for the armed forces. The inmates did a great deal of volunteer work, from indexing, filing, and filling out ration books for the Office of Price Administration and the county, to knitting, sewing, and folding surgical dressings for the Red Cross.

The war had a profound effect on all of society. The Reformatory for Women, like the other social systems under stress, had to make adjustments to carry on its mission. Mahan, an able, innovative, and strong administrator, used her creativity and skills to ease the difficulties.

Staff Shortage

The shortage of staff was the most crucial problem facing Mahan, Clinton Farms, and all correctional institutions during World War II. Female superintendents discussed it at some length at their annual conference in New York City in February 1943. "Several superintendents reported as much as seventy-five percent turnover. The institutions can in no way compete in hours and wages with jobs offered in war plants."

At Clinton Farms the student government honor system allowed for an easier adaptation to the staff shortage. Reliable inmates were depended on in more situations than was usual. They worked alone, without a cottage officer, on night duty; one handled the night shift on the switchboard, and others assumed additional responsibilities where needed in the institution.

Staff shortages during World War II provided the first opportunity to pay summer students, officially "seasonal assistants." Students as volunteers had been encouraged prior to that. One of Mahan's greatest ambitions for Clinton Farms was "to set up a training program for students who wish to specialize in the correctional field." With the exception of one summer, the seasonal assistant positions were funded through the remainder of Mahan's career at Clinton Farms and for some years thereafter.

Through academic contacts at the American Prison Association and the American Association of Social Workers, Mahan sought to recruit interested and qualified students. Sociology departments, through Thorsten Sellin, University of Pennsylvania; Negley Teeters, Temple University; and Walter Reckless, Ohio State University; sent students, some of whom returned to Clinton Farms to fill regular positions or pursued careers in corrections elsewhere.

In the author's first summer at Clinton in 1943, she was joined by the commissioner's daughter, Janet Ellis, who was a sophomore at Hobart Smith College; a senior from Vassar College; and two seniors from the University of Pennsylvania, one of whom returned to marry a Clinton Farms employee and to work there herself for many years.

In the summer of 1945 the American Friends Service Committee of Philadelphia started an institutional unit at Clinton Farms, and seventeen members were employed. Lois Morris, a unit member, remained to work for most of the next thirty years. In January 1946 Antioch College began sending students for their internship program.

At a staff orientation session in the late 1950s Mahan said:

> [T]he main reason we have students every summer is to attract the right kind of young people into this field because other people steer you through community agencies like probation and parole. There are very few who put in a plug for the institutions. I think colleges—I am sure schools of social work—even today, preach that an institution is a dead end. Unfortunately that's true in a great many institutions.... But we are talking about a good institution and that's what everybody wants Clinton Farms to be. It is anything but a dead end. It is the beginning for so many of these people. But we can't have good institutions unless we have good staff.

Not only did Mahan encourage qualified students to work at Clinton Farms, she arranged informal and formal training for them. She met individually with students to counsel and advise them. Often she assigned someone on the staff or asked someone from the central office to arrange a more formal program. Always regular staff were invited and encouraged to attend. According to the 1945–46 annual report, "Dr. Lovell Bixby, Director, Division of Correction and Parole, arranged an excellent series of lectures for the students and the regular staff."

Day Parole

One of the major contributions the institution made to the war effort on the local level was the initiation of "day parole" so that inmates could help local farmers.

Day parole was not a new concept in women's institutions. The Reformatory for Women at Framingham, Massachusetts, which opened in 1877, began "indenture" before the end of the nineteenth century. Indenture allowed inmates to work in domestic service in the community. A few other juvenile and women's institutions started day parole in hospitals, beauty parlors, and stores as well as domestic and farm work during World War II.

Mahan explained its beginnings at Clinton Farms in answer to a question on day parole at a staff orientation in the late 1950s:

> Day parole was started back in the war years, as a matter of fact in April 1941. And that was because there were so few men around, and there was so much need, particularly on a lot of farms. When we started out, groups of girls went to work for several farmers around here who raised tomatoes for the market.

> I think they started out at $1.50 a day for an 8 hour day. The price has gone up to $4.00. From April '41 to April '57—would anyone like to guess the amount of money that this community has invested in Clinton Farms? Day Parole girls? Just make a guess—$112,286. Of that $21,650 has been taken from the day parole earnings to be deposited in the Welfare Fund. [Twenty-five percent of each inmate's day parole wage was deducted for the inmate welfare fund.] So you will see why we can say that the taxpayers' money did not buy the swimming pool.... It was earned by the girls.
>
> When we started this we were on our own. Of course we did get the approval of the Board of Managers. Then it spread to the State Home for Girls and the State Home for Boys and some of the men's institutions. Then when things became more normal in the employment situation in 1946, the privileges were withdrawn by the State Board of Control.
>
> The Board of Managers of this institution is made up of strong individuals. They took themselves down to Trenton, and they said, "We won't have this stopped. This is one of the best things that we have in our program. It is not only the means of partial self-support, but it is good preparation for regular parole." And Clinton got the privilege restored [by the State Board of Control].
>
> As you know it is kept as one of the good honor privileges for those in "good standing," and there are very close safeguards around this. We have a few unfortunate things—one runaway and things brought in that should not be brought in. But on the whole, I think that it develops initiative and responsibility in individuals and is the best way to return them to the community.

Mahan reported on day parole in the 1945-46 annual report and included "some of the girls' own expressions of what this privilege means to them":

> Day parole has helped me to realize that I can be accepted back in society again and that people don't really hold being in Clinton against a girl.... It has made it possible for me to earn something which gives me a certain feeling of security.... I am proud to be in the day parole group because the feeling of trust given me is something that builds up my morale and leaves me feeling a step nearer my goal of freedom.

The success of Mahan's work with the Board of Managers influencing the "powers that be" in Trenton to allow Clinton to continue day parole is noted in the 1946-47 annual report:

> The State Board of Control permitted the institution to continue "Day Parole," restricting it to domestic service under very close supervision. This is still the best intermediate step we know between the institution and regular parole. We

> expect that in a few years those who have benefitted from this practice will be reflected in the statistics of the successes on parole.

Mahan's strong leadership with her board in confronting the State Board of Control to allow Clinton Farms to continue day parole demonstrates Mahan's fight to keep the women's institution from being forced into a male mold. She knew it was a good program. She knew it was carried out in other states, and she trusted her staff, inmates, and the community. Not too many years later men's institutions discovered the benefits of day parole, called it "work release," and institutionalized it throughout correctional systems.

Alcoholics Anonymous

Another important program introduced at Clinton Farms during the war years—though not related to the war—was Alcoholics Anonymous.

In 1944 Clinton Farms became the second correctional institution in the country and the first women's institution to start an Alcoholics Anonymous (AA) group. Mahan, board member Mary Stevens Baird, and Elizabeth Connors, psychologist, heard Bill Wilson, cofounder of AA, speak in New York City in late 1943 and were impressed. They thought the AA philosophy could help alcoholic inmates when they returned to the community. Although there was success with alcoholic inmates in the institution, they returned to alcoholism when they left and went out in the community.

In February 1944, Baird brought Wilson to the annual conference of Superintendents of Correctional Institutions for Girls and Women in New York City. At that time, Mahan and Baird asked him about starting a group at Clinton Farms. He suggested they contact one of the members of the Morristown, New Jersey, group.

As a result, six members of the Morristown group met with inmates at the reformatory on 18 April 1944 and formed the Clinton Farms group. The Morristown group was joined in a few years by other New Jersey groups in coming to Clinton. Connors became the AA institutional sponsor and continued as sponsor until she retired in 1956.

For a few years in the late fifties and early sixties, the Clinton Reformatory for Women's group met once a year with the Annandale Reformatory for Men's group, alternating locations each year. This was initiated by Mahan and Anita Quarles when Quarles was switched from the Clinton Board of Managers to Annandale's.

Each spring the Clinton group held an anniversary meeting. Alumnae often returned for these occasions. In May 1969 the twenty-fifth anniversary meeting of the Clinton Farms group was held in memoriam to Edna Mahan.

AA and day parole were two very important and innovative programs initiated at the Reformatory for Women under Mahan's leadership. Although there were severe staff shortages at this time, there was relatively little disruption of the running of the institution. Inmates assumed more responsibilities and became involved in many volunteer activities toward the war effort. The morale of the institution was high due in part to inmates' and staff's participation in war work. However, the last two years of World War II were perhaps the most difficult Mahan faced in her career at Clinton Farms because of a staff scandal and Commissioner Ellis's death.

The Jayson Affair

Trust was basic to Edna Mahan's philosophy in running Clinton Farms. With long-term inmate Alice T., Mahan's trust was broken many times, yet she never gave up on Alice and was well rewarded for her patience and perseverance. When a long-time trusted staff member broke that trust, she became embroiled in a major scandal that threatened her reputation as well as the reformatory's.

Thomas Jayson was hired as a farmer before Mahan became superintendent. Soon after she took over as superintendent, she promoted him to head farmer because of his hard work, good performance, and loyalty. She trusted him.

In the spring of 1944 an inmate "informed Miss Mahan that [Jayson] had approached her on several occasions promising special favors if she would 'cooperate' with him." Jayson had been a good and trusted employee for twenty years. After some investigation into the inmate's story, Mahan found no evidence to corroborate it. The inmate was demoted, and Jayson was absolved.

On 20 March 1944, Mahan made a notation in her diary that is her first reference to the affair, "WJE [W. J. Ellis] re [T. J.]." On 1 April 1944 there is noted in her diary, "*Bet with HCP re [T. J.]!*" HCP was Mahan's secretary Helen C. Philhower. On the same date in Philhower's diary is "Bet with E.M. re [T. J.]!!" Mahan did not believe the allegation of the inmate. Philhower, who did not share Mahan's trust of Jayson, believed the inmate.

There are no further notations regarding the affair until October, when, according to the *Hunterdon Republican*, "reformatory officials discovered several notes that had passed between [Harold White], farm worker, and one of the inmates." Mahan met with each one of the farmers in question on 5 October 1944: "Asked [White] to resign about D.S. [inmate passing notes with him].... [T. J.]: 'I won't give you an answer right now.' " With the discovery of these notes and Mahan's confrontation with White and Jayson, a full investigation of the case was made.

On 4 November 1944 Commissioner Ellis, Lloyd Wescott (vice-president of the Board of Managers who also oversaw the farming operation at Clinton), and Mahan met with Jayson. Three inmates who had been involved with him came in, separately, and told their stories. Jayson offered his resignation.

Mahan and Assistant Superintendent Cox interviewed many inmates about the affair in the following month. Mahan's handwritten notes of some of these interviews give a picture of what had been going on in the fields and sheds:

> 11/10/44 M. H. [Inmate] Do you want to clear up the mess etc.? "Yes, I believe it—he ain't my type—he said to me one day, Shorty, how about going up in the upper sheds—I said no—of course I knew what he meant—another reason I didn't go in to give him what he wanted was because I was afraid of getting pregnant—I lied to you—I did try to tempt him—I wore a halter and pants rolled up—I wanted to but I was scared—I get caught so easy."
>
> 11/10/44 E. B. [Inmate] Re [T. J.]: about a week after E.G ran away—in pm, [T. J.] said: "Let's go in corn field, Red." No I'm picking apples. Then he asked A.—Went looking—they were laying in the corn. I said come on A.—He said just a minute.
>
> 11/10/44 M. G. [Inmate] Saw [T. J.] have rels. w. D. S. in 2 story shed Aug. '43.
>
> 11/10/44 E. C. [Inmate] Lied at first.—Re [T. J.] affair. "I saw he wanted to get around me so much—I was w. Mrs. Meyers [farm group leader] all the time—I'm not that low that I would go with him"—(denies—then)—"Well, Miss M, he said he would give me cigs & all if I did—I think it was about a month ago—at the sheds—the big shed—afternoon—"I'll do anything in the world for you if you'll suck me off.' "

White resigned and committed suicide 7 December after being questioned by Commissioner Ellis. The case was referred to the Hunterdon County Prosecutor's Office. There were, of course, many conferences with Commissioner Ellis and Eugene Urbaniak, chief of the Bureau of Legal Affairs of the Department of Institutions and Agencies. As reported in the *Newark Evening News*, 14 December 1944, a Hunterdon County grand jury hearing was held 13 December. "Twenty indictments charge [Jayson] with relations with nine inmates." After the indictments were handed down:

> Anthony M. Hauck, Jr., counsel for [Jayson], said last night his client will deny all charges when arraigned in court. He said the proceedings are the result of 'persecution' of [Jayson] because of long-time differences with Miss Edna Mahan, Superintendent.

Commissioner Ellis testified before the grand jury and praised Mahan's handling of the affair.

> Commissioner Ellis of the State Department of Institutions and Agencies...said he thought Miss Mahan deserved credit for her handling of the matter. She brought the girls' stories to the attention of the board of managers, which called in Ellis. He advised turning the case over to the prosecutor's office for investigation.

Although Jayson had submitted his resignation to Mahan on 4 November, he withdrew it a few days later. According to the *Newark Evening News*, "He instituted proceedings with the State Civil Service Commission to withdraw it on the ground it was obtained under duress." The *Hunterdon Republican* reported 1 January 1945; "An appeal by [Jayson]...from acceptance of his resignation last November by Superintendent Edna Mahan was dismissed Tuesday by the Civil Service Commission."

The Jayson trial was held 26 February 1945. He was given a suspended sentence of two to three years at the New Jersey State Prison and fined $500 on an assault and battery count. The prosecution did not press the remaining indictments.

In the midst of the final preparations for the Jayson trial (many Clinton Farms staff were subpoenaed, and Jayson's wife asked others to be character witnesses), Mahan found out that Commissioner Ellis was ill. She visited him 28 February and then went with Gebhardt on 1 March to Buck Hill Falls, Pennsylvania, for a rest. They returned from Buck Hill 6 March, and Ellis died 11 March 1945. His death on top of the Jayson affair was devastating for Edna Mahan.

Two letters from superintendents of the women's institutions at Muncy, Pennsylvania, and Indianapolis, Indiana, show their support and concern for her.

> My dear Edna:
>
> Ruth sent me a clipping from some paper—I don't know what—that you had won out on your case. Now, my dear, cheer up and stop worrying—and trust no man from now on. We told you that it would all iron out right and you would not believe us. [Mahan reported on the case on Feb. 13 at the Conference of Superintendents of Institutions for Women and Girls.]
>
> Good luck to you from now on, and remember, I love you and think you a "*swell gal*"!
>
> Sincerely, Franklin [Wilson]

> My Dear Friend:
>
> One of my former staff ladies sent me clippings about Mr. Ellis's death, and I have had you in mind ever since. He certainly was a very loyal friend to you and I trust that his passing will not throw your present difficulties into "high gear."

> I trust that you will come through without any detrimental physical reactions. Life is too short to have to be worried like you are when what you did was absolutely right.
>
> Since coming home from New York, I am more and more impressed with the idea of retiring from this type of a job. What has happened to you can happen to me, and I do not want to have to take it. I have had a very happy thirteen years here, and am figuring seriously on doing some other type of work that does not carry the heavy responsibilities.
>
> If friends standing by will help any, know that I am thinking of you and praying for you.
>
> Sincerely, Marian F. Gallup

Wescott said the thing that bothered Mahan the most about the Jayson case was that she trusted Jayson, and he had broken that trust. Franklin Wilson in her letter to Mahan advises her, "and trust no man from now on." Trust was at the very core of Mahan's personal and professional philosophy. Clinton Farms could not have been run as an open institution with a student government honor system without trust in inmates and staff. In 1939 in a conference with a long-term inmate, Mahan "told her most things didn't bother me but to lose confidence in a person did."

Her trust and confidence in others is one of the qualities her staff spoke of. She believed in you and, therefore, you knew you could do whatever she expected of you. She had great courage, and she instilled this in others.

Commissioner Ellis had recognized these qualities in her when she first met with him in 1928. His counsel and strong support of her ambitions and her programs at Clinton Farms added to her confidence in herself, her work, and her relationships with inmates and staff. She lost a strong and loving father figure, she told Anita Quarles soon after he died.

Mahan faced many crises at Clinton Farms during her forty years there. The Jayson case was the most devastating to her. Not only did Jayson break her trust, but both he and his wife told the public the charges were false and made up by Mahan to get rid of him. She survived it and was given total support by Reeve Schley, who became acting commissioner until Sanford Bates was appointed 1 June 1944.

Medical Research

After World War II, medical research began at Clinton Farms. The studies came about as a result of personal connections. Emelen Stokes, M.D., of the University of Pennsylvania Medical School served on the State Board of Control of Institutions and Agencies. His brother, Joseph Stokes, M.D., also at the University of Pennsylvania Medical School, summered at Pocono Lake Preserve, Pennsylvania, where the Quarles family spent the summer.

Mahan and the Board of Managers studied very carefully any proposals for medical research that came before them. Some were rejected. After careful investigation and assurances concerning the risks involved, the board and Mahan recognized the contributions inmate volunteers could make to the advancement of medical knowledge and gave approval with the State Board of Control concurring. For those inmates who chose to participate, it was an opportunity to give something back to society. Many inmates expressed this as a reason for volunteering.

The first research undertaken was an ectoparasite study in 1946. Mahan described it in the 1946-47 annual report:

> Through Commissioner Bates and Dr. Emelen Stokes of the State Board of Control, Clinton undertook a nutritional study conducted by the Macy Foundation, U.S. Typhus Commission and University of Pennsylvania. Sixty volunteers selected from all cottages were transferred to Conover Cottage to participate in the study which began in October '46 and ended in May '47. These girls [some staff also volunteered] fed body lice daily. The purpose of the study was to show the relationship between an individual's nutritional state and the ability to breed lice, the theory being that well nourished people do not breed lice rapidly. Special diets for the well nourished and under-nourished groups were supervised by Dr. Paul Gyorgy of the Department of Pediatrics, University of Pennsylvania and Dr. Francis Evans, Assistant Professor of Biology, Haverford College. At the end of the experiment Dr. Frank Fremont-Smith of the Josiah Macy Jr. Foundation and Dr. Gyorgy arranged a banquet for the participants.

No record of the scientific results of this study could be found. The women involved in this research did not face great medical risks. They became very itchy and uncomfortable. They joked about "their lice." They enjoyed the camaraderie and attention of living together in a cottage set aside for them while they took part in the project. They felt satisfaction at the contribution they made. This and the banquet were their rewards.

Desegregation

At the time Clinton Farms opened, segregation in housing and programs for black and white inmates was the usual practice in correctional institutions. A letter to May Caughey from the State Board of Charities, Albany, New York, 19 February 1915, asked her opinion on housing blacks and whites together. It specified as one of the concerns, "on the one hand it is alleged that this practice is harmful because of improper relationships of a serious nature likely to grow up between the white and the 'colored' inmates. On the other hand, the likelihood and the effect of this danger are said to be greatly exaggerated."

In light of the above, the 1913 annual report notes that there are plans for building a cottage for "colored" inmates for which the legislature has appropriated $25,000. "We realize that their treatment will involve many difficulties." There were no black inmates at Clinton Farms when it opened.

Superintendent Caughey wrote in the 1914 annual report:

> The problem of dealing with "colored" delinquents is admittedly more difficult than that of dealing with white delinquents, and therefore, it is necessary to take every precaution to avoid future trouble of any kind. We hope to secure "colored" officers, for we feel that capable "colored" women of education will be able to exert a very beneficial influence over less fortunate members of their own race.

Stowe Cottage for African American inmates, the first cottage built at Clinton Farms, opened in July 1915. Caughey wrote in the 1915 annual report:

> We run Stowe Cottage...almost like a separate institution. The "colored" women have their own school work.... When they work out on the farm, they do so in separate groups under their own officer. They only see the other women at Chapel on Sunday. In doing this we do not wish to be misunderstood. We do not divide the "colored" and white because we feel the former are inferior to the latter, but because they are different races, each with their own peculiarities. As a matter of fact, the Stowe Cottage women are housed in our only new building, and do not suffer one-half the inconvenience of a new institution in its pioneer stage as felt by others. We feel the "colored" women are much happier by themselves. They are more childish and undeveloped in many ways than the white women, and being by themselves, they can make up their own fun and entertainments which are of the sort to make their lives happy and contented. But if they were with the white women, they would not develop this initiative. They would simply follow the white women in their plans. We have been interested to find that the same view is held by our "colored" officers.

The strict segregation of the "colored" and white inmates was reaffirmed by the board at its 11 May 1926 meeting when Cornelia Lounsbury reported there had been note and gift passing between the two, and she "stated that she personally felt the absolute segregation of white and 'colored' was desirable."

The first efforts at integration began as soon as Mahan arrived at Clinton Farms. The board minutes of 11 September 1928 report "that the school expected to have the 'colored' girls in the classes [with white inmates] during the winter instead of in separate classes." Already noted was her success in moving the "colored" babies from a leaky porch at Stowe to the Wittpenn nursery in November 1928 and the objections to this practice that were raised by the Maplewood Women's Club when it visited in 1931.

There were apparently no further efforts at desegregation until November 1945 as reported in the board minutes:

> Miss Mahan asked the Board members to decide whether we should continue to segregate the "colored" in the two separate units—Stowe and Paddock. The consensus was that we might try non-segregation in a limited way and under specific conditions at first. One way is to send "colored" mothers back to the maternity unit instead of to Stowe following delivery. Another way is, if we work out the idea of a pre-parole cottage, to use Paddock where only 30 can be housed and to mix "colored" and white who will be considered for parole within two or three months.

The board minutes of 16 July 1946 report " 'colored' mothers now remain in Wittpenn Cottage following confinement instead of being transferred to the 'colored' unit and 'colored' girls have been working at the barn since June 17th." The May 1947 board minutes report, "On April 12th (1947) negro girls were transferred to all white cottages and white girls were transferred to Stowe. This means that we no longer have segregation."

Lois Morris, head cottage officer in Silzer at the time, recalls:

> It all went smoothly. There was no announcement about it. Miss Mahan talked to each woman who was to move. No pressure was put on anyone. As head cottage officer I received a memo saying who was coming and who was moving out. After the cottages were desegregated, we always tried to have at least one black officer assigned to each cottage.

An inmate wrote to a friend, "Our cottages are all mixed now. I think it is a grand thing. It will make us have better understanding and not so much hate. Paddock has worked out good. I think the other ones will too."

Mahan's friend from California, Walter Gordon, chairman, Adult Authority, California Department of Corrections, wrote her 3 July 1947:

> Sanford Bates forwarded to me a letter in which he quoted an excerpt from your report of your meeting held on May 14, 1947, which, in brief, stated that you had eliminated segregation in cottages under your jurisdiction.

> Needless to say I was most happy to receive this information, and wish to compliment you on your understanding of the problem.
>
> Mrs. Gordon and I have often thought of you, and hope that we will have an opportunity to have a good chat with you at the Correctional Congress to be held at Long Beach in September.

After the institution was desegregated with no problems, Mahan expressed her regret that she had not done this at the beginning of her tenure at Clinton Farms when she moved the black babies to Wittpenn. The board would have resisted this total integration more strongly than they did the babies because of society's attitudes.

There was much controversy and discussion during World War II about integration of the armed forces. This happened after the war. Society, at least in the Northeast, was more able to accept integration of a women's reformatory in 1947 than it would have been in 1915 or 1928.

Postwar Population Boom

Although the inmate population at Clinton Farms remained stable during the war years, it soared at the end of World War II. In 1946 the population reached a high of 451 inmates. An all-time high of 472 was reached in 1948. (The institution's official capacity was 190–200.)

The rapid increase in population was due in part to the fact that service men returned to the jobs they had left to go to war and many women were displaced from the workforce. In addition, the divorce rate peaked in the years immediately following the war as a result of hasty marriages entered into before service men shipped out overseas. Many women were left with no means of support.

Measures used to handle the crowding included double bunking, cots on enclosed cottage porches, a dormitory in Wittpenn basement, and in 1948 the construction of an overflow dormitory.

A programmatic response to the population explosion was described in a *New York Times* article, "Mental Hospital Has Convict Aides," dated 8 August 1950:

> The idea of using prisoners [as attendants for mental patients] was born of necessity three years ago when Trenton State Hospital had a shortage of ward attendants. At the same time, Miss Edna Mahan, superintendent of New Jersey's only women's prison, was pleading for some solution for the desperate overcrowding there.
>
> Today, twenty-eight women, serving terms that range from a few months for crimes such as neglect of children to longer sentences for more serious offenses

> live at Mercer Field, (a Naval Air Station in the war converted to a hospital unit for mental patients) thirty-five miles from Clinton Prison....
>
> "We value this as a good opportunity for our girls," Miss Mahan says. "We don't always succeed, but for the most part we are pleased with the results. For some girls this has made all the difference in the world. They find out they can do this work, handling difficult cases where others have failed, and they get confidence from it."

According to the 1946–47 annual report, "Twenty-five women were transferred to work at Mercer Field on March 15, 1947.... [T]he program is working out quite successfully. Two cottage supervisors from the Clinton staff are assigned to supervise the group at Mercer Field."

The Mercer Field project was engineered by Bixby, deputy commissioner in charge of correction and parole. It was needed by both institutions at the time it opened, and it was innovative. As long as there were surplus inmates at Clinton Farms to transfer to work there it was successful.

But the inmates had to be carefully selected, and when the inmate pool was reduced, it was not possible to find enough qualified inmates to transfer there. Those who went began to complain because they worked long hours, the duties were strenuous, and the pay was low—fifty cents a day. Also, according to Morris, it was hard to find good supervisors to send there, so sometimes ones who were not working well at Clinton Farms were sent.

When the Mercer Field project was no longer able to fill its purpose successfully it was terminated by the mutual consent of Clinton Farms, Trenton State Hospital, and the Department of Institutions and Agencies. It remained in operation through 1953. By this time the Clinton Farms population was averaging 365, and a new cottage had opened in June 1953. Mahan reported at the 25 November 1953 board meeting, "The Clinton population working at Mercer Field has been reduced to 19.... The institution has not been able to refill the vacancies...because of the low population.... In many ways,...this has been one of the best rehabilitative programs Clinton has had."

Runaways and Security

Runaways and escapes present a potential problem to any correctional institution. Where the institution has its inmates in locked cells at night, with high walls and armed officers in lookout towers, the threat of escape is minimized. An institution with few locked doors, no fences or perimeter walls, and relatively free movement of the inmate population continually faces the possibility of runaways. A few runaways from such an institution are expected every year. A large number of runaways present a threat to the system.

Mahan was always concerned about the public's perception of the open institution when there were many runaways or if an inmate who had gained a lot of publicity ran away. In the thirties she wrote in the progress notes of an interview with one such inmate:

> I told her that the minute she began to be tempted to think about running away, she should think about the consequences of her letting herself down, her cottage, me, the institution, Commissioner Ellis, and the State of New Jersey. I told her the state was just waiting for us to lose a girl who had attracted so much attention and prejudice in the public press as she had to have them force us to change our system here. I told her that never again could we give the girls the privileges they receive now if something of this sort happened. She said she realized that and that she never would betray the trust we are placing in her.

Runaways occurred at Clinton Farms from its first year of operation. Demotion and locking had always been penalties for running away. Other procedures varied over the years.

The issue of increased security was raised in the 1945-46 annual report: "A wing of Paddock Cottage...was reconstructed to make eight small secure rooms to house serious problem cases requiring isolation from the group." Paddock Unit opened on 13 April 1946. It remained a small secure unit into the 1970s. Paddock Unit inmates were part of the student government system. They lived and worked as a group under the supervision of a long-term trusted inmate.

The 1946-47 annual report noted:

> Budget requests for 1947–48 will include…a large housing unit. The unit should contain a wing or section of maximum security rooms for difficult problem cases requiring segregation from the group living in open cottages.

There were years when there were very few runaways and others when there were many. In 1947 and 1948, when the institution was extremely crowded, there were many runaways. The board and the staff became alarmed, and on 14 January 1948, two of the board members addressed the entire population and asked the inmates to elect a representative in each cottage to meet with a committee of the board to consider the following:

> 1. Ways to prevent runaways; 2. ways to discipline individuals who do run away; 3. ways to reward cottages having no runaways; and 4. group responsibility and group discipline for runaways.

The recommendations of the cottage representatives were reported to the Board of Managers at its February meeting. At the March meeting of the board the members put into effect recommendations for both punishments and rewards. Punishments included no smoking and no movies for the whole cottage. Cottages that went a year with no runaways were allowed to hang their cottage banner over their fireplace, and they were given a party. Here was an attempt to involve all members of the Clinton Farms community in alleviating the runaway situation.

Some of the honor inmates' reactions to the awards for good behavior were excerpted from letters they wrote in 1949, which were routinely read by a mail censor:

> [*Sophie P.*] We had a wonderful party Wednesday night. Miss Mahan let us see a movie in our cottage. Miss Mahan gave us this party because our cottage being an "Honor Cottage" for over a year.
>
> To top this last night a few girls from each cottage were invited to another party. We saw "Always in My Heart." We had refreshments and smokes. The girls danced and all had a wonderful time. We broke up at twelve midnight.
>
> [*Mabel L.*] Last night was quite something. The student officers and some of the honor girls were given a party. It was quite an affair. There were a lot of us there and Miss Mahan and all of the officers went home after the movies and left us to do as we pleased. It was a wonderful evening.
>
> [*Dorothy B.*] Miss Mahan gave us a party. She is one swell person if only some of the girls would understand her and try to do what is right.

It is impossible to know how much the punishment and reward system did to alleviate the runaway situation. In 1948 when the population reached its peak, a new, temporary sleeping dormitory, Thompson Hall, was opened to house the overflow from three cottages in sixty beds. The east wing of Stowe was reconstructed as a security unit and opened in December 1948. Mahan reported in the Clinton Farms triennial report for fiscal years 1 July 1948 to 30 June 1951, "This section has 13 rooms available for maximum security living. Due to the shortage of staff this unit has always been supervised by reliable inmates."

By 1950 there were only three runaways from the institution. The disciplinary measures were gradually modified as were the rewards for cottages having no runaways. Beginning in 1950, all who ran away from the reformatory appeared in court where they were given a three-year concurrent or consecutive sentence.

Social Workers and Social Work

Although psychology and sociology undergraduate students were attracted to work at Clinton Farms, Mahan, a certified social worker, was less successful in attracting graduate students from schools of social work. Indeed, according to Close (1949), a grudge of Mahan's "is pointed directly at the schools of social work which she believes have not done their proper part in interesting prospective candidates for institutional work. For several years she has tried to interest two of the country's oldest professional schools in sending students to Clinton for supervised field work, but to no avail. 'Who then will train our future administrators?' she asks."

There are two main reasons schools of social work did not send many students to correctional institutions at this time. First, there were no undergraduate social work programs because the Council of Social Work Education did not accredit them. Most of the students who came to Clinton Farms as seasonal assistants or interns were undergraduates.

Second, a correctional institution is an authoritative setting, and some social workers questioned the logic of practicing social casework in such a setting. Herbert Stroup in his 1953 textbook, *Social Work: An Introduction to the Field*, discusses this in his chapter, "Work with Delinquents and Criminals." "Some individuals argue that social casework can scarcely be practiced in a compulsory setting, that it is not a proper restriction upon social casework to have it as an adjunct to the strong arm of the law."

The position of social worker at Clinton Farms was added in 1947 and filled by Leontine "Lee" P. Belmont. A graduate of the New York School of Social Work, Belmont was the first blind student accepted at the school. She was working for Catholic Charities when she heard that Clinton Farms was looking for a social worker. She called Mahan to inquire about the position and told her she had a visual handicap, not that she was completely blind. When she went to Clinton to be interviewed and revealed her true condition, "Miss Mahan had no hesitation about my working there." Belmont had no training for work in a correctional setting. She said there was one course at the school having to do with prisons, but when she was a student, she couldn't imagine who would take such a course. She worked well with Mahan and enjoyed the work. She said "I wasn't in competition with Edna. We worked constructively together. She scared me at first. She was so definite."

Belmont observed that Mahan sometimes gave inmates a hard time. "That's when I first went there. But I saw she was right. She knew her work. Edna had an instinctive feel for people. She could sense when a girl was ready for parole."

In a letter to Mahan dated 4 September 1949 concerning a visit to the Hudson County Jail to see Clinton inmates confined there, Belmont wrote:

> It's so nice to be on vacation but I know after I have a rest I'll be anxious to return to you and 'my girls.'
>
> It's been such a wonderful experience to be at Clinton. Working has its advantages and when you have so many pleasant associations and a congenial atmosphere it is a real joy. You have helped me in so many ways to find myself. In the last few months I have felt this keenly. In the face of such a satisfying personal experience, it is so easy to forget that you have so many others who need to share this too. So, if I do forget sometimes, I'll try not to, I hope you will promptly advise me.
>
> Sometimes I wish that we were not working together because I feel it would be such fun just being friends.

Belmont alludes to the fact that Mahan has so many who need her. It was not only the inmates who needed her. Mahan was extremely supportive of staff with personal problems and spent hours talking with them and helping.

When interviewed, Belmont was asked for her insights on Mahan's inability to get too close to anybody. Belmont said she really didn't know but, "Edna Mahan was hurt deep down in herself. She was sensitive to her environment when she was growing up. She was apprehensive about getting close to people."

During the spring term of 1950, Lee Belmont and Edna Mahan took a course on Karen Horney's theory of neurosis at the New School in New York. They drove into New York once a week for ten weeks. Belmont said, "Edna was interested in different schools of psychiatry. Horney was down-to-earth. She had a much broader view than Freud of women and their accomplishments—women and practicalities. Edna was interested in psychotherapy but in a practical sense."

Mahan, from a practical sense, was concerned with the role of the social worker in a correctional setting. She asked Belmont to put in writing "The Function of a Case Worker in a Correctional Institution." Among the points Belmont wrote are these, which are concerned with issues of authority:

> The case worker must believe in the constructive use of authority; this means not only an intellectual but also an emotional acceptance of this.
>
> The caseworker is a liaison person between the institution and the inmate; she remains objective at all times; she accepts the need for discipline and does not interfere with this.
>
> The case worker permits a discussion of feeling and attitudes, but at no time does she give the inmate the impression that she condones unacceptable behavior. This is extremely important.
>
> The case worker must keep in mind at all times that a good case work treatment program demands that she concentrate her efforts on the individual cases

> and that she does not become involved with institutional procedures that are none of her business.
>
> The case worker must always be mindful that no setting is perfect. She must be tolerant of the imperfections.... She will make note of the negatives, and she will have the wisdom and the good sense to know when and when not to make suggestions to the administration.

Belmont did not have a difficult time working within the authoritarian correctional setting because her prior work with Catholic Charities meant working within the structure and authority of the church. She also had great admiration for Mahan and was willing to learn from her.

Belmont left Clinton Farms at the end of 1950. During the next four years Mahan and the board hired two well-qualified psychiatric social workers in hopes of doing some special projects under their guidance. The new director of psychiatric social work began work on 9 July 1951. She was not able to work effectively within the authoritarian correctional setting, did not inspire confidence in either inmates or staff, and was not a team player. She resigned in August 1955, and the position was abolished.

The second psychiatric social worker, hired in February 1952, had been a faculty member of the New York School of Social Work. Mahan admired her and took a risk in hiring her because she was a recovering alcoholic. Although she supervised a student from the New York School of Social Work for her field work placement from September 1952 to June 1953, organized staff training at the institution, and worked with individual cases, she resigned in January 1954 because of her problems with alcohol. The salaries of the social work positions were used to pay the New Jersey State Diagnostic Center for additional psychiatric services.

Mahan expressed her frustration with social workers' lack of training for work in correctional settings on 4 April 1957 at a meeting of superintendents. She was the last of the superintendents to speak "on what correctional institutions can expect of psychiatric services" and included the following in her remarks:

> Diagnostic Center trained psychiatrists are correctionally oriented. (New Jersey can thank the Lord for this!) They recognize and accept the authoritarian realities. We need them to supervise and teach psychologists, social workers and others who may not have this orientation. Some social workers new to this field have been known to declare that they are the only ones who do not have the punitive point of view!

Miriam Van Waters under Fire in Massachusetts

While Edna Mahan was achieving success and recognition for her work at Clinton Farms, Miriam Van Waters and Framingham came under investigation after an inmate suicide in 1947 that received a great deal of publicity. The ensuing investigations and hearings caused Mahan great conflict between her personal loyalties to Van Waters and her own professional standards.

The inmate suicide in November 1947 was featured in the Hearst newspapers in Boston, which "planted the idea that there was something salacious, if not sinister, about it." The state senator from the inmate's home district insisted the case be reinvestigated even though the District Attorney's and Department of Correction's investigation had found no evidence of foul play (Rowles 1962).

The case might well have run its course in the headlines and faded were it not for the fact that in 1948 a new commissioner of correction, Elliott E. McDowell, was appointed by the governor. The new commissioner's philosophy of correctional treatment was hard-lined, rigid, and opposed to Van Waters' philosophy. He allowed the investigation of her leadership of the institution to go forward full steam. She was accused of such things as running a "loose jail," having a relaxed attitude toward homosexuality, hiring staff who were former offenders, and allowing inmates in indenture status (work release) to work in commercial establishments instead of only domestic service (Rowles 1962).

On 4 June 1948 the commissioner sent a directive to Van Waters "to return to the rules and regulations of October 31st, 1923. At the stroke of a pen we were thrown back into the conditions of a quarter century ago" (Rowles 1962). McDowell used these to build his case against Van Waters. On 9 June 1948, the senator from the inmate's district presented a resolution to the senate "to create a special legislative commission to conduct 'an immediate and thorough investigation of the conduct' of Framingham" (Rowles 1962). An investigative committee was appointed and worked through the summer and early fall. The commissioner and his deputy continued their attacks against Van Waters and kept the affair in the public's eye through the daily press.

While this investigation was going on, Geraldine Thompson, one of Van Waters' long-time friends, came to her defense. She gave Mahan a copy of the "Rules for the Direction of the Officers and Employees of the Reformatory for Women, Framingham, Massachusetts," adopted by the Department of Correction in 1923 to study and comment on.

Mahan replied to Thompson 30 September 1948 that she, Mary Cox, and Elizabeth Connors had studied the rules:

> At the time these rules became effective we understand that Framingham was one large congregate unit. Those of us who operate an open institution have no

> experience on which to base an evaluation of the rules promulgated to govern the staff and inmates in a maximum custody setting. Furthermore, we are aware of the differences affecting the administration in Massachusetts under the present set-up and that in New Jersey where the superintendent has the combined support of the State Board of Control, the Commissioner and the Board of Managers.

The remainder of Mahan's letter refers to some of the Framingham rules that were once in force at Clinton Farms but had changed with changing conditions and times. They also point to some progressive parts of the document. The letter does not lend strong support to Van Waters' case.

Thompson invited Mahan to come to her home to talk about this. There is no indication of how or if the letter was ever used. Mahan wrote her own letter in support of Van Waters 15 October 1948 and sent it to a member of the "Friends of Framingham," a group of citizens who had rallied to help Van Waters:

> Since 1922 I have known Dr. Van Waters intimately.... She was the recognized authority in juvenile delinquency and social work on the West Coast. The many students just out of college who were fortunate enough to have contact with her found her an inspirational teacher and guide. It was through her influence and assistance that I entered the correctional field. Many of her former students and associates have since become known in the field of social work and delinquency in various states.
>
> Not only was she President of the National Conference of Social Work but since she left that field she has earned a national reputation as an able, respected and admired authority in adult delinquency. She has many times served as Chairman of the Committee on Women's Institutions of the American Prison Association.
>
> We all regret that Dr. Van Waters has been singled out to receive such rough treatment after her years of devoted service and inspired leadership. I speak most sincerely for myself and I feel that I can speak for all the women in my field when I say that we hope you and the other people in Massachusetts who know what a real contribution she has made throughout the years will be able to come to her assistance now.

McDowell's attack on Van Waters was relentless in spite of mounting support in her defense. On 7 January 1949 he fired her on twenty-seven charges (Rowles 1962). Ten days later Mahan wrote the following letter to Van Waters from the Inn at Buck Hill Falls, Pennsylvania, where she and Reading Gebhardt were spending a few days (Schlesinger, Van Waters papers, file 201):

Miriam, dearest Miriam—

There is so little to say to bring you comfort. You know I am thinking of you constantly and praying. Your strength for this battle comes from within you. The love and loyalty of your friends are wrapped all around you and "*They*" can not hurt you. I know you would find much—maybe not much—but at least something about all this to be merry about. I can hear your gay laugh as of old when the going got tough!! Given 'em hell! Make 'em like it!! *You will win.*

To my surprise I ran into Geoffrey May in our office the other day—conducting some sort of study. He spoke of you with respect and affection.

Reading says fight the good fight!

Our warmest love to you.

Always, Edna

Close (1949) wrote about the case in an article in *Survey*, "Reform Without Locks":

> One of the country's leading advocates of constructive correctional practices, Dr. Miriam Van Waters, is under fire in Massachusetts. The outcome of the controversy may spell the forward or backward movement of the treatment of women prisoners in the state. Ousted from her position as superintendent of the State Reformatory for Women at Framingham, Dr. Van Waters last month (February, 1949) underwent twenty-six days of hearings before the commissioner of corrections, Elliott E. McDowell, on charges made against her by that same commissioner, who in the end sustained his own previous action.
>
> The famous penologist now has one more recourse in her battle for reinstatement—investigation by a three-man commission appointed by the governor. The commission has already been appointed by the governor and includes: Erwin N. Griswold, dean of the Harvard Law School; Robert G. Clark, Jr., first assistant district attorney of Plymouth and Norfolk counties; and Mrs. Roger J. Putnam, wife of a former mayor of Springfield.

The hearings before the governor's commission began at the end of February 1949 and went on for nine days. The commission's decision, which was handed down a week after the adjournment of the hearings, 11 March, reversed "the decision of the appointing authority" (Rowles 1962). Van Waters returned to Framingham that afternoon.

Mahan's diary on 11 March 1949 carries the notation, "5:15 Re M.V.W. Spencer Miller—Complete vindication!"

Two days later she started a letter to Van Waters (Schlesinger, Van Waters papers, file 208):

Miriam, dear Miriam,

Spencer Miller telephoned me the wondrous news about 5 o'clock Friday. The clouds rolled away. The war was over. We can breathe again. And you can with the turn of the wrist, steer your Framingham onward and upward. My heart is full of Thanksgiving.

March 20

Some crisis kept me from finishing that night and here I am again—late but loving! Maybe my note won't get lost now in among the hordes of others....

Oh, Miriam, you fought the good fight and won as you and I knew you would. You never wavered or lost faith or courage. You will go on to greater heights and you will always be the leader of us all.

My love and admiration always, Edna

Edna Mahan's letters *in support* of Miriam Van Waters and *to* her are very different in tone and in depth of support. The professional letters are not strong letters of support. The strongest point she makes in the letter to Thompson after reviewing the 1923 rules is "the differences affecting the administration under the present set-up at Framingham and that in New Jersey." Under the New Jersey system the commissioner could not fire a superintendent. Mahan was appointed by the Board of Managers and served at its pleasure. When Cornelia Lounsbury was asked to resign in 1928, the Board of Managers conferred with Commissioner Ellis before it asked for her resignation.

Mahan kept her board apprised of any policy change or major change in practice. Usually she had the whole board or one or two members meet with the commissioner, the State Board of Control, or whatever authoritative body or person was necessary to validate or protest a change. She did not act on her own without at least consulting the board. Van Waters could check everything with her commissioner (which records indicate she did), but she did not have the protection of a board when a new and hostile commissioner challenged her.

Not only were Mahan's professional letters of support not strong, when she was asked to go to Boston and testify during Commissioner McDowell's hearings, she declined. In looking through her diary for September, October, and November 1948 there are several calls from Elizabeth Bode, another Californian brought to Massachusetts by Van Waters. She was working with the parole department at the time of the Van Waters hearings. Bode came to visit Mahan in October. They must have talked about Van Waters' problems. There were also calls from individual members of Friends of Framingham asking about hiring people with criminal records to work at Clinton Farms. In reference to one such call she noted in her diary, "Told her no person w. record can be aptd. by CS [Civil Service] in NJ."

Although Van Waters had mentored Mahan early in her career in corrections and by 1948 both were recognized as tops in the field (Austin MacCormick testified to this at the commissioner's hearings), their styles of administration were very different.

Elizabeth Bode, herself a devoted disciple of Miriam Van Waters, wrote Van Waters concerning this on 15 September 1948. She begins, "Dear Boss" and goes on to talk about the attack on her. Then she critically addresses her style:

> You know, Doctor, I've worried about you for years. I know you never wanted to be protected—never believed in it. But all these years you should have had the laws *with* you. Without *fundamentally* altering your methods, and without at all changing your philosophy—I think there could have been more protection for you and what you believed in. You are primarily a great teacher and philosopher. You can set a plan of treatment and inspire those around you to carry it out. But *down the line*, there should be not only those who caught the inspiration but those, who, as well have an ability to "keep the lines straight," to put your plans into practical, clearly understood action. Lots of times I've argued individual procedures with you—but usually my difference with you was not in what you wanted to accomplish but was about the most effective way of accomplishing it. That's all water over the dam. But right now I'll be in there with every strength and facility I have to help you. (Schlesinger, Van Waters papers, file 197)

Lois Morris, who worked with both Mahan and Van Waters, characterized the difference as one in which Mahan took a back seat in situations and Van Waters took a front seat. This is illustrated in a notation from Mahan's diary of Sunday, 2 September 1928, soon after she arrived at Clinton. "Chapel—Didn't sit on the *throne* but w. the rest of the poor sinners." According to Morris, "At Framingham Dr. Van Waters always sat on the *throne* at chapel and chose and directed the girls who participated in the service." Mahan told Morris she didn't believe one person should exert so much control.

Although Mahan's professional support *on behalf* of Van Waters was not strong, her personal support in letters *to* her was. Van Waters and Mahan had built a very close pseudo-family relationship at the beginning of Mahan's career. Van Waters in personal and professional letters to Mahan in the thirties and forties signed off with a family reference. She ends a professional letter dated 4 September 1933, "But most of all I need my daughter, my first child." She wrote Mahan 3 July 1934 about the possibility of exchanging interns and adds at the end:

> Your god-daughter [Sarah, Van Waters' adopted daughter] is in camp in Fairlee, VT. Your sis [Bode] is very well. Your ma misses you.

Mahan had very strong feelings of loyalty, and at this terrible time in Van Waters' career she must have been deeply torn between her personal feelings of love and gratitude and her professional stance that she could not support her methods. Mahan and Van Waters remained friends, worked together on the Women's Committee of the American Prison Association, the American League to Abolish Capital Punishment, and on other issues. But there was never again the very close family relationship.

Personal Life

Edna Mahan always took time from her professional life to enjoy a personal life with friends, to vacation in California, the Pocono Mountains in Pennsylvania, or Mohonk in New York state. Later she built a home on St. Croix in the Virgin Islands.

When she was off duty for an evening with friends in the Clinton area or for a month in St. Croix, she left the reformatory under the direction of the assistant superintendent and other administrative and professional staff. She trusted them and had complete faith in their ability to run Clinton Farms and did not expect to be called for emergencies. Indeed, her vitality as an administrator depended, in large measure, on her ability to leave her professional life behind for periods of time.

Mahan's daily diaries tell not only of her professional appointments, phone calls, runaways, etc., but also her personal activities. In the 1940s she was engaged in an active social life in Hunterdon County. She loved to entertain at Homestead, which she did often. And she was a sought-after guest, because she was attractive, always interesting but never had to be center stage, entertaining, and witty. The successful and talented "lady warden" was admired by the community. The more quiet and reserved Gebhardt was her devoted escort.

The Lloyd B. Wescott family, who in 1936 bought and operated a large dairy farm across the road from Clinton Farms, became very close friends. Lloyd Wescott was appointed to the Clinton Farms Board of Managers in the mid-forties and was a frequent visitor. During his twelve years on the Clinton board, he was a great support to Mahan. His wife, Barbara, was a patron of the arts. His parents, the senior Wescotts ("Sr. W's " in Mahan's diary), and his brother, Glenway, a Pulitzer-prize-winning novelist, were all part of the Mulhocaway Farm complex. They admired Mahan greatly and enjoyed her company. One sister, Beth, and her family lived in the community, and another sister, Beulah, worked in New York City but came to Clinton most weekends. Beth and Beulah were close friends of Mahan's. The Wescott family became another of Edna Mahan's families. In her diary the most frequently mentioned entertaining was with various members of the Wescott family.

Gebhardt's family lived in the community. His brother, Philip, was a county judge who did not share Mahan's philosophy of treatment of lawbreakers. There is occasional mention of dinner with them or some members of the Gebhardt family. But the Gebhardt family never became Mahan's family.

Exercise was very important to her. She often noted in her diary if a Saturday or Sunday went by and she had no exercise. As often as she could, she walked from Homestead to her office in the administration building. Throughout all her years at Clinton Farms there are notes of long walks with someone. In her years with Gebhardt, he was her frequent walking companion around the grounds. Staff said they knew very little about the relationship between the two, but they often saw them out walking together.

She always enjoyed swimming and tennis. There was a tennis court at Homestead until the fifties, when it became difficult to keep up. During the forties she had the little pond by Homestead dredged and cleaned so she could swim in it. In 1957 an outdoor swimming pool was built, and from May to September she was frequently there during the lunch hour or on a Sunday morning.

Horseback riding was a favorite past time. Caroline Wittpenn sent Mahan her horse, Robin, in 1932 with instructions: "He should be ridden with a loose rein and will respond to the slightest indication from the rein or heel turning in any direction wanted." Horses for riding were kept in the horse barn until the 1950s, and Mahan rode regularly with Gebhardt, the Wescotts, staff, friends, or alone. She often lead the annual Clinton Farms circus parade on horseback.

She enjoyed being out of doors. She responded to the seasons and the weather. She loved the snow. She recorded in her diary each year when she heard the first peeper in the pond. The diary often noted rainy and miserable Sundays when she couldn't get out. On the other hand there are such days as Memorial Day 1946: "Gardened and took the sun most of the day. Very hot." She liked to work in the garden, and she always had her own vegetable garden at Homestead. Fresh asparagus just cut and her own tomatoes with fresh dill were two favorites.

Weekends away from Clinton Farms and longer vacations were a necessity. She and Gebhardt went to Buck Hill Falls, two hours away in the Pocono Mountains of Pennsylvania, for weekends. Mohonk in New York was a special spot for vacations. As her mother was getting older, they often spent a month in California visiting her and Mahan's many friends in the Los Angeles and San Francisco areas.

The twentieth anniversary of her coming to Clinton Farms was 14 August 1948. She and Gebhardt were in California, so there was no notice taken of it at that time. However, on 15 December 1948 at a staff Christmas party, she was surprised with a skit recounting events of those twenty years. Morris played the part of Mahan and asked Gebhardt to sneak out some of her clothing. One of the events enacted was removing the bars from the windows of the cottages.

Those first twenty years were replete with her accomplishments at Clinton Farms in spite of constraints imposed by the Depression and World War II. The next twenty years presented more challenges and significant accomplishments as well as prestigious awards.

1. Front and back cover of the "Social Case Mystery Goat Book," in 1923.
2. View from Stowe Cottage to chapel in the 1920s.
3. Edna Mahan in the 1930s.
4. A farm crew in the 1920s. Staff cottage and Stowe Cottage are in the background.

1

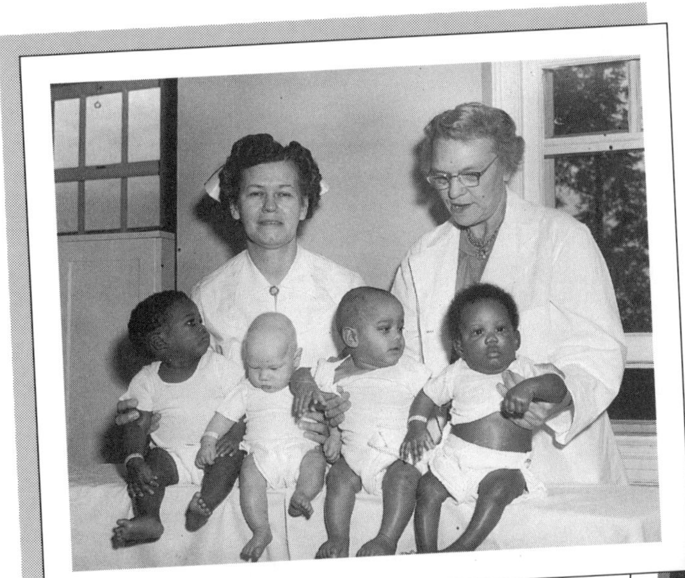

3

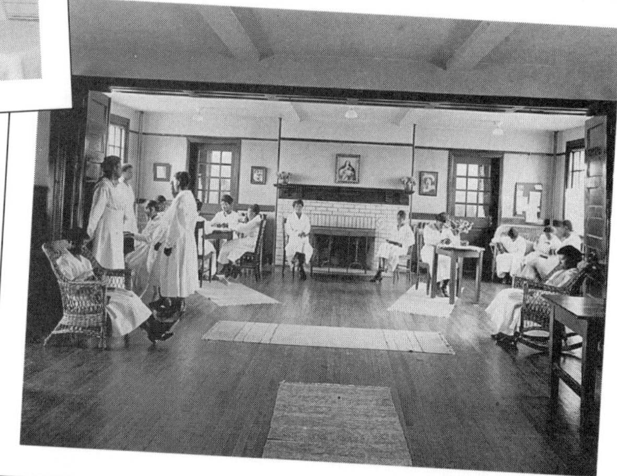

2

4

1. Polio study babies in 1959, with Nurse Florence Darlson and Dr. Agnes Flack.
2. Wittpenn Cottage in 1950. Note the absence of bars on the windows.
3. Stowe Cottage living room with inmates in 1923.
4. Crowding at Clinton Farms in late 1910s.

1. 1957 Clinton Farms graduation. From left, F. Lovell Bixby, Geraldine H. Thompson, Lloyd Wescott, Anita Quarles, Edna Mahan, and Mary Stevens Baird.
2. Clinton Farms 50th anniversary in 1958, W. Marian Anderson.
3. Honorary Degree Rutgers University in 1958. Edna Mahan with Lewis Webster Jones (far right) and other degree recipients.
4. Edna Mahan in her office with pictures of her delinquent friends in background.
5. 1958 Clinton Farms graduation. From left, Anita Quarles, Edna Mahan, Eleanor Roosevelt, and John Tramburg.

1. From left, Edna Mahan and Agnes Flack in St. Croix in 1956.
2. Reading Gebhart on a horse in Circus Parade in the 1950s.
3. Miriam Van Waters in the 1950s.
4. William John Ellis
5. Bee Black and Julie Duane at the classification meeting in 1959.
6. Walter and Elizabeth Gordon in St. Croix in the 1960s.

Chapter 8

The Fifties: "The Golden Age"

After twenty-two years as superintendent of the New Jersey Reformatory for Women, Edna Mahan's leadership as compassionate, innovative, and skilled was unchallenged in New Jersey and the corrections community. Commissioner Sanford Bates wrote her in August 1951 concerning the reformatory's triennial report, 1948–51, "It has some good stuff in it and I am going to turn it over to Chris to see if he can make some kind of a news release out of the material.... In spite of all your troubles and anxieties, you are still running a first-class institution."

In the program celebrating Clinton Farms' fortieth anniversary in 1953, Marie Ellis, widow of the commissioner, wrote, "The 'golden age' at Clinton Farms was ushered in under the leadership of Miss Mahan."

Through the fifties the "golden age" of the reformatory was increasingly challenged by inadequate staffing, crowding, and a changing inmate population. Mahan was secure, however, in the endeavors she undertook there. She believed an open institution meant more than no fences or locks. It meant "permitting participation by the women in community affairs, and at the same time, encouraging the community to take an active interest in the institution" (ACA 1959).

At Clinton Farms interaction with the community—local, national, and international—was manifested in many ways. The fifties presented opportunities to cooperate in important medical research that gave the inmates the chance to make major contributions to medical advancement. It also brought the public's attention to the institution and its inmates.

Changes for the future structure of the Department of Institutions and Agencies were foretold in 1958 with the appointment, by the governor, of a citizen's committee to study and evaluate the department. Edna Mahan and the Clinton Farms Board of Managers took a strong interest in the committee's work.

At Clinton Farms a major change occurred early in the decade with the closing of the institution's nursery.

The End of an Era: The Nursery Closes

The nursery school program at Clinton Farms ended on 1 April 1949 when all the babies were transferred to the hospital from Wittpenn so that more inmates could be housed in Wittpenn. Mahan explained the nursery school and its closing in a letter dated 27 January 1950 to Nina Kinsella, the newly appointed warden of the Federal Reformatory for Women at Alderson, West Virginia. Kinsella had written to Mahan 19 December 1949, "We are reviewing our policies and procedures regarding the care and placement of children born to inmates serving sentences at this institution" and asked Mahan "to furnish us with information...and give us the benefit of your thinking on this subject." Mahan wrote:

> For years we continued to build up the nursery department. Then gradually many of us began to feel quite definitely that this type of institution is no place to rear children. In cooperation with our State Board of Child Welfare [SBCW, formerly the State Board of Children's Guardians] we decided to speed up plans for infants admitted and born here with the result that we now attempt to get them out by the age of 6 months. (Previously we had kept some of them until the age of 2—the legal limit for holding them—and a few beyond that age where there was a question of legal settlement.) In accordance with this new policy we reduced the infant population from eighty-some to the present infant population of nineteen.
>
> We try to determine as early as possible the plan for each infant. We classify the children just as we do the adults. Our first effort is always to find a suitable home with the immediate family or relatives. After all such placement possibilities are exhausted we then commit the child to the care of the State Board of Child Welfare for foster home placement. We never do anything about the adoption of children direct from the institution being convinced that this is the function of a child placing agency.
>
> We now have in attendance at Classification meetings a representative of the State Board of Child Welfare who interviews the mother and helps us to work out plans for each child, whether the child is going to relatives or State Board for foster home placement.

After World War II questions were raised as to whether a correctional institution was an appropriate place for children to spend the first two years of their lives. "It was the tone in the community at the time," according to psychologist Connors.

This tone for change was prompted by practical concerns. Connors pointed out the expense of maintaining and running a good nursery program. In addition, the quality of the program depended on the personnel running it, and it was sometimes difficult to get good staff for the nursery program. The most urgent practical reason for closing the nursery was because the institution was crowded after World War II, and the nurseries in Wittpenn were needed to house inmates.

To help close the Wittpenn nurseries, SBCW agreed to cooperate and accelerate plans to place babies in foster homes by the age of six months. An SBCW worker was assigned to attend classification meetings and to help work out plans for the babies.

Continuing to Fight Segregation

Edna Mahan is first listed as attending the American Prison Association Congress (its annual meeting) as an official delegate from New Jersey in 1929. Although she did not attend every congress until her death in 1968, she became an increasingly active and respected member of the association. She served on the Board of Directors from 1938 to 1949 and again in 1955. She was a member of the Executive Committee 1942–45, 1948, 1949, and 1955. She participated on many committees throughout the years. A short article, "Introducing," that appeared in the November-December 1940 *Prison World* presents three female penologists and concludes about Mahan: "Miss Mahan at the present time is a member of the Executive Committee of the American Prison Association, and over the years has been particularly active in increasing the effectiveness of the Association."

During the years Mahan was most active in the association, E. R. Cass was the executive secretary (1929–62). He ran the association as his personal organization. Some of the reform-oriented men prominent in the field of penology and leaders of the association at the time Cass was executive secretary included Bates, director of the Federal Bureau of Prisons, later commissioner of Institutions and Agencies in New Jersey; Austin MacCormick, professor, School of Criminology, University of California-Berkeley, executive director of the Osborne Association, and formerly with the Federal Bureau of Prisons; and Richard A. McGee, director of corrections, California. Mahan was the female member of this group. Martha Wheeler described her:

> Edna was one of the men. The men enjoyed saying they didn't understand women and were glad one came along to make suggestions. Edna had courage. She had a willingness to go ahead when other people wouldn't. Edna was really quite shy. She made her impact from the wings.

The Warden's Association, an affiliate organization of APA/ACA almost from the beginning, was seen as the most influential and powerful group within the parent association for many years. According to Eaton (1962), "Many of the working committees of the American Correctional Association were dominated by wardens who were punitive and traditionalistic in their outlook." In 1950 the Warden's Association demonstrated its power in a controversy over the location of the 1951 congress. Bates and Mahan protested.

Walter A. Gordon, chairman of the California Adult Authority and a member of the American Prison Association, was not allowed to stay at the Statler, the host hotel in St. Louis at the 1950 congress, because he was black. There must have been others who were refused lodging, too. As a result the membership adopted the following Resolution at the business meeting:

> Congress Location
>
> Whereas, It has been called to the attention of the Congress now in session that certain members arrived at the conference under the impression that they would receive the accommodations and courtesies that other members received, and
>
> Whereas, Upon their arrival these accommodations and courtesies were not extended to them, therefore, be it
>
> *Resolved*, That the American Prison Association sincerely regrets the occurrence of this situation which caused certain of its members considerable inconvenience and embarrassment, and be it further
>
> *Resolved*, That the Association declares it shall be its policy hereafter not to hold its Annual Congress of Correction in any city which denies equal treatment and directs its committee on Time and Place to act accordingly. (APA 1951)

There is no record in the proceedings as to who proposed the resolution. Edna Mahan did not attend this congress, but felt strongly about racial discrimination and did not hesitate to take action to rectify injustices. Walter and Elizabeth Gordon were also personal friends.

Sanford Bates did attend the congress and tried to have the 1951 congress—scheduled for Biloxi, Mississippi—changed to another location. Bates sought Mahan's help in this. She notes in her diary 16 October 1950 (three days after the end of the congress), "SB write Ed Cass re St. Louis!" On 24 October she notes, "Phone MSB, ASQ, KK [board members] re Resolution" and on 27 October, "*Take letter to SB*."

Her letter to E. R. Cass was dated 6 December 1950:

> Dear Ed,
>
> You must be miserably unhappy about the conference at St. Louis. It is cruel and senseless that fine citizens like the Walter Gordons should not have been welcome at the Statler Hotel. I should think the thing that would bother you more than anything else is the fact that the American Prison Congress is committed to meeting in Biloxi, Miss. next year. It is difficult to understand why the Executive

Committee and the Board of Directors did not change the place of meeting after the St. Louis fiasco.

I did not renew my membership in the organization this year and I shall not do so as long as these conditions prevail.

This makes me as sad as I hope it does you.

Cordially,

N.J. Reformatory for Women
Edna Mahan, Superintendent

As Bates's letter to Cass (dated 18 October 1951) indicates, Cass tried to persuade Bates to come to Biloxi:

Dear Ed:

Thanks for your letter of October 16, and I appreciate the spirit in which you made the request that I send a message to Biloxi.

I do not have to tell you of my profound and lasting interest in the American Prison Association; however, there are certain influences in it which I do not like, which I think are definitely reactionary, and as to which I think someone should make a protest that can be understood. The reason I am not going to Biloxi is because certain members of the American Prison Congress have stood by and permitted one of our members, an American citizen and a distinguished individual, to be practically thrown out of the hotel. In spite of that, they not only campaigned but brought pressure to bring the Congress the very next year into the deep South, where everybody who knows anything knows that even such a distinguished gentleman as Walter Gordon will not be treated equally and will not be permitted to live at the same hotel with the rest of us. That I cannot approve, and that is the reason why I am not going to Biloxi.

Feeling as I do about the matter, I think it would be more or less improper for me to try and convince them that there was some other reason for my not going. As a matter of fact, I am tremendously busy, and we have budget hearings three days next week, but I am afraid I will not be able to tell the good southern wardens that I am not coming for any reason except the real one. I do not care to make any issue over it or get into any arguments with anyone. I would like to spend a few days in the South, but I am not going to let my personal preferences stand in the way, in this one instance, of expressing my adherence to what I think is a profound principle.

In doing this, Eddie, I think I am showing greater concern for the future and standards of the American Prison Association than either by going or by writing the kind of letter which you suggest.

I keenly realize the difficulties that you have been under in trying to keep the varying elements together—which has not been an easy job.

> I have worked through thick and thin for the American Prison Association and I shall continue to do so, and I am sorry that in this instance I cannot do as you suggest.
>
> Very truly yours,
>
> Department of Institutions and Agencies
> Sanford Bates, Commissioner

The 1951 congress went on in Biloxi carrying out its usual business without Sanford Bates and Edna Mahan. It did not meet in the South again until 1959 in Miami, at which time there were no problems.

Separation from Gebhardt and Mother's Death

Probably one of the reasons Edna Mahan did not attend the 1950 APA congress was that she and Reading Gebhardt were separating. Her daily diaries contain clues foretelling this. In July 1950 she went to California alone to visit her mother, who was not well. Gebhardt took his vacation alone in August. After his return there are several references to long talks with him. On 22 October 1950, she wrote, "R. left 8 pm." There are four notations in the diary between that date and the end of the year concerning two calls from Gebhardt and two afternoons when he came to the Farms and they rode together.

According to Lloyd Wescott, "Edna and Reading were not close." Lillian Kornitzky, teacher from 1937 to 1943 and director of education 1943 to 1955, said, "The staff didn't talk about them much. They observed they didn't seem to talk to each other very much. They walked around the grounds together. Miss Mahan called me to her office to tell me she and Reading had separated." Another staff member who attended parties in the community where Mahan and Gebhardt were also guests recalled as they were getting ready to leave at the end of the evening, Gebhardt would say, "I've got to get my baby back home."

In her early life there was ambivalence and confusion about marriage and men. There have always been great pressures for women to marry, and marriage was expected to provide a woman with security and companionship. As Mahan was launching her career, she wanted both. After a brief and stormy marriage to Richard Steinmetz, Gebhardt, an established lawyer from one of the most highly respected families of the Clinton community and a lover of nature and the outdoors, would appear to be an ideal partner for Mahan.

By 1950 Edna Mahan's security was her career. Reading and his family did not provide her the family she sought. Though she wanted companionship, she told a friend years later she became bored with Gebhardt. He wanted to take care of her, but she did not need to be taken care of. It came to the point where she could no longer tolerate this. She told Anita Quarles, "I just couldn't have him around the house any longer."

Reading was devastated by the separation and eventual divorce. Mahan was supportive in maintaining contact with him and keeping in close touch with his family members and friends to be sure he had all the help he needed. They remained friends, and in later years often went to dinner together.

The critical illness of her mother followed six months after her separation from Gebhardt. She received a call 2 April 1951 saying that her mother had had two heart attacks. She did not go to California at this time. She received word 28 September 1951 that her mother was in critical condition, and she left that evening for Los Angeles. She remained with her mother two weeks and returned to Clinton on 17 October. She returned to California in late May 1952 after receiving a phone call on 25 May. Her mother died in Hawthorne 10 June. Funeral services were held there two days later, and Edna accompanied her mother's body to her birthplace in Yreka where she was buried.

These were difficult years for Edna Mahan. Although she was relieved to be separated from Gebhardt, they had been married for fifteen years, and the end of the marriage represented a failure in her personal life. The death of her mother soon afterward was an emotional loss. She had visited her mother in California regularly. Her mother's death represented a cutoff from her early life and friends.

There are only two personal letters among her papers that refer to these events in her life. An old friend from Corcoran wrote, "Was sorry to hear of your Mother's passing. It does make a happier remembrance to know you were with her at the last." In 1953 she received a letter from one of her Boston friends, "Margaret told me when your mother died and I was sorry that you were so far away from her during her illnesses—and I know you haven't been as happy as some in your married life, and I am very sorry for that."

There is no indication of the depth of her feelings of loss. She had great compassion for others, and it must have been a particularly lonely time. In earlier years her spiritual mother, Van Waters, was her confidante and consoler. But there were no letters offering love and support during this period.

Her diary notes show her need to have others around. She had dinner almost every evening with friends: Mary Cox in the staff dining room and Beth Wescott James at Homestead or at Beth's home are the most frequent references. Beulah Wescott Hagen and other friends were weekend companions.

No longer tied to vacations in California, she visited the Caribbean. She picked out St. Croix in the Virgin Islands as a spot for yearly vacations. Mahan was introduced to St. Croix by Hunterdon County friends, Hugh and Pris Hilder, who had bought a home there. By 1954 Mahan bought her own property and began to build a house. She loved the place and from that time on went there once or twice every year. Often she spent six weeks between February and March there.

She soon became an active member of the community. The daily diaries she kept while there are full of lunch, cocktails, and dinners with individual friends, a few couples, or large parties. She reciprocated at her house, where she always had friends from home visiting.

Walter Gordon became governor of the U.S. Virgin Islands, and Mahan often saw him and his wife when they were on business in St. Croix. Mahan took an interest in the Richmond Prison on St. Croix and the warden, Thomas Martin.

When Agnes Flack, the resident physician at Clinton Farms appointed in 1954, came to St. Croix to visit a few years later, she discovered a small forgotten leper colony there. She and Mahan worked assiduously until it was closed in 1958.

At Clinton Farms the demands and challenges of her work were constant. At the beginning of the decade the reformatory was in the midst of one of the most interesting projects ever undertaken there: medical research on infectious hepatitis.

Infectious Hepatitis Studies

Beginning in 1949, a series of studies involving infectious hepatitis was done at the request of the Army under the supervision of Joseph Stokes of the University of Pennsylvania School of Medicine. The State Board of Control and the Clinton Farms Board of Managers approved it after careful review of any risks involved. Eight studies were conducted from 1949 to 1953 and involved over 150 inmate volunteers.

Alice T. was a member of one of the first volunteer groups. She recalls she was given what was known as a "hot shot" of hepatitis serum. "We were not told this at the time. Others of the group were just given a glass of orange juice. We did come down with hepatitis one week after taking the serum."

Infectious hepatitis is caused by a virus and is therefore unaffected by antibiotics. Unlike other viral illnesses, such as influenza and polio, infectious hepatitis cannot be transmitted to laboratory animals for study. Therefore, human volunteers were needed to be infected with the disease.

Werner Henle, a member of the medical team from the University of Pennsylvania, gave an "Address on the Jaundice Project" at the Clinton Farms graduation exercises on 27 June 1951:

> I have been looking forward to this day to see finally Clinton Farms and to meet the groups who have cooperated, for the past several years, so splendidly with us in our mutual efforts to bring under control infectious hepatitis, a disease which as yet may go unchecked through civilian and military populations.... It is no

> military secret that infectious hepatitis has added to the untold hardships facing our men at the Korean Front.
>
> Everybody has the greatest admiration for your willingness to volunteer in these studies, to submit to the disease which often is long and unpleasant and causes you many a miserable day.... Long discussions and debates precede each project here at Clinton. We ask ourselves, "Can the answer be obtained by some other means? Is this experiment absolutely essential? Is it worth the risk our volunteers are taking?" And only when all agree to the need for the experiment will it finally go through.
>
> It is unfortunate that at the present time there is no other way than the use of volunteers in order to arrive at solutions for many urgent medical and I might say military problems concerning infectious hepatitis. We have been asked often by doctors and research workers, "How do you get individuals to volunteer?" and they are amazed when they hear of the response from your group, the large number who have volunteered without any promises, benefits, or remuneration. They are impressed, as we all are, with your courageousness to go through this ordeal in the hope that others, the men at the front and people elsewhere may benefit by your sacrifice.
>
> This is outstanding, I believe, and reflects the excellent spirit of the institution, which in turn, reflects the leadership and understanding of Miss Mahan....
>
> So you can see that your sacrifices certainly have not been in vain. We have made slow but steady progress in the understanding of the disease, and we can see at the horizon a possibility to prevent it. And I feel you and we can be proud of these achievements.

There were risks for the inmates who volunteered. They became seriously ill and felt miserable for a long time, some well after the study ended. While they participated in the study they were isolated in the basement of Wittpenn Cottage. They did not complain. There were deep feelings of pride at the significant contribution they made to the military, medical research, and society. More than one inmate expressed satisfaction that she had been able to make some reparation for the crime she had committed. There were no other rewards.

Polio Vaccine

Another significant medical research project was undertaken at Clinton Farms in the fall of 1955 and continued until 1966. This was the development of an oral vaccine to immunize babies against polio. Research had been underway elsewhere for over five years to develop a lifetime immunization against polio with a live virus that could be taken by mouth. However, only adults had been used in the study up to this time. The purpose of the research undertaken at Clinton Farms "was to feed the virus to the infants at the earliest possible age under scientifically controlled conditions in order to determine the effectiveness of the vaccine as the infant matures" (Hotchkiss 1956). Again it was Stokes who initiated the project. He called Mahan on 22 June 1955 to discuss it. The board minutes of October 1955 report:

> Dr. Stokes visited the institution on September 24th and October 8th. Today Dr. Andrew Hunt of the Hunterdon Medical Center and Dr. Agnes N. Flack, resident physician, met with the Board to present the plan and to answer questions. The members unanimously approved the project with the concurrence of the State Board of Child Welfare, State Home for Girls, and North Jersey Training School. Dr. Bixby will ask Dr. Stokes or his representative to attend the State Board of Control Meeting on October 21st to obtain formal approval.

The State Board of Control authorized the clinical testing of oral immunization against polio with mothers and babies at Clinton Farms with the understanding "inmates' participation in the trial will be entirely voluntary and that appropriate written permission will be obtained in each case." In this study inmate aides were trained and paid for their work as assistants.

Hunt and Flack reported to the board on the clinical progress of the polio vaccine project 8 February 1956:

> There has been no evidence of any illness and the children have gained weight normally. They have received extra mothering from the nurses and attendants. A registered nurse is on duty at all times. The inmates who are assisting (in the care of the babies) learn sterile techniques and receive $10. per month each from the Lederle Laboratories. The results so far have been extremely successful, according to Dr. Hunt.

The board minutes of 18 March 1966 reported that the polio project would be closed down as of 30 April 1966. Thomas E. Norton, assistant to the director of the Wistar Institute in Philadelphia, notified Mahan of this in a letter of 6 March 1966, which read in part:

> Needless to say, it has been eleven years of a very pleasant relationship, and it is no exaggeration to say that the work at Clinton went far in its contribution to a live virus polio vaccine. The scientific data that came out of the Clinton studies were used not only by us, but by other people in the field, and added to the knowledge of polio vaccination in babies and the relationship between polio strains. They were not the sort of studies that make the headlines, but nevertheless, they were the kind of studies that must be done before the headline-making final results.

Again there were no rewards for the infants or their mothers. All members of the Clinton Farms community—inmates, staff and their families, and board members and their families—were given the oral vaccine if they wanted it. Mahan reported in 1956 "that most of the inmate mothers have accepted the studies wholeheartedly and many of them have made specific requests that their children be included in the research program" (Hotchkiss 1956).

Medical research studies were allowed at Clinton Farms and other New Jersey correctional institutions with the approval of the State Board of Control under careful supervision and with the voluntary consent of the inmates. Researchers sought inmate populations because the necessary controls could be handled more easily than with an outside group, some of whom might drop out of the study before it was complete.

But such research sometimes put inmates at considerable risk. There is always the possibility of coercion and misuse of the inmates. Today correctional institutions are prohibited from allowing inmates to participate "in medical or pharmaceutical testing for experimental or research purposes" (ACA 1990).

The Guidance Center

Clinton Farms coped with the serious crowding and discipline problems in the last half of the forties with the addition of Thompson Hall, which opened in October 1948, as a temporary overflow dormitory, and Paddock and Stowe east wing security units. However, new permanent inmate housing was desperately needed. The last cottage to open for inmates was in 1930 when the average adult population was 192.

A letter to Commissioner Bates dated 9 September 1947 from the Clinton Farms visiting psychiatrist, Joseph G. Wilson, addressed the need for a disciplinary unit and detailed the psychological and psychiatric make up of the inmate population necessitating this. In 1950 the board sent the commissioner a general plan for the "Guidance Center," and Mahan wrote in the Clinton Farms triennial report for the fiscal years 1 July 1948 to 30 June 1951, "From Bond Issue funds Clinton Farms will receive...a Guidance Center (close custody building)."

The Guidance Center officially opened on 8 June 1953. Lois Morris, who served as the first head cottage supervisor there, had gone to the Reformatory for Women at Framingham, Massachusetts, to work in 1951. Mahan called her early in 1953 and asked her to return to Clinton Farms to run the Guidance Center.

Morris recalled that the Guidance Center was sold to Commissioner Bates on the need for a "secure cottage." It contained forty single rooms in two wings, twenty rooms in each. One wing was designed as maximum security with a toilet and basin in each room and prison locks on each door as well as on the door opening into the wing. The other wing was medium security with a common bathroom and regular locks on the doors. There were bars built into all the windows.

A work room was located in the Guidance Center as well as individual conference rooms and a multipurpose room for leisure-time activities. Like the other cottages, it had its own kitchen and dining room. There were rooms for staff upstairs.

An open house was held before the building was occupied so each inmate could see it. Mahan told inmates at cottage honor meetings that the new cottage would be available with single rooms and those wishing to move there could apply by writing her a note. No doors were locked, not even the front door.

Commissioner Bates, who fully expected the building to be run as a locked unit, came to inspect it on 14 June with two foreign visitors. Morris recalled:

> Miss Mahan called me to come to her office to meet with the commissioner and his visitors before taking them over to the building. She then told Bates it was open, nothing was locked, and it was not being used as maximum security. With that the commissioner turned to his guests and said, "What do you do with a woman like that?"

Austin MacCormick wrote in a letter to Van Waters on 7 August 1953, "I had a very pleasant visit at Clinton Farms when I spoke at their 40th Anniversary celebration and wish you could have been there. The way Edna is running the security building is one for the book!"

During the summer there were several runaways from the Guidance Center. As a result all the exterior doors to the building were locked. At the 23 September 1953 board meeting Mahan reported on the Guidance Center:

> An average of 36 girls are housed there. On the whole things have gone fairly well under the plan of permitting the girls to request placement in the new unit.... A number of transfers have been made to and from the building to stabilize the group. The maximum security rooms have been in use on occasion. It is still too soon to tell exactly how this unit will function, but in view of the fact that the hospital is no longer used for maximum security and because it is no longer necessary to transfer inmates to Hudson County Jail, we are confident that the building will serve many useful purposes.

The Guidance Center functioned as a close security cottage for nine years. All inmates housed there had single rooms. Unless they were locked in one of the disciplinary rooms, they circulated with the rest of the population in work assignments, classes, leisure activities, etc. An institutional sewing room was opened in the space provided for an in-house work department. Inmates assigned to work there were not limited to those living in the Center.

Fortieth Anniversary

On 25 June 1953, 400 guests assembled to observe the fortieth anniversary of Clinton Farms. A buffet supper was served to staff, former staff, student officers, former Clinton Farms residents, board members, and outside guests. The whole population was invited to the ceremonies after supper. Service awards were presented to staff members. MacCormick was the principle speaker. The *Hunterdon Democrat* reported:

> "I say categorically that this is the best institution for women in the United States and in my opinion the best correctional institution for either men or women in the United States."
>
> These words from Austin H. MacCormick, executive director of the Osborne Association and national authority in the field of prison administration, marked a high point in the program....
>
> Mr. MacCormick reviewed the history of prison administration and noted that the period of greatest accomplishment in that field coincided with the 40-year history of Clinton Farms.... He noted also that the 40 years of history at Clinton Farms were not normal years, but years of recurring emergencies which complicated problems of prison administration as they did other problems of government and economics.
>
> The speaker noted the completion of a maximum security building at Clinton and said he had "dreaded to come and see it." He said that the new building...is one of the most secure for women offenders in the United States, but the security of the building lies in the attitude of the girls and of those who put them there. "The real test," he declared, "is in the desire of the girls to live up to what Miss Mahan expects of them."
>
> The Clinton Farms Board of Managers presented a reproduction of a Queen Anne silver ink stand to Miss Mahan as a gift from "friends" to commemorate the completion of her twenty-fifth year.
>
> Miss Mahan responded with informal remarks in which she said she "would accept the gift as a tribute paid Clinton Farms, and not for myself." She said that whatever had been accomplished was possible "because of the teamwork my staff around me has shown for so many years." Mahan also said that the State of New Jersey had made the work of Clinton Farms possible by reason of its enlightened administration of prison affairs under Commissioners Ellis and Bates and the citizens who had served unselfishly on the policy-making and administrative boards. She contrasted conditions of twenty-five years ago when workers at the institutions received only maintenance or $50 per month for their services and when parolees could expect no more than $5 a week in domestic service. She said that "we get in return from the girls what we expect of them" and that Clinton Farms had been operated on that basis....

> Girls of the institution served a buffet supper and also attended the ceremonies, joining loudly in the applause when a number of the officers of the institution were called forward to receive service pins and awards.

On this gala occasion Mahan downplayed herself and gave the staff and the department much of the credit for the success of Clinton Farms. The inmates were allowed to attend the ceremonies and mingle with the other guests.

Bringing in the Community

Mingling with the community was an activity Edna Mahan liked to promote. The reformatory was not only open in the sense that inmates weren't locked in, the community was not locked out. Mahan encouraged outside individuals and groups to come in and participate in some way or just visit to see what went on.

In 1959 Mahan wrote, "The community can be a vital source of help to the institution's program.... The institution should feel a part of the community and conversely the community should feel a genuine interest in the institution" (ACA 1959). Clinton Farms under Mahan's leadership was a part of the community, and Mahan inspired the community to feel a genuine interest in the institution.

Clinton Farms was Mahan's accomplishment, and she loved to show it off to all who would come. Practitioners in the field came from all over the world; scholars were invited to study and send students as interns. Many volunteers served as Sunday school teachers, art teachers, and "friendly visitors." Graduations in June were a big occasion, and well-known women such as Marian Anderson, Margaret Mead, Frances Perkins, and Eleanor Roosevelt were among those who came to deliver the commencement address.

Christmas pageants were held in December and circuses in the summer. A picnic and fireworks were held on the Fourth of July. No matter what the occasion, the focus was the inmates. The events acknowledged and highlighted the work inmates did and served to foster their pride. Invitations for major events were issued far and wide from the governor to friends in the local community. And Mahan was unassuming as she displayed her accomplishment.

An early effort to bring in the community was the Friendly Visitor program. Friendly Visitors visit inmates who receive no mail or visits. The program was suggested to the Board of Managers in 1939 by Sir Alexander Patterson, commissioner of prisons in England. A small nucleus of women recruited by board members began visiting prior to World War II. The program was stopped during World War II and started again in 1947. By the mid-fifties there was a group who came to the institution regularly. Orientation sessions were given twice a year, and they became a small but important group who visited at least once a month, remembered birthdays and holidays, and enjoyed circuses, ball games, and Christmas pageants with inmates.

In 1948 the Soroptimists International Club of Hunterdon County was organized, and Mahan was a charter member. Membership in the Soroptimists was limited to business or professional women who were executives, administrators, or owners and was by invitation. Mahan was active in the Soroptimists, serving as a director and as president in 1950. The charter dinner was held at Clinton Farms in 1948, and chapter meetings were held there periodically over the years. Mahan actively sought appropriate women for membership.

In 1950 the Community Garden Club of Hunterdon County organized a chapter at Clinton Farms. This was the first garden club in a correctional institution in the country. The club held monthly meetings in Thompson Hall. Members of garden clubs from nearby communities came to each meeting to instruct the inmates in flower growing and arranging. There were many flower gardens around each cottage that were cared for by Garden Club members. A flower show was held each year. During holidays colorful decorations enhanced dining tables and offices. Mahan and the president of the Community Garden Club screened inmates for membership in the club, which always had a waiting list. It was a privilege to be a member of the club.

The American Association of University Women (AAUW) initiated a Hunterdon County Chapter in 1958. Mahan was a charter member. AAUW met at Clinton Farms periodically and held covered dish suppers and white elephant sales there. Again, Mahan encouraged women, particularly members of her staff with a bachelor's degree who qualified, to join. She knew the importance of these groups to professional women for networking and support.

The institution worked with other community groups. In the late forties when money was being raised for building the Hunterdon Medical Center, the inmates raised $1,000 by charging admission to the circus and to a glee club concert.

Once the medical center was open it became the institution's referral source for all medical problems that could not be handled at the institution.

Clinton Farms raised money every year for the local Cancer Society drive, and the inmates made cancer dressings. Red Cross blood banks were held regularly. In the fifties the blood banks were organized and run by Alice T.

Christmas and Christmas Pageants

Christmas pageants as an annual event were first held at Clinton Farms in 1928, Mahan's first Christmas as superintendent, and continued after her death in 1968. By the late 1930s these were occasions to show off the institution to personal and professional friends beside the members of the Board of Managers. The January

1939 board minutes report, "December 21st and 22nd—Many guests attended both performances of the Christmas Pageant, *Once in Bethlehem.*"

Lillian Kornitsky recalled that the education department was responsible for the pageants. "Miss Mahan always invited the board, central office people, local friends and dignitaries to the pageant and to her house for dinner beforehand. All the inmates would be in the auditorium waiting, but the show couldn't go on until Miss Mahan and her guests arrived. I had to remind her each year that the girls got restless." The author remembers the pageants as lovely occasions and was always pleased as a little girl when her mother took her along. In later years, the buffet dinners at Homestead preceding the performance were festive occasions.

Other activities took place every Christmas season, including carolling by cottage groups or outside groups invited to come in, midnight mass in the chapel, and the distribution of gifts in the cottages. Outside stores and organizations were solicited each year for contributions of appropriate gifts. The Salvation Army, the Soroptimists, and church groups brought gifts for every inmate. Mahan each year wrote out a Christmas tag for the gifts for each woman in the institution.

She loved Christmas and always spent it at Clinton Farms. She gave gifts to all the children of staff who lived on the grounds. In later years she spent most of the day working at the switchboard with Morris so staff could be home with their families. Friends who visited from New York made a foursome for bridge at the switchboard. The 25 December 1960 diary notation "Lunch at swbd. w. Lois. Bridge! Walk in late afternoon to all cottages. LM to dinner w. J&JP [New York friends]" was typical.

Christmas was a sad time for most inmates who had to spend it at Clinton Farms. Mahan did all she could to let them know she understood this and to make it as festive as possible. She tried to share a small piece of the day with them.

Graduations: "Accomplishments Are the Stepping-Stones of Life"

Graduations each June were the most formal ceremonies at Clinton Farms to which the outside community was invited. Whether the speaker was a well-known public figure or a member of the Board of Managers, it was an occasion to recognize inmates who had achieved eighth grade diplomas, high school equivalencies, beauty culture licenses, home economics certificates, and power sewing certificates. Invitations were sent to families of the graduates, members of the State Board of Control of Institutions and Agencies, central office staff, superintendents of other institutions, as well as friends from the local community. All the Clinton Farms residents were invited to attend. A reception was held afterward for graduates and guests.

The graduates and their achievements were the focus of the ceremonies. The president of the Board of Managers and the director of education presided over the ceremonies.

Eleanor Roosevelt first visited Clinton Farms in 1956 to attend the graduation exercises on 21 June. *The Welfare Reporter*, a publication of the Department of Institutions and Agencies, gave the following account:

> Rain drove the annual Clinton Farms graduation exercises indoors, but otherwise failed to dampen the enthusiasm of those who took part on the stage and off. Mrs. Eleanor Roosevelt was a guest of honor, as was Mrs. Anna Kross, commissioner of the New York City Department of Correction. Both shared the task of addressing the class of sixteen women who were being graduated from the eighth grade. Ten others received awards for choir service, eight certificates in home economics, twelve licenses in beauty culture and thirty in recognition for power sewing.
>
> Each member of the class told what the academic training she had received meant to her. Mrs. Roosevelt picked up this thread in an informal address which had strong personal references in it. Accomplishments, she told the girls, are the stepping-stones of life and nothing more than an opportunity to advance.

Roosevelt (1956) wrote of the graduation in her newspaper column, "My Day":

> I went out to Clinton State Farms in New Jersey, a state institution for women last Thursday at the invitation of my old friend, Mrs. Geraldine Thompson....
>
> It is interesting how, in visiting this type of institution, one almost immediately feels a change in atmosphere. But the atmosphere at Clinton Farms is not that of a prison. No girl is locked in. All go about freely....
>
> The inmates are given opportunities to learn, and they sense the value of education, in character training as well as in academic achievement.... Everyone learns a skill.... They do the work of the institution and they do it well....
>
> But the remarkable thing was the feeling of all the girls for the superintendent. When her name was mentioned she was cheered—a reaction that is not always accorded the warden of a penal institution.
>
> The educational director arranged for each girl who was being graduated from eighth grade to make a little statement on the value of what she had learned....
>
> One girl, in speaking of the value of arithmetic, said it was easier to meet problems in life when you had been trained to analyze a problem in arithmetic because, in facing other problems, you worked them out much the same way.

Though the honored guests or graduation speakers were not always as prominent as Eleanor Roosevelt, the graduation ceremonies were similar each year. The graduates and their achievements were the focus of the occasion.

After graduation came the circus, which started organizing early in June. Each cottage selected representatives for the general planning committee, which chose the theme. Shopping trips were made to purchase materials for decorations and prizes. The maintenance staff cooperated by providing vehicles for the floats and carpentry services for making booths and the various items needed for the floats, games, and skits. They often put on their own skit, which was kept secret and was always one of the highlights of the day. The 23 September 1953 board minutes report on the annual circus, held on 18 July:

> Music was furnished by the Brown and Lynch Post American Legion Band of Phillipsburg. Guests included Mrs. Quarles and Mrs. Montgomery of Plainfield, a free lance writer; Mrs. Burch [board member] and about 30 members of the Metropolitan Baptist Church of Newark came by bus; Mr. and Mrs. Charles Leatham of Trenton; two representatives of the Essex County Sheriff's Office; Mr. Dworetz of the Passaic County Sheriff's Office and his wife. A picnic supper was served to the girls and guests on the lawn back of the administration building.

The circuses were put on under the direction of the education department until 1958. By this time the Homesteaders had become a well-established club on Clinton Farms. They put on the carnival beginning in September of that year.

The Homesteaders

The program that brought more of the community into the institution than any other was the Homesteaders Club and softball team. Although Clinton Farms had a softball team that played games every summer with many groups, such as the Clinton Farms staff, the correctional officers from Annandale Farms (the nearby Reformatory for Men), or the neighboring team from the Wescott's Mulhocaway Farms, it was not an organized group and did not play a regular schedule in a league.

In 1956 a Hunterdon County Women's Softball League was being formed. Membership of the Clinton Farms team in the county softball league was initiated by the new resident dentist, John F. Ackerman, who joined the staff in January 1956. The board minutes of January 1956 report, "He was referred by Dr. John Cain of Phillipsburg and Dr. Ferderle J. Fisher, Supervisor of Dentistry for the Department." Cain, Edna Mahan's personal dentist, was a longtime friend of Ackerman's. Ackerman was a recovering alcoholic who had lost a lucrative practice and was in need of a job. Mahan, with the concurrence of her board, hired him.

It was a risk that paid off well for Clinton Farms for the next twenty years. He accomplished so much in his first six months that the board noted at its 11 July 1956 meeting, "The Board members are delighted with Dr. Ackerman's work in the dental field and his interest in the whole institutional program. The President asked to have a letter written commending him for his first six months' achievements."

Not only was Ackerman a superb dentist who trained many inmates to become dental assistants, he became involved in the life of the institution. He took over the leadership of the Alcoholics Anonymous group from Connors, who retired in June 1955. He became coach of the softball team and was instrumental in having the team accepted into the county league. According to the 1963–64 annual report of the Homesteaders Club:

> The Homesteaders was started February 29, 1956 by a group of girls who wanted to play softball with some degree of organization with outside competition. They chose their own name, elected their own officers and wrote their own By-Laws, with the purpose in mind to play ball, sponsor activities for the benefit of all the girls on the Farms and help themselves by helping the other fellow.

For the Clinton Farms team to become a member of the county league, the other teams in the league had to agree to play all their games with the Homesteaders, home and away, at Clinton Farms. Most of the league meetings were held at Clinton Farms because inmates were elected officers. The local teams and their supporters came to the reformatory once or twice a week during the softball season and played with the inmates of Clinton Farms or sat in the bleachers next to them cheering on their teams. The local community had more access to Clinton Farms and its inmates than had ever before been possible.

The softball games attracted many guests beyond the local community. On Memorial Day 1957 Governor and Mrs. Meyner were spectators along with Cain, who was an old friend of theirs.

Annual Homesteaders softball banquets were held each fall, and outside guests were invited. Awards were presented for highest batting average, most runs scored, most home runs, best defensive player, most improved player, most valuable player, best sportsmanship, and outstanding cheerleader. Bertha Venable, beauty culture teacher, organized and coached a group of cheerleaders who performed at every game and led occasional pep rallies.

The Homesteaders held a meeting once a month. According to the 1963–64 annual report, "The girls learn parliamentary procedures, self-expression, and many for the first time realize their individuality as a member of such a group." There were many nonathletic members.

They had many extra-league games with the Lions and Rotary Clubs and Junior Chamber of Commerce of Phillipsburg. The games were usually followed by a hot dog roast with visiting team members at the Homesteaders' outdoor fireplace, which was donated and constructed by the Lions Club. Cain was largely responsible for these activities.

The club also sponsored many activities for the Clinton Farms population, such as carnivals, dances, and parties. They paid for expenses in connection with these as well as for their equipment by cake sales and white elephant sales that were held in the Clinton Farms auditorium and advertised in the local community.

Alice T. was a key player on the team and in the development and running of the Homesteaders Club as well as the county softball league. She had organized the Clinton Farms teams for many years prior to the formalization of the Homesteaders. She was highly respected by other inmates. She worked well with Ackerman and encouraged his efforts in establishing the county league. They had a great deal of admiration and respect for each other. The success of the Homesteaders as an organization was as much due to Alice as to "Doc" Ackerman.

Alice T.: Years of Leadership

From 12 July 1948 when Alice was elected to the Honor Group at Stowe until 14 July 1959 when she left the New Jersey Reformatory for Women on parole, Mahan's progress notes for Alice are shorter and the tenor of them is very different from the notes of her first ten years. Alice became a leader in many Clinton Farms activities. Mahan asked Alice for suggestions on such things as recreation, and she sought her help in influencing inmate behavior and opinions. Alice told Mahan when she was aware of runaway plans and other potential trouble. She was among the first inmates to volunteer for the hepatitis study, and she was in charge of the group of volunteers who lived at Wittpenn Dormitory. Alice helped organize and run the blood drives that were held at Clinton Farms at least twice a year.

She was an editor of the inmate newspaper *Us Personified.* In this role she was able to influence opinion and behavior among inmates. Mahan sometimes suggested topics for editorials such as on 25 July 1952, "I saw [Alice] to suggest writing an editorial re girls getting parolees to smuggle out letters."

In 1950, Alice and the three other editors of the paper wrote an inmate handbook, *About You and Clinton Farms*, which was given to each new arrival. The introduction, "Our Superintendent Greets You" explains the purpose of the handbook and tells a little bit about Clinton Farms:

> "Why don't you give the new girls some information about Clinton Farms on arrival?" was asked so often that the girls themselves decided to do something about it.
>
> This booklet expresses group thinking and group action. It was written for you by four editors of the girls' paper based on material submitted by the entire population. We hope it will help you to see your new home through the eyes of those who came before you. We hope you will do something here to help those who will follow you. If you give your best, you will be doing much to keep Clinton Farms a good institution....
>
> The Court may have sent you here for "punishment"; the community may think you should be exhibited as a public example to keep others from committing offenses; we need your cooperation to continue to show society that it can best be protected by the rehabilitation of girls like you in an institution like Clinton Farms.

Alice provided leadership for the Homesteaders Club and its many activities. Ackerman wrote in a recommendation for Alice for her consideration by the State Parole Board in 1959:

> I have been in almost daily contact with [Alice] since 2/29/56, the birthday of the Homesteaders. The beginning of this organization, its continued success and what it means to Clinton Farms and stands for today can be attributed to—better than 90%—the efforts of [Alice].... She is a natural leader—on the playing field and off. Our problems of getting the girls to work and play hard and to the best of their ability are solved or at least aided by her leadership and example. She can cope with their moods and "snap them out of it" even when she is hindered by problems of her own.
>
> She has organized and executed the white elephant sales, the carnival, the dances, the lectures, hot dog roasts when we entertain outside organizations such as the Lions Club, the Rotary, the Central Office, etc. No task seems too big for her if it is in the interest of the Homesteaders, the girls and all of Clinton Farms. I am lacking in superlatives to describe her leadership, enthusiasm, ability and cooperation.... This association, her loyalty, devotion and help, is truly treasured by me.

Alice recalled the honor meeting at Stowe in 1951, when her cottage-mates said they wanted her as their student officer. She refused, not feeling she was ready for such an honor. Mahan looked at her and asked, "Can't you accept a challenge?" Alice became a student officer and continued living in Stowe until February 1954 when Mahan arranged for her to live on the unsupervised floor of Paddock with other long-term inmates. She assumed increasingly more responsibilities in her work assignments. In 1953 she was working in the laundry and on Sundays supervised a group of volunteers who did the baby wash for the hospital. In the spring, summer, and fall she supervised the lawn group. In August 1953 Mahan asked her to take over as dairy supervisor when the staff member in that position was not able to handle it. On 15 November 1954 when the inmate delivery truck driver had to be removed for medical reasons, Mahan arranged to have Alice add that duty to her regular work.

On 18 November 1954, three days after taking over the delivery truck duties, Mahan asked Alice to move downstairs to Paddock Unit and take over the responsibility of running it. The former long-term inmate supervisor had been paroled. Alice was surprised at the request but said she would be glad to do it if Mahan thought she could. She told Mahan she did not want to stop driving the delivery truck. For the remainder of her time on Clinton Farms Alice was supervisor of Paddock Unit and drove the delivery truck. Some of the crew on the truck were residents of the unit.

Driving the delivery truck, Alice circled the grounds at Clinton Farms several times each day. Many times inmates who were having problems spoke to Alice about them and sometimes asked to come to Paddock Unit to live or at least to work on the truck with her. If Alice thought she could help, she spoke with Mahan and, with Mahan's approval, arrangements were made for the switch.

Driving the delivery truck also put Alice in a position to know very quickly everything that happened on the grounds and to pick up on rumors and bits of gossip. Although she had enemies among the other inmates, for the most part she was extremely popular. There were always undercurrents of resentment among the staff that Mahan would do anything Alice asked. Some were envious of her ready access to the superintendent. However, most of the staff admired Alice for the change she had made in her adjustment and in all the work she accomplished at Clinton Farms.

In 1957 Alice, the Paddock Unit residents, and the Homesteaders corresponded with some of the lepers at the leper colony in St. Croix after Mahan and Flack told them about the colony. Alice first wrote an introductory letter on 26 March 1957:

> Dear Folks,
>
> I could call you all by name but for my first letter I'd rather speak to the group and as time goes by, my group and I will write individual letters. When I speak of my group, I am referring to 14 young ladies who are living in a small Unit under Student Supervision. We are part of Clinton Farms and we are all residents. We just like small group living and are privileged to live this way.
>
> When Miss Mahan, our Superintendent, returned from her vacation, she told of her visit to your colony and we were most impressed. As usual, she has permitted us to share her friendship with you, and we are hoping to build one of our own in due time. We love people and I'm sure your little group does too. We'd like very much to hear from you, as a group or individually.

> Our weekend was spent collecting books, magazines and most anything that we felt you might like and enjoy. This to us was a pleasure and I and the group hope that it brings just a bit of sunshine into your lives.... You will be hearing from us often and we will be sending boxes approximately twice a month. Thank you for letting us chat with you. We hope you will write real soon, for we are very anxious to hear from you. Just know that we are your friends, and we hope you will accept us as such.

They continued to correspond and send packages until the colony closed in 1958.

In the summer of 1958, Mahan asked Alice's assistance in another arena. She asked her and whomever she selected to talk to the staff orientation group in August. Alice wrote a friend, "I can talk about anything with no interferences.... I like this. It is an honor." There is no record of what went on in the meeting. It is, however, an indication of the high regard Mahan felt for Alice and her understanding of the feelings and needs of the inmates, and it is an indication of the respect the staff had for her, or Mahan would not have asked her to speak before them.

Alice appeared before the State Parole Board several times. Although she expected the first few denials, after the fourth one she was disappointed and discouraged. She talked with Mahan over two hours of her depression at the thought of never being paroled. Alice accepted Mahan's explanations for the denials. When leaving the office, Alice said to Mahan, "Call me when my parole date is set. Other than that, don't bother me."

In July 1959 Alice got the news she would be paroled. Her reactions on being told were to call her family, friends on the inside and outside, and then she went and rang the chapel bells. She was ecstatic and asked Mahan to share it with her "for like you tell me, you have earned it! Share it with me in knowing you at long last accomplished your mission which makes you radiantly happy. It really is showing!"

Later in a letter to Mahan, Alice noted she was surprised at all who shared her happiness over her parole and how wonderful it was to know that so many people at Clinton Farms felt she was worthy of her parole. She goes on to write:

> What can I say to you at this time to convey my true feelings? You who are not only known to me as the Superintendent of Clinton Farms but as one of the greatest women I have ever known. This is not flattery, Miss Mahan. I feel all that I am saying and it comes from the deepest part of my being. Admire you? I do! Have faith and confidence? Truly I do and at times, "Blind faith" for I know that behind everything you do, there is a reason. Despite our former "Rough" years, and I can see the "Why" of many of your actions and then there are some situations that I just chalk up to experience and your lack of "know." For all our years of knowing each other I wish to say thanks, a deep sincere thank you for what you have helped to make of me. Thank you too for permitting me to have the Unit, for the faith and confidence you have in my judgement and decisions. I

> will never forget you Miss Mahan and be it here or out there, I will still be "on call" when needed. Right now I've got a lump in my throat as big as you and I know it's time to quit.... [M]ay good health enable you to continue the work program that so badly needs you and that you so thoroughly enjoy.

On the day that Alice was to leave Clinton Farms a press conference was arranged to have some control over the publicity her leaving would generate. Many newspaper reporters called about it. These reporters and more were waiting in the board room of the administration building before the conference. Ackerman, Mahan, and Wescott were with Alice.

Alice's first months on the outside required many adjustments. She wrote Mahan a few months after leaving Clinton Farms:

> I miss you so much that there is quite an empty spot in my life. It can't be filled and I've stopped trying to do so. The 14th of November I've been a civilian for 4 months and believe it or not, I'd rather be "HOME." Freedom offers me no compensation for what I had. Sounds mad I'm sure, but 'tis so true. No, I'll not return but just don't think I'm the happy one. You filled my life with everything that meant something, something fine and worthwhile—now, is it to be found out here???
>
> I will always keep in contact—you are one person I will never forget.

In her last six years of incarceration Alice was an important member of the Clinton Farms community. Because she worked so well with many of the more difficult inmates and because she had tremendous energy and was willing to help anywhere she was needed or anyone who needed anything, she had a great deal of influence and power. When she left Clinton Farms she was a parolee working and living in new surroundings. Her parole officer was a woman who held her clients closely to all rules. Alice had no influence or power in her new surroundings.

Alice showed her concern for the problems the institution was encountering with the young, unsettled population of the 1960s in a letter to Mahan dated 7 February 1962. She starts her letter by saying she had just heard that five of "our young ladies" were transferred from the Newark jail to the Flemington jail:

> I will never understand the situations that exist today. I'm only sorry that all this is happening and I'm not there to be of some help. Conceited aren't I to feel that I could be of any value! There must be some way to cope with these rascals—apparently hasn't been found yet, yes?...Chin up, better days are coming!?!?!

Alice's offer to come help was sincere. She had had considerable success working with some of the more difficult inmates. She must have felt a sense of frustration that she was not allowed, by law, to go back to Clinton Farms to work and to help Mahan. The letter shows her sense of commitment to Clinton Farms and Mahan more than eighteen months after she left.

Alice adjusted well in the community she settled in. She has led a productive and worthwhile life working and contributing to the community and giving strong support to many individuals.

In a June 1989 interview, Alice said, "Miss Mahan made Clinton Farms a place where human beings could become a part of society—not a house of horrors." Although there were other women committed to the reformatory who arrived burdened with national publicity, and there were many who presented great challenges to Mahan whom she liked, in whom she saw potential for change, and who assumed leadership positions, there was no one who took over as much responsibility as Alice did. When she left, the business manager figured it would take three full-time paid staff to take her place.

After Mahan died, Reading Gebhardt, who served as her lawyer, called Alice and asked her to come to his office on some matters concerning the settlement of Mahan's will. Alice was floored when she found that Mahan had left her some money. When she asked Gebhardt why, he replied, "She was fond of you and because of all you did for the Farms." Alice started to cry because of the generosity of Mahan in remembering her in her will but more so because she was not permitted to see Mahan before she died. Mahan did not wish to see anyone in her sickly condition. Alice said her love and devotion to Mahan left a part of her life void, but she would have to go on without her.

"We Can't Have Good Institutions Unless We Have Good Staff"

One of Edna Mahan's greatest strengths in her forty years as superintendent was her ability to balance the increasing control and formalization of all institutions into a common male mold by the State Department of Institutions and Agencies with the special needs of the Reformatory for Women. Her efforts to raise salaries, improve working conditions, and create parity for her staff with staff at men's reformatories exemplify this.

When she arrived at Clinton Farms in 1928 staff morale was low. She had to make some immediate changes, and she worked with the Board of Managers during her first years to raise the general caliber of staff. Staff meetings of cottage supervisors were held on a regular basis, and in later years staff orientation sessions were organized. She kept an open door for staff and supported and mentored them. She wanted to develop and hold good staff. Those who did not work out were asked to resign if they did not leave of their own accord.

Mahan's efforts on behalf of staff had two thrusts: (1) to make them comparable to staff working in men's correctional institutions by improving salaries and working conditions for staff and (2) to attract well-qualified staff to work in the women's institutions. Concerning the first, Close (1949) wrote, "Men prison guards, whose main qualifications are brute strength and the ability to shoot, are paid on a scale that begins twice as high as that of cottage supervisors, whose strength must be of the spirit; and Miss Mahan resents that."

During the Depression of the thirties there was little Mahan or the board could do to improve salaries for staff. At the March 1940 board meeting there was the first discussion of the differences in wages and hours for female employees at Clinton Farms and correctional officers in men's institutions. "Our matrons and relief officers work practically 24 hours a day [the shifts were 12 hours but at least one matron was required to live in each cottage] and receive $50. to $70. a month plus maintenance. Male guards in the reformatories for men work 8 hours and receive a minimum of $150. per month."

Efforts by Mahan and the board to upgrade salaries and working conditions continued through the forties and fifties. There are references to these in board minutes every few years. Letters were written to the commissioner and the Civil Service Commission pointing out the inequities. The New Jersey Reformatory for Women wasn't the only women's institution in the country with these concerns. Minutes of the Conferences of Women Superintendents of Correctional Institutions for Women and Girls report on salaries and working conditions at almost every annual conference.

In 1951 the shift to an eight-hour day was made at Clinton Farms, but a cottage officer still had to live in each cottage. In August 1955 Mahan and the board included the male correctional officers' and female cottage officers' salary ranges with the "Statement to be Taken with the Clinton Farms Budget Requests, 1956–1957" to highlight the differences. Board minutes in 1956, 1957, and 1958 indicate continued efforts to address salary inequities and request needed new positions. It was not until 1965 that male correctional officers and female cottage officers were paid on the same salary scale.

Although Mahan and the board labored long to correct the salary inequities between men and women working in comparable positions, there was no effort to change the title of the cottage officer to correctional officer. In "keeping faith with the founders" of Clinton Farms, there was the enduring recognition of the unique needs of female offenders, which were best met by qualified female staff.

Edna Mahan's continuing concerns and efforts to improve salaries to attract qualified women to work in correctional institutions may be summed up in her words at a staff orientation in the late 1950s:

> Young women will not choose a career in correctional institutions until salaries compare favorably with community opportunities. The taxpayers benefit, the public gets better protection and offenders earn their freedom sooner with more chances of success on parole when they are exposed to the best institutional program the state can provide. The quality of the staff determines the value of the program. I would say that over and over to you in capital letters.

Summer seasonal assistants were continued after the war and provided an excellent means for attracting capable young women to corrections. In 1958 no money was appropriated for seasonal assistants. Mahan requested from the central office, the budget bureau, and the Civil Service Commission seven seasonal assistants for the summer of 1959. The April 1959 board minutes note, "The Board urges approval of these positions since college students are given an excellent opportunity to become familiar with the correctional field through summer employment."

Although Mahan did not hand-pick the students who came to work as seasonal assistants and she accommodated the children of friends, colleagues, and Clinton Farms staff, she knew that all of them had the potential to work in the correctional arena. She refused to take students for purely political expediency. One day in the mid-sixties while the author was talking with Assistant Superintendent Morris in her office next to Mahan's, Mahan could be heard saying to someone on the phone, "Well, you just tell the governor he can go to hell!" When asked the reason for that expletive, she said the governor wanted to send summer students to accommodate political friends.

Student conferences were another effort to introduce students to correctional work. In early January 1959, Morris and the author suggested in an informal conversation with Mahan a weekend conference on correction be held to which junior and senior students and faculty from nearby colleges in New Jersey and Pennsylvania would be invited. The main purpose would be to interest college women in the correctional field. Mahan was immediately enthusiastic about this and brought it to the attention of the board at its January meeting. "The Board and Dr. Bixby endorsed the plan and urged the institution to begin this Spring."

The first conference was held the weekend of 10 April 1959. Thirty-eight students from ten colleges attended. Thirteen students arrived Friday afternoon and spent the night in staff rooms in cottages. The program included panel discussions of staff and inmates, a keynote speaker (Edward Galway from the United Nations Social Defense Section), tours of the institution, and informal talk with inmates and staff at meals and coffee breaks.

The participants were enthusiastic about their experience and urged it be repeated. One-day conferences were held in the spring for over ten years. The attendance grew to over a hundred students. MacCormick, director of the Osborne Association; Bates, retired commissioner of Institutions and Agencies; and Anna Kross, New York City commissioner of correction, were frequent participants along with staff from the New Jersey central office and other state institutions. Panel discussions were lively and sometimes heated as the students challenged the experts.

Rutgers University developed its own school of social work in the mid-1950s. In 1956 Mahan wrote Dean Wayne Vasey of Rutgers in regard to having students assigned to work at Clinton Farms. No Rutgers social work students were assigned field placements at Clinton Farms. However, in the early sixties the first Clinton Farms staff member was sent to the school of social work under the state "Extended Learners Program."

The staff member chosen was Marilyn Davenport, who had come to work at Clinton Farms in 1959 as a cottage officer. In 1960 she was promoted to classification officer and two years later assumed the position of supervisor of cottage life. While she was in this position, Mahan told her Clinton Farms would be eligible to send a staff member to the School of Social Work. "You're the only one qualified, and we want you to go." During this conversation Mahan alluded that Davenport could be the next superintendent of Clinton Farms. Davenport did complete her Master of Social Work degree at Rutgers and returned to her position as supervisor of cottage life. She was appointed superintendent after Mahan died.

Staff Orientation

There is no record when staff orientation first took place at Clinton Farms. It was probably in 1946 when the American Friends Service Committee established an institutional unit at Clinton Farms and a program was arranged for them. This was after World War II when the staff became larger and more diversified.

An orientation program was never formalized at Clinton Farms while Mahan was superintendent. The position of training officer did not exist. Mahan asked different staff members to take on this responsibility and tried to see that there was at least one program a year. The programs varied in length and content. New staff were required to attend, and all staff were encouraged to attend. Wherever possible in the cottages, student officers covered so that the cottage officers were free to attend.

Mahan tried to attend each session of an orientation program, and one session was devoted to her presentation. Much of her wisdom and philosophy concerning the inmates and the running of Clinton Farms was set forth in these meetings. At one orientation session in the late 1950s, she asked staff to write questions for her and submit them to her ahead of time. One of the questions ("What is the administration's attitude toward chick playing?") dealt with lesbianism, which has always been a controversial topic in women's institutions.

Mahan's discussion of lesbianism in the institution is frank and illustrates well her ability to talk easily and openly with staff in a group setting even on emotional and sensitive topics:

> There are several things I'd like to say about this, and one is that in my evolution at Clinton Farms we have gone through various stages of thinking about this problem, and anybody who tells you it isn't a problem is not facing facts.... Whenever you shut one sex up together, you're going to have certain types of unusual behavior.... The need to be loved, the need for attention is so great in most of our girls, it is not at all surprising that there are all sorts of manifestations. The thing that I worry about in this connection is the attitude of the staff toward this, the fear that they will sit in judgment on them.
>
> Now, maybe this is not a topic for discussion here, but I think in some of the older people's minds there will also be a question about masturbation. As a matter of fact when I was growing up this was a crime. Today psychiatrists and most other people who have tried to study human behavior say that every little boy masturbates and most little girls masturbate. Well any staff member who fills the minds of the girls with the evils of masturbation, the fact that you are going to go to a mental hospital, the fact that you will never find anybody to marry you, doesn't belong here.
>
> I think we can speak equally frankly about homosexuality. In a free society people worship as they choose. In a free society you may be a lesbian or a homosexual if you choose.
>
> As the superintendent of this institution, I have discussed this frankly with the girls. When the committee of girls wrote *About You and Clinton Farms,* they took me to every cottage to hold discussions. This was one of the subjects that I was asked to discuss in every cottage.
>
> What can I say? I don't want to be like the superintendent in Massachusetts [Miriam Van Waters] who was accused of fostering homosexuality. I don't want to punish people for what an older woman said to me once, "Oh, Miss Mahan, why do you worry about this? It's a game we play while we're in jail." Now somewhere in between—and this is the conflict that the administrators have in so many areas in trying to do what the public demands and what the institution hopes for. I said to the girls when it was discussed with the whole group in every cottage. This is a public institution supported by state funds. It is the duty of the Board and the administration to have as decent conditions as possible in public institutions. We hope that you will conduct yourselves in a way that you will not be harmed and that you will not harm anybody else.
>
> Now what more can I say? It is a fact that there are aggressively sexual deviates. It is our business to make it impossible, or as nearly impossible as we are able, to keep them from harming other people. That is why we have some single rooms in most cottages. If anything very serious happens, we have to take

> disciplinary action. We have tried to make them realize that this is something that doesn't go.

Mahan's forthright presentations to staff—individually, at staff meetings, or at orientation sessions—were appreciated. They did a great deal to enhance her image with staff and to ensure their support of her philosophy.

In her forty years as superintendent there were increasing constraints imposed by the formalization of the bureaucracies of the State Department of Institutions and Agencies and the Civil Service Commission. When these bureaucracies provided the means for more and better qualified staff, Mahan used them while insisting on the institution's autonomy in hiring individuals and using them for the specific needs of the Reformatory for Women. In her endeavors to improve salaries and conditions for staff, to attract and train qualified staff, and to remove quickly staff who were detrimental to the program, the Board of Managers worked with her. Commissioner Ellis backed her and was her strongest ally. Bates continued this support while he was commissioner as did Bates's successor in 1956, John Tramburg.

Chapter 9

The Late Fifties: Conflict and Change

Ten years after the end of World War II the United States was in a period of relative calm and prosperity. The world experienced great change and upheaval as a result of the war. Technological advances were occurring at an unprecedented rate, and these affected all of society. In the United States baby boom babies were beginning to put strains on the educational, mental health, welfare, and correctional systems.

In the last half of the fifties the Clinton Farms board minutes take note of a number of meetings that foretell changes to come. Between 1955 and 1957 there was a public hearing and a meeting of the boards of all the correctional institutions concerning parole rules and policies. The increasing number of drug addicts coming to the institution prompted the board to appoint a committee "to consider the problem of narcotic addicts in a correctional institution."

At the State Board of Control meeting in January 1957, President Lloyd Wescott "[r]eported that Mr. Frank Walsh, past president, Commissioner Tramburg, and he had met with the Governor and the legislative leaders to discuss with them the appointment of a Long-Range Study Committee of the Department."

This meeting resulted in the appointment by Governor Robert B. Meyner on 10 January 1958 "of a Commission of six citizens of New Jersey...to examine the Department of Institutions and Agencies and to report as to how its organization could be improved" (Commission to Study the Department of Institutions and Agencies 1959). Governor Meyner wrote Archibald Stevens Alexander, grandson of Caroline Stevens Wittpenn, "It would be appreciated if you would be willing to accept Chairmanship on the Commission." Alexander's wife, Jean, was a member of the Clinton Farms Board of Managers.

Wescott was the moving force behind the Alexander Commission, as it came to be called. He served on the Board of Managers of Clinton Farms for thirteen years.

In July 1956 he was appointed to the State Board of Control. Wescott was elected president of the board in November 1956.

Wescott was a leader in Hunterdon County and the state for fifty years. According to his 1990 obituary in the *Hunterdon County Democrat,* he was "a leading dairy farmer in the county...and the moving spirit of the Hunterdon Medical Center.... [He served] 16 years as president of the Board of Control in the State Department of Institutions and Agencies, president of the New Jersey Agricultural Society, an official of the state and national health and social welfare organizations, and trustee of the New Jersey Ballet and the New Jersey Symphony."

He had been a friend as well as a board member of Clinton Farms from the early 1940s. His family became Edna Mahan's family, and a warm personal relationship developed between Edna and Lloyd.

The work of the Alexander Commission at first was greeted with enthusiasm by Mahan and the Clinton Farms board as an opportunity to look closely at their own structure and the institution, set goals for the future, and send forth their own recommendations on boards, parole, and the institution. They had already started doing some planning on their own. In November 1957 a meeting was called at Clinton Farms by Director of Correction and Parole F. Lovell Bixby "to discuss the correctional needs of girls and women in this State for the future." At the December board meeting a committee was appointed "to work with Miss Mahan and members of the staff on this project." This committee met 13 January 1958 "to consider changes which might be desirable in handling of female offenders in New Jersey by 1975."

Little did they anticipate that two of the recommendations of the commission would erode the powers of the local boards of managers and precipitate dissension and divisiveness among the commission members, the State Board of Control, and the Department of Institutions and Agencies.

By the time the Alexander Commission was beginning its work in the spring of 1958, Edna Mahan received word of a high honor to be bestowed on her: an honorary degree from Rutgers University.

Doctor of Humane Letters—Public Servant and Humanitarian

On 14 March 1958, Lewis Webster Jones, president of Rutgers University wrote Mahan:

> It is with the greatest pleasure that, acting on the authority of the Board of Governors of Rutgers, The State University, I invite you to accept the honorary degree of Doctor of Humane Letters at the University's Commencement Exercises on Wednesday, June 4, 1958.

> With this report of the formal action of the Board goes its sincere hope that you will accept. May I add my own personal hope that you can come, and tell you how delighted I shall be to confer the degree upon you.

Sebastian DeGrazia, professor at the Eagleton Institute of Politics at Rutgers, nominated Mahan for the degree. Lucia Ballantine, who later married DeGrazia, told him about Mahan and her work at Clinton Farms and arranged for them to meet. One of DeGrazia's professional interests was women in politics, and he recognized Mahan as an appropriate candidate for the degree.

Mahan replied to President Jones's letter on 25 March:

> Thank you so much for your gracious letter of March 14, 1958.
>
> How can I say anything but "yes"? It will be with pleasure and humility that I accept the degree on June 4, 1958.
>
> I am deeply touched that my adopted State wishes to confer this honor upon me.

The details of the commencement evening included an early supper for the honored guests at the president's home where "you will meet your 'escort,' a Trustee of the University, who will present you for the honorary degree during the Exercises." The citation reads:

> EDNA MAHAN
>
> Public servant and humanitarian. As superintendent at Clinton you have served thirty years with distinction, establishing Clinton Reformatory as one of the foremost institutions in which a humanely conceived society seeks to rehabilitate rather than to punish those who have broken the law. For your years of service, society is in your debt.
>
> By virtue, therefore, of the authority vested in me by the Board of Governors of Rutgers, the State University, I hereby confer upon you, *honoris causa*, the degree of Doctor of Humane Letters.

Among the nine degree recipients were Justice William J. Brennan, Jr., of the U.S. Supreme Court, formerly chief justice of the New Jersey Supreme Court, and the current chief justice of the New Jersey Supreme Court, Joseph Weintraub. Mahan was the only woman.

Mahan accepted eight tickets for the commencement ceremonies. No one remembers whom she invited or if she invited anyone. The ceremonies were held in the Rutgers stadium where there was ample room in the bleachers for guests without reserved tickets. In her modest way she made it clear to her staff that this was "no big deal" and they were not to come. There was considerable debate among them as to whether or not they should go anyway. The author and her mother, board member Anita Quarles, attended the ceremony with Agnes Flack and Eleanor Reppert, director of education.

The *Flemington Democrat* of 5 June 1958 reported the following account in "Edna Mahan Gets Honorary Degree On 'Routine' Day":

> Yesterday was just a usual routine sort of a day for Miss Edna Mahan of Clinton Farms.
>
> "I'm busy with my usual Wednesday classification meeting," she told a reporter who called her up at 8:40 a.m. "Call me later." At noon she was still busy with her staff, discussing the new girls and the problem cases at the State Reformatory for Women of which she is head.
>
> "Guess I'll be running down to Rutgers with my coat tails flying," she remarked ruefully. And that was Miss Mahan's comment—the only comment—on the honor to be accorded her later in the day, when Rutgers University would bestow on her the honorary degree of Doctor of Humane Letters at its commencement exercises.
>
> If the publicity-shy superintendent insisted on no comment, her staff felt differently.
>
> "You can say we are all delighted and we think it's an honor that's long overdue!" said Miss Beatrice Black of the parole staff.

In spite of her humility, Mahan was pleased at receiving the honorary degree. Wescott made sure all her friends knew of this honor by hosting a large party at his home on 14 June. With her cooperation he sent invitations and personally wrote notes to her New Jersey friends as well as those all over the country, including her longtime California friends, Walter and Elizabeth Gordon, who were then in the Virgin Islands where he was governor. Many cards and letters were sent from inmates and staff, friends from her Boston days, professional friends from the American Correctional Association, and New Jersey colleagues, including former commissioner Sanford Bates and present commissioner John Tramburg. Governor Meyner was unable to attend as he was away for Naval Reserve training.

Austin MacCormick, who was busy finishing up the academic year at the University of California-Berkeley, wrote Mahan on 27 May 1958:

> A letter came from Lloyd Wescott telling me that you are getting an L.H.D. from Rutgers, and asking me to the June 14 party in your honor at his house. I can't come, but I'll be thinking of you....
>
> It is a wonderful honor and one you deserve on every count.... I know you never think of yourself as distinguished, but you really are and you might as well

face it. If you were looking at the record of anyone else who had accomplished as much as you have, you would whip out the old "Honoris causa" scroll pretty fast. So face your greatness, Doctor, and wear the degree in humility and happiness. It carries only one obligation: when somebody asks "Is there a doctor in the house?" you have to be ready to operate.

With love and awed admiration,

Austin

Eight administrative and professional staff members presented her with the following homemade certificate:

TO
EDNA MAHAN, OUR PAL
also
DOCTOR OF HUMANE LETTERS
THIS IS AN INTERNATIONAL CERTIFICATE GOOD AT A
STORE OF YOUR CHOICE
ANYWHERE
FOR FIFTY DOLLARS

At the Clinton Farms commencement exercises on 11 June 1958 Eleanor Reppert read the following:

THE HONORARY DOCTORATE is conferred by universities and colleges upon those persons who have made an extraordinary contribution in their field of service to mankind. Most institutions confer this degree on very few individuals—deeming it of the highest merit; a distinct honor to be conferred only upon the most worthy.

I believe we should understand this significance of Academic Degrees in order to more fully appreciate the recent honor bestowed upon our Superintendent at the Commencement Exercises at Rutgers University.

The only woman in a distinguished group of men, Miss Mahan received her degree as a "public servant and humanitarian—having established Clinton Reformatory as one of the foremost institutions in which a humanely conceived society seeks to rehabilitate rather than to punish. For your years of service—society is in your debt."

Such an honor deserves no less than our own expression of appreciation and recognition.

A standing ovation followed Reppert's recognition of Mahan's award. The honorary degree was framed and hung in her office behind her desk.

The dinner in her honor at the Wescotts was a gala affair that she thoroughly enjoyed. The *Democrat* took note of the occasion:

> Such nice things have been happening lately! Last Saturday evening Edna Mahan was the guest at a dinner party at Lloyd Wescott's most attractive and unusual home to mark especially the recent honor she received from Rutgers University.
>
> Lloyd entertained fifty-six guests among whom were Dr. and Mrs. Webster Jones of Rutgers University, Commissioner John Tramburg who heads the Department of Institutions and Agencies, and former I. and A. Commissioner Sanford Bates. Also among the guests were a number from out-of-state.
>
> Miss Mahan who heads Clinton Farms, received the honorary degree of Doctor of Humane Letters at commencement exercises there and everyone felt she really deserved it.
>
> After dinner there were brief speeches and congratulatory messages for Miss Mahan and the rest of the evening was enjoyed by the guests in just being sociable.

Receiving the honorary degree was a high point in Edna Mahan's life. The institution was running smoothly. The inmate population was relatively low. The beginning of the Alexander Commission was a time for planning for the future, which Mahan and the board saw as a possibility for more resources and the opportunity to enhance the Clinton Farms philosophy.

Wescott's admiration for Mahan was highlighted by the party he gave in her honor. In 1989 he said, "There are few people in the world that I admired more than Edna Mahan.... There was something majestic about her—great dignity. She had a pride about herself but didn't show it."

Mahan's thirtieth anniversary at Clinton Farms was 14 August 1958. The officer's club held its annual picnic at the pool on 16 August. The August 1958 board minutes state, "The highlight of the party was the presentation to Miss Mahan of thirty silver dollars in honor of her thirtieth anniversary at Clinton Farms on August 14th."

Clinton Babies Studied

Even after the Wittpenn nursery was officially closed, problems with placement of the babies continued. In November 1956 a meeting was held at Clinton Farms to reevaluate the maternity unit of the hospital. Besides Mahan and resident physician Agnes Flack, there were in attendance representatives from the State Home for Girls, the North Jersey Training School, central office staff from Trenton, SBCW, and all the female parole officers except one. (The State Home for Girls and the North Jersey Training School sent their pregnant inmates to Clinton Farms for delivery.) The 12 December 1956 board minutes report, "the most significant event (of the meeting) was Mr. Alloway's agreement to have the State Board of Child Welfare workers investigate the placement plans for all infants born in Stevens Hospital [named in 1944 for the many members of the Stevens family who maintained interest and support of Clinton Farms]."

Despite efforts to have SBCW remove babies from Clinton Farms by the age of six months, this often did not happen. There was no program in the hospital for the babies. The hospital staff was not used to having older babies and did little except attend to their medical needs.

Mahan and the Board of Managers were increasingly concerned as to what were the best plans for the care of the babies born at Clinton Farms. They proposed a study of the Clinton Farms babies. Mahan wrote to Bixby, deputy commissioner of the Department of Institutions and Agencies, 2 August 1955 asking his advice and help:

> Since the opening in 1913 to June 30, 1955 a total of 1569 infants have been born in our hospital or admitted with their mothers under 2 years of age....
>
> I share with the Board of Managers the belief that a careful study of what has happened to these children over the years following their coming into the world at Clinton Farms would be a very interesting and valuable contribution to our knowledge in the field of social adjustment generally and delinquency more specifically.
>
> Do you think the Department would be interested to explore the possibilities of securing a research grant from some foundation to finance a follow-up study of our babies? I am sure that our records at Clinton together with those of the State Board of Child Welfare and the Central Parole Bureau would offer a solid foundation for such a research project. We would be happy to give every cooperation to any University group or other suitable agency that would undertake such a study.

There is correspondence over the next three years with Joseph Stokes of the University of Pennsylvania Medical School, the Turrell Fund of New Jersey, and Andrew Hunt, Jr., director of pediatric services at Hunterdon Medical Center, concerning the study and funding for it. There were frequent references in board minutes, including the following on 11 June 1958:

> *Study of Child Care Program*
>
> On June 4th Mrs. Boutelle [board member] and Miss Mahan met with Dr. Hunt of the Hunterdon Medical Center, Dr. Plotkin of the Wister Clinic and Dr. Julia Duane of Pipersville, Pa. to discuss plans for such a study. Dr. Duane, a friend of

> Dr. Hunt's is a pediatrician and would be interested in undertaking this assignment. The Board members are enthusiastically in favor of such a study. This would be an excellent opportunity to evaluate the present methods of the physical care of the infants in Stevens Hospital; hopefully it would include an appraisal of foster home placement of children by the State Board of Child Welfare. Out of this might come desirable, modern methods in procedures for dealing with infants born in correctional institutions.... Dr. Knocke [board member] will confer with Dr. Hunt to determine the amount of money needed. Dr. Duane will be available for this project by the middle of August. She will be employed on a per diem basis and would work under the Hunterdon Medical Center staff specialists.

Although grant money was not found for this study, the board was anxious to start it. At its 9 July 1958 meeting board members agreed:

> [T]his study should begin in August with Dr. Duane working one day per week at $60. per day. She would be paid from the Special Services account if the Department approves the request. The Board instructed Miss Mahan to request the sum of $3000. per year for the next 5 years beginning with the 1959–60 budget to complete this vitally important study.

Duane was to study the physical and emotional care of the baby in the institution in relation to the next step in the baby's life and the relation of the pediatric care of the baby to the mother's situation. This would be accomplished through a study of cases of babies at Clinton Farms and in the community with the mother or other relative or in foster care. The board also hoped to make a study of training provided to foster home caregivers to the babies and children of mothers incarcerated at Clinton Farms.

The board pointed out the following:

> Obstacles [to care of the babies in the hospital] so far have been that in spite of the general recognition of the need for a better program for children born in institutions, the whole problem has been by-passed and submerged in the general (and absolutely necessary) medical concerns of an institution's hospital, and the relatively isolated child welfare departments with many demands on very limited personnel hours. No one was ready to begin and where to begin was unclear.

Duane began work in September 1958. She said in a 1990 interview that when she first went to Clinton Farms there were many babies in the institution and child welfare wasn't moving them.

> For the most part child welfare authorities were a block to any planning much less creative planning for the babies. And the hospital staff was difficult to work with. No effort was made to help the mothers concerning the care of their babies. The mothers were allowed to work in the nursery after their babies were born, but if they proved unsatisfactory, they were dismissed. No effort was made to help them understand how to care for the babies.

On 12 November 1958, Duane met with the board to discuss her observations:

> So far she has concerned herself principally with the physical care of the infants. She has found few pathological cases. The infant population totals 22 at present with 17 of these participating in the polio-mumps-measles survey. The children in the survey receive a fair amount of attention but they too are comparatively quiet and non-active. She feels that more personnel would be required to keep them fully activated. Dr. Duane plans to begin a course of instruction for the mothers here on the physical and emotional care of children.

She met with the board again on 14 January 1959 and reported that the babies were more responsive since they all had rattles and were using the playpens in the nursery. The classification committee discussed with her the need for special work with mothers committed for neglect charges. As a result Duane was working with the director of education on the possibility of taking Wittpenn cottage for "the special supervision and training of neglectful mothers." Two courses would be starting—one on the care and training of children and the other on the emotional aspects of child care.

Besides the mothers whose children were born at Clinton Farms, there were many other mothers in the population. A significant number of these were committed for neglect of their children. The board first noted concern about these commitments at the 9 May 1939 meeting when the attorney general brought to their attention "that the statute definitely provides for a 1 year term only."

At the 14 May 1940 board meeting neglect cases were discussed again. "At the present time there are 44 women [approximately 15 percent] in the institution committed on the charge of Neglect of Children.... The Board members are interested in knowing what steps should be taken to promote legislation to provide for a 3 year indeterminate commitment on this charge." The superintendent was asked to get Commissioner Ellis's suggestions.

The 1945–46 annual report details the board's concerns and the changes in the law that were made in 1944:

> Until 1944 mothers who were found guilty of cruelty or neglect of children were subject to a term of imprisonment not to exceed one year and the incarceration

> was either in a county jail, penitentiary or the reformatory. The Board of Managers and institutional authorities became increasingly concerned about the impossibility of effecting an adequate and successful program of rehabilitation for these mothers in the short period of time available under this sentence. Through the combined efforts and cooperation of several judges of courts of domestic relations, staff members of the Central Office and Clinton Board members, amendments were enacted declaring Neglect a misdemeanor and providing for a 3 year indeterminate sentence. In addition to providing a longer period of training in the institution there is the added advantage of continuing these cases on parole supervision during the period of community adjustment.

At the time the term for neglect cases was changed to a three-year indeterminate sentence, there were few community facilities available to refer these cases to. As a result judges sentenced them to the reformatory. The board's and Mahan's desire to keep them for a term longer than one year goes back to the ideals of the female reformers of the nineteenth century who "claimed that if given a chance to bring their feminine influence to bear, the fallen could be redeemed and made into true women" (Freedman 1984).

Although Mahan and the board were "keeping faith with the founders" in their efforts to redeem their charges, they also kept in touch with the New Jersey Welfare Council and SBCW on community issues concerning the mothers, fathers, and children. Within the institution, efforts were made through the education department to teach domestic science classes and incorporate aspects of parenting in other education classes.

In July 1957 a "Study of Neglect Cases" was made by SBCW of the "56 women who were in Clinton Farms for neglect of children at the end of July 1957. These women came to Clinton from 14 of the 21 counties of New Jersey. The 56 mothers had a total of 260 children under the care of the State Board of Child Welfare."

In the chapter "Women's Institutions" in ACA's *Manual of Correctional Standards* (1959), Mahan spells out the controversial nature of the subject—which continues to be controversial today—and her recommendations for resolving the controversy:

> Mothers and their babies deserve special mention since the care they need is one of the highly controversial subjects for women and girls. The problem is confounded by the fact that institutions receive women who have demonstrated their incapacity to raise their children adequately as well as mothers who must eventually assume the care of a child for the first time and who have shown their inability to handle their own lives in a satisfactory manner. Whether the birth of children shall take place in the institution or the community hospital is a controversial point. Arguments are presented on an emotional rather than a realistic

> basis. If the institution gives tender, loving care, then it is better than a poor foster home.
>
> The most scrupulous study should be made as to how these cases should best be handled for the benefit of mother, child and society. Psychiatric-pediatric orientation should be brought to focus on these mothers, whose supportive needs are so great. In a long-term sense, foundation or government backing must be provided for research in the best treatment for this kind of family breakdown to prevent recurrence, and how to protect the individuals concerned as well as the community. In the meantime, a program should be implemented under the direction of a pediatrician concerned with emotional aspects of child care. Mothers, both married and unmarried, should be given full opportunity for training in caring for their children. Children need love and affection, and should be taught how to play. This is as important as their need for vitamins and cleanliness. The closest scrutiny must be made of foster homes. Many damaged personalities result from a series of unsuccessful foster home placement.

It was not until Duane arrived in 1958 that more concerted efforts were made to address the needs of the mothers. According to Duane, "Essentially none of the women young or old knew how to care for children." At the time Duane started work at Clinton, mothers visited their children in Stevens Hospital only once a week, which was a surprise to the board. "Dr. Duane reported to Miss Mahan that she had discussed this with Dr. Flack and that from now on the mothers of children in the survey will be permitted to visit once a day."

Besides the parenting classes, Mahan assigned Duane individual mothers to counsel about their children and mothering. However, a special program in Wittpenn for "supervision and training of neglectful mothers" was not established.

Duane said she felt she accomplished a lot in her work at Clinton Farms. Besides the pediatric care of the babies in the hospital, the parenting groups, and individual counseling with mothers, she worked with child welfare authorities to help them become more sensitive to the needs of the babies.

She worked with hospital staff so that more effort was made to play with the babies. She convinced hospital staff accustomed to a medical focus of the need for individualized attention for the babies, including daily interaction with the mothers. In her quiet way she produced many changes in the care and handling of the babies at Clinton Farms and in planning for them when they left.

Duane loved working at Clinton Farms. She was committed to it and went there three days a week even though she was paid for only one day and never received an increase in all her years there. She said in an interview, "I have a strong sense of service. Edna Mahan was a great support, and Clinton Farms was a fun place to work." Duane continued her work at Clinton Farms for more than ten years.

In 1962 Flack retired, and it was difficult to find a certified obstetrician and gynecologist to replace her. These services were, therefore, provided by the Hunterdon Medical Center. For several years mothers went to the medical center for delivery and returned with their babies to Clinton Farms. The babies remained in the nursery until placements were made for them. Under Duane's supervision mothers and babies had several months for bonding, which had become recognized as essential.

During the seventies, the nursery at Clinton Farms was closed. Mothers were taken to the Hunterdon Medical Center for delivery. Unless there was a complication, they were returned to the Clinton Farms hospital the next day, and the babies remained in the medical center until relatives picked them up or SBCW made arrangements for their placement in foster homes. Mothers and their babies had no time for bonding. This became the practice in women's correctional institutions that at one time had nurseries, with the exception of Bedford Hills, New York.

Recommendations of the Alexander Commission

Before the report of the Alexander Commission was released officially, the proposed recommendations were circulated to boards, institution heads, and state officials. There was immediate reaction on the part of the Clinton Farms board members and Mahan. The proposed recommendations were probably sent out the last week of September 1958. Mahan's diary notes several conversations with board members in the days that followed concerning the commission's recommendations.

The New Jersey Institutions and Agencies Study Commission (as it was officially known) included in its report mental health, retardation, correction and parole, welfare, the central office, and citizen participation. Recommendations specific to each one of these as well as recommendations affecting the whole department were contained in the report. It was the recommendations dealing with citizen participation that came under the strongest fire because most of the power and authority local boards held were to be transferred to the commissioner.

The recommendations included strengthening the powers of the commissioner, increasing the authority and membership of the State Board of Control, and establishing advisory divisional councils under the State Board of Control. In addition, the commission recommended that the local boards of managers no longer be given the power to manage or set policy for their institutions. They should serve in an advisory capacity only.

The power to appoint and remove the heads of institutions and agencies was to be the commissioner's subject to the approval of the State Board of Control. "When the Commissioner recommends and the State Board approves a change in the head of an institution or agency, the Local Board should be consulted and given at least fifteen days' notice before final action by the State Board."

Parole authority of the local boards of managers as it existed was to be transferred to a "Citizens Parole Board, appointed by and subject to the authority of the State Board of Control and vested with final parole powers over indeterminate sentences." The Citizens Parole Board was to be composed of "persons selected from each Local Board now having parole power."

Two members of the commission, Archibald S. Alexander and William H. Jackson, dissented from the other four members on these two issues. Their "Statement of Dissent" is included in the commission report.

Mahan and the board members fought the recommendations of the majority in every way they could conceive. The board members who had worked so well with Wescott for thirteen years on the Clinton Farms Board of Managers were puzzled and angry that their once strong ally would so quickly give up the authority and powers of the local boards. Mahan felt a sense of betrayal by Wescott, and their personal and professional relationship would never again be as close as it had been.

In light of their many years as friends and neighbors, working together at Clinton Farms and his great admiration for her, it was wrenching for her when he strongly supported the majority position of the Alexander Commission Report. Although Wescott was concerned with progressive change, his personal ambitions as head of the State Board of Control prevented him from keeping a balanced view of how the change should be accomplished. The impact of the differences between Mahan and Wescott became apparent as they moved into the sixties and began to implement changes and new programs.

Mahan and the board members knew that the authority and power invested in the board ensured Clinton Farms could remain a unique institution focused on the needs and the treatment of female offenders. The institution could not be forced into the male correctional mold. The enlightened leadership of Mahan could not be threatened as Van Waters' was in Massachusetts.

The changes called for in the commission's recommendations were not carried out until almost a decade after Mahan's death because of the considerable opposition to it and the extensive changes that were called for. A productive outcome at Clinton Farms of the Alexander Commission Report in the years immediately following its recommendations was the self-study it initiated.

At the 5 February 1959 board meeting Geraldine Thompson spoke with the members about the commission's study. "She is particularly anxious to have a brief history of Clinton Farms given to the committee since Clinton antedates the establishment of the Department of Institutions and Agencies by at least five years." Three board members met at the institution 11 March to put together the history with excerpts from the first annual report of the Board of Managers in 1913 and the paper written by Mahan in 1950, "To What Extent Can Open Institutions Take the Place of the Traditional Prison?" These statements accentuated the uniqueness of Clinton Farms in relation to men's institutions. They were added to the recommendations the board prepared in January, and the document was given to the members of the Alexander Commission, who were present at the March board meeting.

The recommendations the board made for "handling female offenders in New Jersey by 1975" included the usual need for additional small cottage units to provide individual rooms, more psychiatrists and psychiatric social workers to provide individual counseling, a separate unit for treating alcoholics and narcotic addiction as psychiatric and medical problems, and closer cooperation with probation and parole. Two of the recommendations speak to new types of programs for women and juveniles.

> Small "Community Training Centers" should be established in several areas of greater population density in the state. These Centers would be under the direction of the Superintendent of Clinton Farms and would be staffed by personnel trained at Clinton Farms. Their purpose would be to provide a stepping stone between the protected prison environment at Clinton and living in the community on parole. It is planned that the inmate could be on day parole to work and return to the center for sleeping, some meals, and for counselling and supervision, until she has demonstrated that she is ready for the greater freedom and responsibility of a regular parole. It is hoped that under this set up the Parole Officer would become acquainted with the inmate and would start planning for regular parole. If possible local mental health groups would be encouraged to work with the centers, and community interest and support would be encouraged.

The above anticipates the halfway house, which by 1975 was a reality in New Jersey and most other states. The board, in its strong belief in Mahan, recommends that the direction of the centers should be under the Clinton Farms superintendent and staffed by Clinton Farms-trained personnel. The board also recommended a small residential group center "for selected members of the younger age group" modeled after the Highfields program for boys.

At the end of the history and recommendations the board added the following:

> In achieving these changes we feel that it is most important to preserve the basic philosophy of Clinton; namely, that while protecting the community the inmate be treated as an individual, in trouble and with personal problems, within the framework of the prison community. The institution will try to help the individual to face and understand her problems, to overcome her troubles, and to gain a firm sense of values, so she can return with self-confidence to the community as a useful, productive citizen.

Staff members were encouraged to contribute their suggestions and recommendations. As classification officer, one of the author's main responsibilities was inmate work assignments, so she spent time analyzing the population and the types of work assignments and their supervision and prepared her own recommendations pertinent to these issues.

By the time the report of the commission was officially released on 24 August 1959, the author had decided to leave Clinton Farms and pursue doctoral studies, but she was urged to write Governor Meyner to say that her decision to leave Clinton Farms was in part due to the recommendation concerning appointment of superintendents and directors of institutions by the commissioner, which would open them to political appointees and threaten career service. A letter was sent 29 September 1959, and a reply dated 14 October 1959 was received that strongly defended the commission's recommendations. The letter was signed by Governor Meyner with the initials "LBW" in the lower left corner.

The board and Mahan over the next few years gathered more material to bolster their strong opposition to reducing the authority and powers of the local boards. In April 1961, Mahan asked the author, then in graduate school, again for suggestions for the whole institution and its programs. She particularly asked her to write a statement on the parole process at Clinton Farms since the author's other main responsibility while employed there was to prepare case summaries for both parole boards. Mahan and the author were both convinced that the local board procedures, at least at Clinton Farms, were much more thorough than those practiced by the state parole board.

The author's statement recommending that parole powers for inmates serving indeterminate sentences remain with the local Board of Managers addressed the differences in the case summaries prepared for the Clinton board as opposed to the state parole board:

> For two and a half years.... I wrote case summaries of every girl who was being considered for parole whether she was serving a determinate or indeterminate sentence. In writing these case summaries I was required to dig fully into the folder of each girl who was being considered for parole by the Clinton Farms Board of Managers. They insisted upon knowing all the details of the circumstances leading to the girl's commitment as well as all pertinent facts of her stay on the Farms. Although I started out writing complete summaries for the State Parole Board [at Mahan's request], I was soon informed they didn't require all that information. They preferred a routine set outline which was considerably easier to write but never gave the complete picture of the girl. I had to sneak in extra things such as AA and Homesteaders. It was obvious that the same care and consideration was not exercised by the State Parole Board in deciding who should be paroled as was exercised by the Clinton Farms Board of Managers.

The Alexander Commission Report generated a great deal of debate, healthy exchange of ideas, and self-examination of New Jersey's institutions and agencies. It set the direction and structure of the change to be accomplished by the middle of the seventies. In 1958 the commission did not foresee the incipient civil rights movement becoming the major force of social change that affected all society in the next two decades. Actually, when the Division of Correction and Parole asked Clinton Farms to outline a plan of diagnosis and treatment of the female offender in New Jersey for 1975, one of the assumptions it made was that there would be no major social change that could presumably affect criminal behavior.

The civil rights movement and the women's movement that began in the 1960s brought about major changes in society that affected criminality and the treatment of female offenders. The Alexander Commission set the Department of Institutions and Agencies and its components, including the Reformatory for Women, on a course for change.

Fighting for Women's Institutions

Edna Mahan did not always, as Martha Wheeler put it, "make her impact quietly from the wings." In dealing with her male colleagues in the American Prison/Correctional Association there were times when she was outraged, and she was direct and sharp in her criticism. Her revision of the chapter on women's institutions in the 1954 *Manual of Correctional Standards* illustrates this. It is an example of some men's lack of understanding of the differences in working with female offenders and putting women's institutions into the mold of men's.

The American Prison Association in 1946 published for the first time a *Manual of Suggested Standards for a State Correctional System.*

> These standards were developed in answer to the requests of the governors of various states, correctional officials and legislative and civic organizations, and...proved helpful in the initiation of many improvements in the adult correctional systems of the United States and Canada.

At the 1951 congress a resolution was adopted specifying "that a committee should be appointed to review and revise the Manual." After reviewing the scope of the 1946 manual, "The decision was made to include 12 additional chapters to cover subject matter considered essential" (APA 1954). A separate chapter on women's institutions was one of the additional chapters.

Mahan was appointed a member of the committee to review the 1946 *Manual of Suggested Standards.* (One other woman from community corrections was also appointed to the committee.) Austin MacCormick was appointed a member of the committee and also served as one of six members of the editorial committee. MacCormick and Mahan worked together over the years not only in the American Prison Association but also the Osborne Association. Their correctional philosophies were similar, they admired each other, and they were good friends. The chapter on women's institutions was written by MacCormick "using freely material given to me by Edna" (MacCormick 1962). The chapter is indeed a reflection of her thinking and her practices.

At the 86th Annual Congress of Correction, August 1956, a committee to review the 1954 *Manual of Correctional Standards* was authorized. Mahan was again appointed to the committee—the only woman. MacCormick also was on the committee and was again a member of the editorial subcommittee. Mahan was given the responsibility for the chapter on women's institutions. Although she made no substantial changes to the chapter in the 1954 manual, she did make several significant additions.

She added an opening paragraph, which is a strong statement on the women who run the institutions:

> Penology was advanced considerably when some of the states began to build separate institutions for women.... Many of them are run by women who have made this a career service with very little political interference. The personnel requirements have always been reasonably high and well trained young women were attracted to live and work in these institutions.... Women superintendents like to experiment, to try out new methods and to use new techniques. (ACA 1959)

She also expanded on some of the discussions of essential elements, most notably personnel, and under "Medical Services" the handling of mothers and babies. In a paragraph on salaries and working conditions she adds, "Women should be paid on an equal basis with salaries paid in the best men's institutions. Women supervisors should be on a forty-hour week basis for their own well-being as well as for those they supervise." She adds at the end of the personnel section:

> Any progressive institution will be the better for offering training opportunities to promising college students. Several members of the administrative staff at one institution formerly worked there as students during summer vacations. If the quality of the staff is to be raised generally throughout the correctional field, this practice must be increased and encouraged. (ACA 1959)

This chapter is the best and most comprehensive published statement of Edna Mahan's thinking and philosophy on the treatment of female offenders. It is no wonder then that she was so irate at its editing by a member of Richard McGee's staff. McGee was chairman of the committee to review the 1954 *Manual of Correctional Standards*.

The committee for the revision of the *Manual of Correctional Standards* met in New York City 18 February 1959. This was the last meeting of the group, and they were under some pressure "to have the manual completed and printed in time for distribution at the Congress of Correction in Miami on August 30th" (McGee 1959). Mahan was not present. She was vacationing at her home in St. Croix. Committee members had received, prior to the meeting, drafts of all chapters but three. Members would be forwarded drafts of these three as soon as they could be duplicated. Committee members were to review them and submit comments in writing. The chapter on women's institutions was one.

The minutes of the meeting note:

> Chapter XXVII, Women's Institutions, has been received. Inasmuch as committee members have not had an opportunity to review the chapter the comments concerning this chapter should be placed in writing. **It was agreed that this chapter should be prepared with a primary focus of indicating those aspects which are different in the institutions for women offenders** [Emphasis added].

Further on in the minutes:

> General discussion followed and it was agreed that it was the sub-committee's responsibility to incorporate into the final draft the spirit of the proceedings here today, and to proceed with integrity but that it would not be necessary to again clear with the authors of the various chapters.

On 25 March 1959 McGee sent the following letter to members of the committee for revision of the *Manual of Correctional Standards*:

> Gentlemen:
>
> Enclosed are rough drafts of Chapter 27, "Women's Institutions" and 1, "Development of Modern Correctional Concepts." The original draft of Chapter 27 has been revised considerably by the staff consultant in order to reduce duplicating other material in the Manual.
>
> In accordance with my letter of March 20th, it will be appreciated if your comments and suggestions are received by April 3rd.
>
> Very truly yours,
>
> Richard A. McGee, Chairman

The revised version of Mahan's chapter bore little resemblance to the version she had sent to McGee in February. Her twenty-five, single-spaced pages had been reduced to fourteen double-spaced pages.

The editor states in one of the opening paragraphs:

> Although different from an institution for men in many respects, the administration of a women's institution is almost identical in many areas. To examine here all of the elements necessary for the successful operation of a women's institution would mean duplicating much of the rest of this manual. To avoid this, we have listed and discussed only those "essential elements" which have special implication for women's institutions. Other than the differences hereafter related the operation of a women's institution requires almost the same approach as does one for men.

Mahan listed the following fifteen "essential elements":

- building and grounds
- personnel
- reception, orientation, and classification
- medical services
- psychiatric and psychological services
- social education
- academic education
- vocational training
- educational personnel, budget, and facilities
- library
- leisure -time activities
- community relations
- student government
- religion
- discipline

The editor cut this to six "essential elements": physical plant, staff, medical (including psychiatric and psychological), vocational training, leisure-time activities, and plant maintenance program, all the rest being the same as those for men.

To the editor's credit he left in all but the first of the paragraphs Mahan had added to the 1954 edition. However, discussions of student government or inmate advisory councils, which were used successfully in many women's and juvenile institutions, were totally left out.

The editor added his own diagnosis of women's medical and psychiatric needs. His discussion of "Medical, Psychiatric and Psychological Services" starts with the following two paragraphs:

> It goes without saying that most of the elements essential to an adequate medical program in a men's prison apply equally well to a women's institution. But here, comparison between the medical needs in the two institutions ends. Not only is woman susceptible to practically all of the illnesses common to man, but she is subject to diseases peculiar to her sex and the disabilities incurred in procreation. The latter, indeed, far exceed the illnesses shared with men. Any numerical comparison, therefore, between the medical needs of a women's correctional institution and those for men can be extremely misleading.
>
> The medical staff of a women's institution, therefore, must be versatile and experienced to cope with the many problems encountered, but must be particularly versed in either one of the two major fields of medicine—psychiatry and gynecology—which form the predominate medical need of women committed to an institution.

The editor makes no mention of inmates' babies. His interpretation of women's medical needs as primarily gynecological or psychiatric is stereotypical. He suggests at the beginning of the chapter in a discussion of the problems with justifying a separate institution for women in states with very few female inmates, "The possibility of housing a state's women prisoners at the State mental hospital should not be overlooked." This solution is advanced in the chapter on "The Physical Plant of Institutions" (for men) in the 1954, 1959, and 1966 editions of the manual.

This emphasis on the psychiatric nature of women's problems is one of the issues that disturbed Mahan. Whereas the editor categorizes psychiatric and psychological services as "essential," she categorizes them as "valuable resources." Mahan's interest in Karen Horney and a feminist psychology of women as well as her use of psychiatric services at Clinton Farms point to her lack of sympathy to the editor's statements.

In the discussion of the physical plant the editor incorporates most of Mahan's essential points, but he edits out sentences that emphasize the importance of these to the rehabilitative goals of the institutions. He omits any mention that some institutions for women have no perimeter fences or security protection on most of their cottages. He adds at the end of his discussion:

> The power plant and service facilities should be outside the security area in a correctional institution. In an institution for men this is so the facilities will not be destroyed in case of trouble; in a women's institution, it is essential in order to reduce the contacts between craftsmen and the inmate population.

Mahan underlined this paragraph with large exclamation marks on her copy. In her discussion of personnel she writes:

> Most of the workers in a women's institution will be women but it is desirable to employ some men in professional and skilled roles such as teachers, psychologists, medical officers and the various maintenance trades. They must obviously be selected with utmost care, especially on grounds of personality and character.

Two notations on Mahan's 31 March 1959 calendar allude to her and Bates' reactions to this chapter: "Wired Dick [McGee] re chapter! Bates phoned from N.Y.C. re chapter." Her wire to McGee:

> What is the feminine of castrate? This is what the condensed chapter on women's institutions is now. I will have no part of it unless included as originally submitted. What can you do?

Copies of the telegram were sent to MacCormick and Cass, and she had spoken to Bates over the phone.

Bates, who was also a member of the revision committee, sent McGee his comments on the chapters in a letter dated 3 April 1959:

> Dear Richard:
>
> I have received the three remaining Chapters of the Revised Manual of Correction....
>
> With regard to the women's Chapter I find several omissions. There is nothing about classification and the preparation of case histories. There is nothing on the use of student councils or inmate organizations, which are used to good advantage in many women's institutions, nor is there anything about what to do with the disturber, the destructive recalcitrant or psychopathic women—a novice on reading it might expect there were none such. What kind of quarters are proper for discipline or seclusion. Should there be a humane system of administering discipline (punishment). We all know there are many difficult personalities to be handled. The whole Chapter describes a women's prison as a pleasant garden type resort—and after all there must be rules and women like men must get accustomed to obey them. It is just as important to learn self control as to learn how to curl (or uncurl) their hair....
>
> Sincerely,
> Sanford Bates

R. K. Procunier, assistant editorial consultant for the committee to review the 1954 manual, wrote Mahan from California 1 April 1959 saying McGee had discussed with him her telegram and referred it to him because he "was assigned the editorial work on this chapter." He apologizes for not checking with her because of the deadline for completion. He goes on to write:

> At this time, our objective should be to edit this chapter within the framework set by the committee. As I understand it, we are to omit any material from the chapter that would be duplicated in another chapter, however, not at the expense of clarity. On the other hand, we are to emphasize features and standards of particular importance to Women's Institutions.
>
> Our need now is to have you suggest further revisions to emphasize those program aspects and standards which apply.
>
> One way of approaching this is for you to compare the two versions of the chapter and let me know right away what I should do in order to make the resulting material acceptable. If you will do this, I will make every effort to bring the two together so that our objectives will be met.

After receiving this letter Mahan wrote to MacCormick on 6 April 1959:

> Dear Austin:
>
> I hate to keep pestering you about the Chapter on Women's Institutions but I feel that you may be able to resolve the present difficulty. Here is a copy of the telegram I sent Dick after receiving the revised chapter. The reply came from R.K. Procunier which is no help at all. He simply says that the chapter has to be revised within the framework set by the committee.
>
> In this morning's mail I get a copy of a letter Sanford wrote Dick in which he says in part: "The whole chapter describes a woman's prison as a pleasant garden type resort—and after all there must be rules and women like men must get accustomed to obey them."
>
> I say again that unless the Chapter is included as I revised it I will have nothing further to do with it and it might just as well be left out completely as to be put in the way this guy has condensed it....
>
> Please do what you can about the Chapter.
>
> Cordially,
>
> N.J. STATE REFORMATORY FOR WOMEN
> Edna Mahan, Superintendent

She must have felt some relief when she received a letter from MacCormick dated 8 April 1959 saying he had called McGee and told him "that since there is only one chapter on Women's Institutions in that big Manual, it is justifiable to duplicate or overlap some material in other chapters."

On 17 April 1959 Mahan wrote McGee:

Dear Dick:

Once again I am appealing to you to include the Chapter on Women's Institutions as I submitted it. The dissected revision makes no sense at all for anyone (and I think most women working in institutions for girls and women as well as Board members) who wants to get a fairly complete picture of the women's angle.

Most of the procedures in a women's institution are quite different from those in the large male prisons. To keep referring to other chapters where there might seem to be duplication is not valid and destroys the continuity of the chapter. It seems to me that the few more pages than were allotted in the original draft might well be salvaged as a chivalrous gesture to the ladies.

So again I say PLEASE include it as is or eliminate the Chapter altogether.

If you are opposed to this perhaps Ed Cass would consider issuing it as a separate appendix to the Manual....

Cordially,

N.J. STATE REFORMATORY FOR WOMEN
Edna Mahan, Superintendent

On 22 April 1959 Edna Mahan with two other officials of the New Jersey correctional system embarked on a trip to Europe to meet with officials and study prison systems in several countries. Her anxiety about the outcome of the chapter was expressed in the following letter she sent to MacCormick:

Dear Austin:

On the eve of my departure I want to ask you to do me a favor. I will not be very happy until I hear what has happened to that famous Chapter. As soon as you know anything definite could you have your secretary write me a note? You can reach me in England from the 12th to 29th of May:
c/o Miss Molly Mellanby

Prison Commission
Horseferry House
Dean Ryle Street
London S.W. 1

or in Geneva from June 15th to 18th at:

Hotel Beau Rivage
13 Quai deu Mont-Blanc.

THANK YOU, THANK YOU.

Affectionately,

N.J. STATE REFORMATORY FOR WOMEN
Edna Mahan, Superintendent

There is no record of MacCormick writing her in Europe. On 23 April 1959 McGee wrote Mahan the following letter, which she did not receive before leaving for Europe:

> Dear Edna:
>
> I am glad to have your letter of April 17th. Our editorial committee, which includes Austin MacCormick and others who are working on the job of hammering the Manual into shape for the printer, will meet on April 29th.
>
> There is much merit in what you say about a fuller chapter on women's institutions, even though there may be some duplication, for it is entirely probable that many of the readers of this chapter will not care to make frequent cross references. Our chief concern should be, I believe that there be no fundamental conflicts on questions of broad policy.
>
> In any event, I assure you that we will do our best to come out with a manuscript which you will not wish to disown. In short, I might say, "Keep your bodice buttoned." This is female for "Keep your shirt on!"
>
> Cordially yours,
>
> RICHARD A. MCGEE
> Director of Corrections

On 4 May 1959 a letter was sent to her at Clinton Farms from the editorial consultant saying, "You will be happy to know that the chapter on women's prisons has been restored to the Manual substantially as you had submitted the draft."

Edna Mahan was one of the last of the female superintendents who was able to run her institution as envisaged by the early female reformers and put into practice by many of the first female superintendents. The chapter on women's institutions in the 1959 edition of the manual represents her best written work on the subject. She fought to have it remain her thinking, not the thinking of the less progressive male establishment. Her more progressive male colleagues in the association supported her.

European Prison Tour

Before the fifties ended, Edna Mahan enjoyed her first trip to Europe, a combined professional and personal journey. Apparently the trip was first talked about when Sir Lionel Fox, chairman of the prison commission, London, and M. Paul Conril, secretary general of the Belgian Ministry of Justice, were visiting in America and were entertained by Mary Stevens Baird. F. Lovell Bixby wrote Conril on 29 January 1959, "The European trip which we discussed jokingly in Mrs. Baird's apartment when you and Sir Lionel were here seems to be developing into a reality...."

Correspondence found among Mahan's papers include copies of letters to Baird written in the fall of 1958 from people she knew in Europe regarding plans for the trip. Also included among these papers is a handwritten list of questions and notes by Mahan for "M.S.B. 1/19/59" concerning details of the trip such as who will make the arrangements, countries to visit, institutions to see, and people to meet with. There is also the notation "M.S.B. & L.B.W. make it right w. Commissioner. (He wants a decent report.)" According to her diary she conferred with Baird and Bixby about the trip over the phone several times in the next few days.

Bixby, Ralph Brancale, director of the New Jersey Diagnostic Center (and his wife), and Mahan were to visit correctional institutions and meet with officials in France, Belgium, Holland, Denmark, Sweden, and England to study their methods. Kenneth Kassler, an architect with an interest in corrections, joined the tour in Sweden. Bixby made all the arrangements for the professional appointments. Baird's secretary and travel agent made all the travel plans and hotel reservations. Ken Kassler and the State of New Jersey financed the trip. Baird had originally planned to join the group in London but was unable to do so.

The group left New York for Paris 22 April 1959. Mahan was joined in London on 23 May by Beulah Wescott Hagen. The trip officially ended 29 May in London. While the others returned to New Jersey, Mahan and Hagen flew to Rome. Besides Italy they traveled in Switzerland, Austria, Spain, and Portugal. Although this part of the journey was primarily pleasure, Mahan also visited institutions for female offenders in all the countries except Switzerland. Their trip ended in Lisbon on 26 June when they departed for New York.

Among Mahan's papers are three file folders full of materials concerning the European prison tour. One file contains her handwritten daily notes, mostly on hotel stationery, of each day's happenings and her impressions. A second file holds all the brochures and reports she obtained from the institutions they visited, and the third file has all the official correspondence, travel itineraries, and the draft of a 117-page report about the trip, presumably the "decent report" for Commissioner Tramburg.

Bixby wrote the draft. Mahan made many corrections on it in her own handwriting. The descriptions follow fairly closely her handwritten notes, which he must have used, and there are many blank spaces throughout the manuscript with the notation "space for E.M." There is no copy of a final report. It was probably never completed, for Mahan kept copies of reports and papers she wrote or had considerable responsibility for.

The draft contains descriptions of many of the institutions they visited, some of which were considered very progressive, and the many people they met. It is interspersed with Mahan's impressions of the places and the people as well as the institution's surroundings. It tells of the social events they attended and the people who entertained them. It is unfortunate it was never completed, for it is a descriptive and insightful day-by-day account of the tour.

The European prison tour indicates the high regard New Jersey's State Board of Control of Institutions and Agencies held for Bixby, Brancale, and Mahan and the pride the State Board of Control had in the institutions they ran. Although the primary purpose of the tour was to study methods of treating offender populations, these three traveled as correctional ambassadors from New Jersey, which was proud of its progressive institutions.

It was another high point in Mahan's career and in her life. It is unlikely Baird would have arranged such a trip were Mahan not part of it. Baird gave her a great deal of advice on places to visit throughout the countries she toured with both Bixby and the Brancales and later Hagen. She wrote personal friends throughout Europe advising them of the prison tour and hoping arrangements could be made for personal visits. Geraldine Thompson wrote Mahan a letter of introduction to Lady Astor in London and had Eleanor Roosevelt write the Queen Mother. On 29 May 1959 the private secretary to Queen Elizabeth the Queen Mother wrote to Mahan in London:

> I am writing to you at the bidding of Queen Elizabeth The Queen Mother to tell you how very sorry Her Majesty is that it has not proved possible for her to see you while you are in London.
>
> Actually, Her Majesty only received Mrs. Roosevelt's letter two days ago, when she was away on a visit to Wales, and has learned to her regret that you are leaving London at the end of your visit today.
>
> Finally I am to tell you how much Queen Elizabeth hopes that you have enjoyed your time in London, which Her Majesty trusts you have found interesting and informative.

On Mahan's return to the United States, she wrote Her Majesty Queen Elizabeth the Queen Mother how disappointed she was "not to have met you, but you will be happy to know that everyone at the Home Office was most courteous and helpful when we came over from New Jersey to study the English penal institutions. We were deeply impressed by the work which is being carried out by the Prison Commission."

"Stay Home and Run Your Own Dam Prison"

Mahan was away on the European tour over two months. Earlier in the year she spent a month at her home in St. Croix. This was the greatest amount of time she had spent away from Clinton Farms since first coming to work there. As always she had complete confidence in her staff. Josephine Hull, assistant superintendent, was competent, respected, and well-liked. The Board of Managers met as usual, and the work of the institution was carried on smoothly. She was, however, missed because her presence was dynamic and she was fun. The classification committee missed her particularly at their weekly Wednesday meetings and sent her the following cablegram, composed by Ackerman, while she was in Europe:

Stop running around inspecting "clinks."
When you're away we think it stinks.
"No wandering" should be your decision.
Stay home and run your own dam prison.

On her arrival back at Clinton Farms, Ackerman penned the following rhyme to greet her:

Please nice "Boss Lady"
Ne're more roam.
Mahan alive!
We're glad you're home.

The "Boss Lady" returned to a very busy summer and fall schedule at Clinton Farms. There was the day-to-day running of the institution, which had no grave emergencies at this time, but it was never routine.

The summer and early fall of 1959 were warm and sunny. Mahan loved to sunbathe and swim in the outdoor pool that had been built in 1957. She swam at lunch time or in the late afternoon regularly that summer. On Sundays she often spent a couple of hours at the pool in the mornings before it was opened to the population. She was often joined by the author, parole officer Bee Black, and Lois Morris and on Sundays by any house guests she had. On Sunday 2 August 1959 she wrote in her diary, "Gorgeous day—sun with no humidity. Sunned by pool 10:15 to 12:45. Picked peaches and corn. Caught up on papers. No business for 1st time since I came home."

As always she enjoyed dinners, often cookouts, with local friends. She spent some weekends at Stony Brook, Long Island, with Gertrude and Bob Hawley with whom she had become friends through Beulah Hagen. She built in time away from her desk and the institution to better cope with the heavy demands they brought.

The "Boss Lady" also spent more time socializing with the Clinton Farms staff. Every summer a group went to Ebbets Field to watch the Brooklyn Dodgers play, and she often came along. A few of the staff enjoyed deep sea fishing off the Jersey coast and persuaded Mahan to try it. Once she did, she looked forward every summer to the outing and the bluefish she brought back.

Not long after her return from Europe there are references in her diary to "Bix's" (Bixby's) illness and hospitalization. He apparently suffered depression and alcoholism. He fully recovered from both. In spite of this and strong support of some board members and superintendents of institutions as well as Board of Control members for him to continue as director of correction and parole, he was eased out by Commissioner Tramburg and Wescott. He remained in state service, however. He was appointed to do a study of all the courts in New Jersey and produced a superb report before he retired.

Bixby's replacement was Lloyd McCorkle, who was brought to New Jersey by Bixby to introduce guided group interaction programs in the institutions. McCorkle was the first director of the pioneer Highfields program for male juvenile delinquents, which used guided group interaction methods. Guided group interaction is group therapy that combines "psychological and sociological approaches to the control of human behavior. The psychological approach aims to change the self-perception of the [juvenile] from a delinquent to a nondelinquent.... The insight of sociology is to reverse the process by which the group inducts the [juvenile] into delinquency and compels him [or her] to continue it. In guided group interaction, the influence of the group is directed to free the [juvenile] from being controlled by delinquent association and to give him [or her] the desire and inner strength to be autonomous" (McCorkle, Elias & Bixby 1958).

Mahan notes in her diary on 15 September 1959, "Mr. W. [Wescott] admits Mac [McCorkle] will be over correctional supts." This presaged a major change for correction and parole, for though McCorkle was a bright man and made significant contributions to the correctional field, most directly in New Jersey, he was not the sensitive, supportive, warm person Bixby was. Mahan did not look forward to working under him.

In her forty years at Clinton Farms, Edna Mahan concentrated on keeping faith with the founders in running an open institution based on a philosophy of reformation rather than punitive discipline. William J. Ellis, the first commissioner she served under, understood the philosophy of Clinton Farms and backed and counseled the young superintendent in her endeavors. Later commissioners supported her. The Board of Managers was as crucial to carrying out the ideals as were the commissioners.

As Mahan approached the sixties, work on the Alexander Commission's recommendations and planning for the future of Clinton Farms were priority items of her last years of work. The sixties also held crises that threatened the reformatory's ability to continue as an open institution with a student government honor system.

Chapter 10

The Sixties: Courageous and Hopeful

Courageous and hopeful was how Lloyd Wescott described Edna Mahan in a tribute to her at the fiftieth anniversary of Clinton Farms in June 1963. In these years, which were to be her last, this description seems to be particularly appropriate, for the challenges to continue the institution as open and with a student government honor system were the greatest they had ever been. Mahan never lost hope that her methods could succeed with inmates sent to her because she was always willing to try new approaches.

The changing inmate population was accompanied by the changes called for in the Alexander Commission report that would dilute the autonomy of the boards of each institution and force them into a common mold. Also, the top administrators in the Department of Institutions and Agencies changed. Bixby had been replaced by McCorkle as director of correction and parole in 1959. Commissioner John Tramburg died unexpectedly in 1962, and Lloyd McCorkle was appointed commissioner. Albert Wagner, who had worked his way up through the New Jersey system, became director of correction and parole. He was a "stick to the rules" administrator who lacked the vision Bixby had.

Mahan was now the leading name in corrections in New Jersey. The American Correctional Association recognized her for outstanding work in the correctional field by bestowing on her in 1962 the Certificate of Merit and in 1963 the Edward R. Cass Correctional Achievement Award. Her reputation in Europe was increasing. In June 1960 she attended the Second United Nations Congress on the Prevention of Crime and the Treatment of Offenders with the official U.S. Delegation. The fiftieth anniversary of Clinton Farms marked Mahan's thirty-fifth year as superintendent.

Despite her national and international reputation, she had no aspirations for higher positions. She wanted to be able to run Clinton Farms as a place of human dignity where each inmate could learn that to be free is to be responsible. She fought to continue her work and "keep faith with the founders" in spite of changes in the state bureaucracy. During her last years she continued to fight for the autonomy of her institution and to create new programs for female offenders in New Jersey. She worked to meet the challenges presented by the changing inmate population, which several times created bad publicity for the institution. In spite of the increasing demands of her position, she was able to spend more time away from Clinton Farms in St. Croix and with friends on Long Island. She knew Clinton Farms was in the capable hands of Assistant Superintendent Lois Morris (Josephine Hull resigned in late 1960), Marilyn Davenport, supervisor of cottage life, and the other top-level administrative and professional staff.

Alexander Commission Recommendations

Controversy over the recommendations of the Alexander Commission continued through the sixties. An article in the *Newark Evening News* dated 19 February 1960 refers to two of the issues Mahan and the Clinton Farms board opposed:

> The board of control of the State Department of Institutions and Agencies is split over a recommendation that the boards of managers be relieved of power to appoint their own superintendents.
>
> The board of control voted 5–2 yesterday to back the Alexander Commission suggestion that heads of state institutions should be appointed by the commissioner.
>
> Board President Lloyd B. Wescott said that two Board members, Mrs. Mary Baird and Dr. Frank J. Hughes, favored keeping the power with the local boards of managers.
>
> Wescott reported that the board still has failed to set its policy on the...recommendation that boards of mangers be reduced from policy-making to advisory boards.
>
> A two-man minority of the six-member Alexander Commission...favored retention of the policy-setting local boards. The Alexander body was unanimous, however, on giving the commissioner the power of appointment of superintendents.

Mahan met or talked with Baird, Anita Quarles, and her own board members to continue the fight to keep the Clinton Farms board autonomous. She asked the author to send to the editor of the *Newark Evening News* the same letter she had written to the governor the previous September. The letter appeared in the newspaper on 11 March 1960.

These efforts paid off for Clinton Farms. An article in the *Morris County Daily Record* dated 21 February 1961 refers to "a plan to abolish the Citizen Boards of Managers which run New Jersey's three male reformatories...and replace the three...7-member boards at the Jamesburg, Annandale and Bordentown reformatories...with a single 15-member super board." This single Board of Managers for the men's reformatory complex became effective 1 January 1964 (Wagner 1965). The Reformatory for Women's Board of Managers retained its policy-making and parole powers until after Edna Mahan's death.

In the same years of the work of the Alexander Commission and the controversy that followed its report, a proposal for a residential group center for delinquent girls modeled after the Highfields program for boys was presented to the Clinton Board and Mahan.

Turrell Residential Group Center

After World War II, Bixby brought McCorkle to New Jersey to develop rehabilitation programs based on guided group interaction. McCorkle had used this method during World War II working with prisoners in the navy. In the summer of 1950 the Department of Institutions and Agencies, with financial help from the New York Fund, opened the Highfields Project on an experimental basis for two years. McCorkle was appointed superintendent for this period. The Highfields program was found to be successful for the male juvenile probationers sent to it. Guided group interaction programs were also introduced in some of the adult institutions including Clinton Farms. (McCorkle trained staff there in the method.)

In 1958 a bill was passed by the legislature and signed by the governor that allowed the department to establish other residential group centers. Several additional programs for men were opened throughout the state. In early 1958 "the Turrell Fund offered...the funds for the construction of a residential group center for delinquent girls" (McGrath 1963). It was to be located at Allaire on the grounds of the Arthur Brisbane Child Treatment Center. This was the first addition to the state's facilities for female offenders since Clinton Farms opened in 1913.

The planning for the program was first reported to the Clinton Board of Managers by Wescott at its 14 May 1958 meeting. On 23 July 1959 the State Board of Control developed a tentative proposal for the operation of the Turrell project. On 18 November 1959 McCorkle, now officially director of correction and parole, met with the Clinton Farms board to discuss the proposal, including Mahan's role in the project. The State Board of Control's proposal suggested Mahan be in charge of the planning for the Turrell Project. At the board meeting:

> Dr. McCorkle indicated that if this project were placed under the direct supervision of Miss Mahan it would require at least half of her time. Since her responsibility to the Clinton institution is on a full-time basis, Miss Mahan stated she is unable to accept the responsibilities outlined in the State Board's proposal of July 23.

Mahan did not wish to have the planning for the Turrell Project as one of her major responsibilities. McCorkle had introduced guided group interaction at Clinton Farms in the late forties and trained some staff to run the groups. However, the program did not last long there because it did not appear to be as effective with female inmates as it was with male inmates.

If Bixby had still been director of correction and parole, Mahan may well have taken it on to see if it could be adapted for juvenile girls. However, she did not enjoy working with McCorkle, and she would be more subject to his control if half her time was devoted to the Turrell Project.

It is unclear who wanted Mahan to play a major role in this. A safe assumption is Wescott. In a letter written by Wescott to the Clinton board concerning Turrell, he expresses his consternation at the board's and particularly Mahan's reluctance to become involved in Turrell in a significant way.

Mahan, probably with board member Sara Holmes Boutelle's help (Mahan's diary notes on 7 December: "Phoned SHB re Turrell etc."), drafted a statement of the conditions under which she would work with the project and spelled out other issues relating to the planning committee for the project. These are contained in a typewritten rough draft with corrections in both Mahan's and Wescott's handwriting. They were discussed by the Clinton Board on 9 December before being shown to Wescott.

> Miss Mahan informed the members today that she is eager to cooperate in the Turrell Project under the following conditions:
>
> 1. That she serve as a member of an initial planning committee and as chairman if it seems advisable.
>
> 2. That the membership of the planning committee include two members of the Clinton Board, The President of the Board of the State Home for Girls, Miss Sheley, Superintendent of the State Home for Girls, Mrs. Juanita Cogan, Rutgers School of Social Work and a member of the Board of Jamesburg, Mrs. Stevens Baird of the State Board of Control.
>
> 3. That the Committee appoint the Director who would be responsible to the Committee.

Conditions four through eight deal with planning the operation of the project and developing programs, establishing relationships with juvenile court judges, determining the selection of the girls, budget and personnel needs, and evaluation of the project.

The ninth and last condition states: "That the Committee function in the existing pattern of local boards." It ends with the following statement concerning Mahan's role:

> The Board of Managers of Clinton Farms believes that Miss Mahan's unique talents, background, and training particularly suit her to contribute to this challenging new project, and agree to her participation under the conditions outlined above. It should be stressed, however, that Miss Mahan's primary responsibility is to her position as Superintendent at Clinton Farms, and that any new commitments should not interfere with the discharge of her primary duties.

This is a carefully worded statement that acknowledges the importance of the Turrell Project and Mahan's unique qualifications for contributing to it. It also addresses two issues of controversy in the Alexander Commission report: the appointment of the director and the role of the planning committee. The board takes the responsibility for stating that "Miss Mahan's primary responsibility is to her position as Superintendent" and she can't take on commitments that will interfere with that.

This statement was given to Wescott after the board meeting. According to Mahan's notes, there was a great deal of discussion about the Turrell Project in the next two months between her and the board and Wescott. Wescott called her on 12 December, "re keeping the Turrell memo over the weekend" and a week later, "Mr. W. came at 10:15 w. new proposal." He phoned again regarding Turrell on 22 December and on 26 December he "arrived w/o notice. Discussion of McC—etc." On 5 January Mahan had lunch at the Hunterdon Medical Center with Lib Schley, Sara Boutelle, Frederick J. Knocke, and Jean Alexander, all board members. "Dr. K will tell Mr. W. of the revised statement." On 7 January, "Mr. W. phoned re action on Turrell. Told him FJK [Knocke] is going to see him re." On 8 January, "Lib phoned—Dr K. phoned re his talk w. Mr. W." Mahan went away on vacation to St. Croix 9–31 January.

On the morning after she returned from St. Croix she had calls from Schley, Mary Baird, and Lucia Ballantine (Jamesburg board member) about the Turrell project, for there was a Turrell committee meeting scheduled at Clinton Farms on 2 February. According to a rough copy of the minutes taken by Mahan's secretary, with corrections in Mahan's handwriting, those present at the meeting included McCorkle, who presided; Albert Elias, who worked under McCorkle at Highfields and then took over from him; Lloyd W. Lussier of Brisbane Child Treatment Center; Mahan; Schley, president of Clinton Farms board; Harold Starr, Clinton psychologist; Helen Sheley, superintendent of the State Home for Girls; and Nancy Riker, president of board from the State Home for Girls.

The proposed program for the Turrell Residential Group Center was presented to the members and discussed categorically, including budget, medical care, recreation, architecture of building, treatment methods, research program, admission policies, and the need to educate judges. There was a great deal of discussion concerning the necessary criteria for the appointment of the director.

> Dr. McCorkle presented to the Committee the tentative specifications it is felt by the department are requisite in the choice of a director for the program. He asked the Committee to study the specifications carefully and present to him...names of persons thought to be qualified. He reported that the Department personnel was in process of being screened for possible applicants.... He also said that he would follow up contacts of his own outside the Department to get a line on qualified applicants. He particularly urged all members of the committee to contact personally any workers in the field who would be qualified and who might be interested in the directorship.
>
> Dr. McCorkle repeatedly stressed his anxiety that a suitable director would not be found in time for the opening of the Center on July 1. When asked by the Planning Committee what would eventuate in such circumstances, he stated that the Commissioner himself would then find someone. He also stated that neither he nor the Commissioner were in agreement with the Planning Committee on the criteria they had set up, and that the Commissioner was inclined to substitute his own criteria. Miss Sheley then asked Mr. McCorkle why, if the Commissioner was going to ignore the criteria established by the Planning Committee, it was worthwhile for the Committee members to continue to give their time and efforts for the next several months in trying to find a director and other personnel and plan for the opening of the Center, only to have their planning set aside by the Commissioner. Mr. McCorkle repeated that the Commissioner did not consider the present criteria practical but that he wanted the Committee to continue its efforts to find a suitable director by May 1. In the event that the Committee is unsuccessful in finding a director within the prescribed time the Commissioner will then revise the criteria.
>
> The feasibility of having a male director for the Center was discussed at considerable length, and there was disagreement among the participants. Miss Mahan, when asked her opinion, said such an appointment would present problems; that community reaction would be adverse and that the parents of the girls might object. She said that there would certainly be problems connected with having a male director, and that an unmarried man could certainly not be considered....
>
> After considerable discussion it was agreed that every effort would be made to find a woman candidate, but that a married man might be acceptable if he met all the other requirements.

At the bottom of the last page Mahan wrote, "Dr. Mc & A.E. are interested in a man in Ohio." From the discussion about the director it can be seen why Mahan did not want to work under McCorkle on this project. He made his name in the correctional field with residential group treatment centers using guided group interaction as the treatment model. Most of his work had been with men, and Mahan was not convinced of its effectiveness with women.

Mahan, Sheley, and some others of the committee could not accept his disregard for their criteria for the director. One of these criteria was that the director should be a woman. Though McCorkle states that "neither he nor the Commissioner were in agreement with the Planning Committee on the criteria they had set up," it was he who was not in agreement. John Tramburg's experience and expertise were in the field of mental health. McCorkle worked with men—in the Navy, at Highfields, and after that as warden at the New Jersey State Prison in Trenton. His insensitivity to the need for a female director of a small residential group treatment center with eighteen girls between the ages of sixteen and eighteen was incomprehensible to most members of the committee. He stated if they were not able to find a director by 1 May, the criteria would be revised, and presumably McCorkle would appoint the man he was interested in.

Mahan actively tried to find someone to be director. She called her friend Elizabeth Bode, superintendent of the Industrial School for Girls in Massachusetts, as well as other friends in the field. A young woman she had met in England came over and stayed a month at Clinton Farms and the State Home for Girls, although in the end Mahan decided not to recommend her for the position.

There were committee meetings in the spring and summer. Graduation was held at Clinton Farms on 9 June, and Mahan left the next day to spend over a month in St. Croix. On 18 July she spoke at the quarterly meeting of the St. Croix Chamber of Commerce on "juvenile delinquency and what to do about it." She returned to Clinton on 19 July.

The search for a suitable candidate continued through the fall. On 22 October 1960 when the Turrell dedication was held, a director had not yet been appointed. However, when Turrell admitted its first residents and began program operation on 16 February 1961 a female superintendent, Rosemary McGrath, was there. The Turrell Residential Group Center was launched successfully. Edna Mahan remained involved in an advisory capacity, and the turmoil concerning her role in it disappeared.

Two-and-a-half years after its opening McGrath (1963) wrote that the program was constantly being evaluated and modified for the girls as Mahan knew it would be:

> Because Turrell is new and limited knowledge is available about the operation of group centers for female adolescents, we have had to constantly evaluate and modify the ways in which we handle the problems presented by our residents. In the future we hope to be able to minimize returns to court. Undoubtedly, as our experience grows we will learn to recognize problem areas sooner, thus enabling us to avoid situations in which there is no recourse but to remove a girl from the program. Along these lines we plan to embark upon research which will help us to understand some of the factors which make it impossible for some delinquents to complete our program.

Second United Nations Congress on the Prevention of Crime and the Treatment of Offenders

In the midst of the Turrell directorship search, Mahan left Clinton again, this time to accompany the official representatives of the United States to the Second United Nations Congress on the Prevention of Crime and the Treatment of Offenders in London, 8–19 August 1960.

The first international prison congress was held in London in 1872 under the leadership of the Reverend Enoch Wines. (Wines had organized the National Prison Association in the United States in 1870.) From the London congress in 1872 grew the International Prison and Penitentiary Commission, which held meetings every five years, except for war years, until 1950. In 1955 the United Nations sponsored the congress, which was held in Geneva. The 1960 congress was hosted by the United Kingdom and was held in London.

There were three categories of participants attending the congress: governmental delegates, nongovernmental delegates, and individual participants. Among the U.S. delegates to the congress were Alexander Aldrich, Lucia Ballantine, Sanford Bates, James V. Bennett, Edward R. Cass, Sheldon Glueck, and Frank Loveland.

Cass, Ballantine, Bates, Loveland, and others including Edward Galway of the social defense section of the United Nations wanted Edna Mahan to attend. Arrangements were made for her to accompany the U.S. delegation as an individual participant to prepare a report on the congress for the American Correctional Association meetings to be held in Denver at the end of August. Mary Baird financed Edna Mahan's expenses.

Friday, 5 August 1960, the day before she left for London, a Turrell committee meeting was held at Clinton Farms in the early afternoon. At 4:00 p.m. Mary Baird brought Austin MacCormick and his wife Patty to visit and no doubt talk about the upcoming congress. Mahan went to dinner at a friend's in the evening and stopped on the way home to talk with Morris, who would be in charge at Clinton while she was away.

Early on 6 August she and Agnes Flack, who accompanied her to London, left Clinton Farms for London. The next day she met Sanford Bates and Ed Cass before going with them to a meeting with the U.S. delegates.

Mahan took careful notes of all the sessions she attended, including the names and countries of individuals who spoke. In her official report on the congress she describes Church House, where all the sessions took place, as "an attractive building of the Westminster Abby group, reconstructed after the last war." She notes that "The two weeks of faithful attendance at the formal sessions were relieved and enlivened by a number of occasions when participants had an opportunity to associate informally with those of other nations" (Mahan 1960). These included receptions, a bus trip to Trinity College, Cambridge, for a garden party, services of Thanksgiving at the Church of St. Martin-in-the Fields, and visits to institutions. Though her time was primarily devoted to the congress and its activities, she also met friends for lunch and dinner, visited the Tate Gallery, and went to the theater.

She returned home on Saturday, 20 August, so she had Sunday to spend a couple of hours in the office, swim and sunbathe, call friends, and have Gebhardt for supper. Her next week was a busy one, for besides the day-to-day activities and meeting with staff, inmates, and classification, there were runaways on two nights, the budget hearing on 23 August, and many hours working with Miriam Woodruff, her secretary, on the United Nations Congress report for the Denver ACA meetings.

On 29 August she left for Denver. Her "Report on the Second United Nations Congress on the Prevention of Crime and the Treatment of Offenders" was one of the general session addresses of the Ninetieth Congress of Correction.

She left Denver on 2 September and was met at Idlewild Airport by Flack. She notes in her diary, "Back at RFW by 1 am 9/3. They were looking for 2 runaways from Center."

On 3 September four inmates ran away from Silzer. The runaway problem had become acute in 1960. There was a total of ninety-one, an all-time high and more than twice as many as any previous year in the history of the institution.

In 1959 and 1960 the average daily population at Clinton had dropped slightly below 300, which eased many of the problems due to crowding. This did not last. The population began to increase: in 1960–61 the average daily population was 335 with the highest count of 357. By 1965 it was 390 (Wagner 1966).

Change in Inmate Population: "Some Personalities Coming to Us Today Cannot Adjust to an Open Institution"

At a staff orientation in November 1962 Mahan introduced her remarks with some historical background about Clinton Farms. She noted that the founders always intended it to be an open institution:

> We have been able through most of the years to operate as an open institution; we have always had runaways but only a small percentage. Our population has been larger than it is today. During the war it went over 400, but we had fewer runaways. We have always had a few isolated problems.... In the immediate past we have had certain unfortunate incidents due to the great increase of juvenile offenders (in the 16–17 years bracket) most of whom are also very disturbed personalities....

> The Department of Institutions and Agencies has come to our assistance in sending the more assaultive, more destructive girls to other places. We have six girls in the Mercer County Jail and two in the Morris County Jail.
>
> Throughout the years I have always felt that everyone could be reached and helped if we worked long and patiently enough to find the right spot. Some personalities coming to us today cannot adjust to an open institution. It is very disturbing to note the many lawless youngsters we are receiving who have no respect for anyone or anything.

During the fifties an increasing number of juvenile delinquents were admitted to the institution. In 1950, 28 percent of the inmates were between the ages of sixteen and twenty-one; by 1960 this had changed to 51 percent. These were the beginning of the postwar baby boom babies, and they had a major effect on the open institution and student government. Juveniles were committed directly from the courts, and many were transfers from the State Home for Girls, which was unable to cope with them.

Budget requests almost every year made note of crowding and the need for additional staff. The budget request for 1956–57, written in August 1955, highlights the increasing number of State Home transfers and juvenile court commitments:

> We must study our whole training program in terms of vocational needs of the younger girls.... Cottages intended for twenty-five house fifty to sixty. Every type of problem is magnified when there is no privacy.... If the Reformatory for Women is going to continue in business with any degree of success, those who can do something about it will face the facts and take action.

The "Opening Statement Supporting 1963–1964 Budget Requests," written in July 1961, starts out, "Clinton had the usual problems of overcrowding and shortage of personnel." The statement ends, "With the marked increase in the commitment of young inmates comes inevitably the urgent need for closer supervision and more individual attention in both cottages and work departments." With the sixties also came an increase in the number of inmates convicted for narcotics and narcotic-related offenses, and these inmates needed closer security and supervision.

Mahan described these young inmates in the 1961–62 annual report, dated 31 July 1962:

> During the past several years there has been a significant increase in the number of disturbed, aggressive, and assaultive inmates admitted to this institution. These problem cases have so disrupted the effectiveness of the traditional program that only by removing them from the open cottages can acceptable standards of rehabilitation and custody be maintained.

In late 1960, Mahan, Morris, psychologist Harold Starr, and Center Head Cottage Supervisor Iola Coles had discussed further security measures for Center. However, no one was prepared for the flimsiness of the walls between the rooms. In September 1961, an inmate "managed to go through the walls of four rooms in a surprisingly short time" using a knitting needle. Some structural improvements were made to the building after this. Mahan stated in the 1961–62 annual report:

> It is obvious that a long term program must be implemented *at Clinton* for those who require close custodial care.
>
> On the recommendation of the Central Office and with the concurrence of the administration and the Board of Managers at the July 18, 1962 meeting at which Dr. McCorkle with Mr. Wescott and Mrs. Iselin of the Board of Control were present, the East Hall of Center is now being operated as a self-contained unit under a new staffing pattern which includes the use of male corrections officers.

The above was written and signed by Mahan on 31 July 1962. On 17 August, when the staff on the east hall of Center complained to Mahan about the profanity and abusive language of the inmates, Mahan ordered a radio removed from the cellblock. After that four inmates in separate cells smashed through the hollow tile between the walls, smashed wash basins, and damaged the iron beds, which they used as battering rams. All the inmates had to be removed from the wing, and those who needed maximum security were boarded in several county jails throughout the state.

This incident caused considerable publicity and generated an influx of central office staff to Clinton Farms. Many of Mahan's personal and professional friends called her from all over the country in the next few weeks, primarily to offer support. Evidently there was also some concern these troubles would lead to her leaving Clinton Farms. On 24 August Henry David, a department psychologist, called Starr and asked, "Is the lady discouraged enough to leave?" She definitely was not.

Although there were many people and details that had to be dealt with, she managed it all. The staff carried on the running of the institution. Lois Morris's birthday was 18 August. Friends of Mahan's from New York who were frequent weekend visitors arrived as scheduled that day, which was a Saturday. They all went out to dinner for Morris's birthday, and on Sunday Mahan entertained them all for dinner and bridge. On 22 August she accompanied other members of the department on a previously arranged visit to the women's correctional institution in Muncy, Pennsylvania, to look at the managment and construction of the security unit there.

The author returned to Clinton Farms at this time to live with Morris and start doctoral research. She saw Mahan almost every day and talked with her often. Mahan's concerns were to provide a secure and safe environment for all at Clinton Farms and to develop programs that were geared to the younger, more volatile inmates. This required additional staff and additional buildings. Mahan notes in the 1963–64 annual report the need for more treatment staff "if Clinton is to have a more therapeutically oriented program" and the need for "a trained vocational counsellor who can develop new programs for the unskilled, unmotivated young people."

The east hall of Center was reopened in the spring of 1963 after extensive repairs and renovation. The wing was completely rebuilt and reinforced. A fenced-in exercise yard was built behind Center with direct access from the east hall. It served as a closed maximum security unit with a male correctional officer on duty with a female cottage supervisor for each shift. It was run as a maximum security unit, inmates living there having no contact with the rest of the population. Runaways and severe behavior problems did not cease to exist. The number of runaways was reduced, and there was a secure unit for those inmates who could not adjust to the open setting.

After the crises in Center with the subsequent publicity, the Department of Institutions and Agencies in 1963 recognized the needs of Clinton Farms for new facilities by including six new buildings in a departmental bond issue, which was approved by New Jersey voters in November 1964. These included a multipurpose school and recreation building with a gymnasium, maximum security unit, unit for the psychologically disturbed, two regular cottages, and a central food service building. None was in use before Mahan died. The multipurpose school building, which opened in 1973, was named Edna Mahan Hall.

Edna Mahan never lost her belief and faith in an open institution with a student government honor system for the majority of the inmates. In the "Statement Supporting the 1963–64 Budget Requests" she wrote:

> The majority of the inmates still benefit by the program of Clinton Farms with its traditional philosophy of an open institution where the emphasis is on student government. For the few who can not conform, Center will be the answer. When the program there is thoroughly accepted and running smoothly, it will undoubtedly have a healthy, stabilizing effect on the whole institution—girls and staff alike.

In the 1963–64 annual report she stated, "Student Government at Clinton is undergoing a test of its effectiveness because of the great changes in the characteristics of the inmate population. It is still, however, one of the most constructive instruments for promoting inmate morale, self respect, discipline and responsibility."

For the forty years Edna Mahan was superintendent of Clinton Farms it remained an open institution with a student government honor system. During most of these years crowding was severe. Except for her first few years at the institution, staffing was inadequate. In her last ten years the inmate population changed to a majority of younger inmates, many of whom were aggressive and assaultive. In addition there were a significant number of narcotic users committed.

Three commissioners, Ellis, Bates, and Tramburg, supported her philosophy and advised her in making adjustments at the institution to carry it on. In the final analysis, however, its longevity and success at Clinton Farms was due to Edna Mahan's belief in it and commitment to it as well as her leadership skills and personal charisma, which affected almost all who came in contact with her.

"One of the Old Timers of the ACA"

In September 1962 in the middle of the crises in Center, Mahan went to Philadelphia for three days of the American Correctional Association's annual congress. She received a Certificate of Merit, which the American Correctional Association presented for the first time to eleven of its members, at a banquet on 20 September. Edna Mahan, Women's Correctional Association, was one of two women honored.

The Certificate of Merit reads:

> Selected by the Affiliate body of the Mother Organization of which they are a member. The American Correctional Association here in Philadelphia, Pennsylvania, on September 20, 1962, at the 92nd Annual Congress of Correction proudly recognizes for their service to the field of correction and for their diligent efforts to adhere to the Statement of Principles of the American Correctional Association....

Her citation reads:

> *Edna Mahan*
>
> As the youngest appointee to the Superintendency of the New Jersey Reformatory for Women and one of the "old timers" of the American Correctional Association, Miss Edna Mahan sets an example for others in correction through her devotion, imagination, integrity and intelligence. Serving as an enthusiastic and active member of the American Correctional Association on the Board of Directors and on its executive committee she was influential in reactivating the Women's Correctional Association. Edna Mahan is a dynamic, forceful and enthusiastic penologist who shows a rare combination of administrative skills and philosophical [sic] insights combined with an ability to maintain through the years a flexibility and willingness to try new approaches.
>
> Acknowledgement—Certificates courtesy of the Illinois Department of Public Services. Gold Lapel Ensignia Pin courtesy of the Aluminum Plumbing Fixture Corporation.

She received many letters of congratulations on this recognition. One was from Howard B. Gill, founder and guiding spirit of the Norfolk (Massachusetts) Prison Colony in the 1930s and a longtime friend of Edna Mahan's from her Boston days:

Dear Edna,

Now that the Plumbing Trade has given you a Gold Insignia, may I join the chorus in recognition too!

Of course, it wasn't necessary for the State of Illinois *or* the Plumbing Trade to proffer either certificate or insignia for me to recognize the outstanding woman in corrections in the U.S. This Willem and I did many years ago as I recall it—one day when you were sick in bed and Willem mounted the suit-case stand to deliver encomiums on a young and beautiful lady penologist. Now I see they refer to you as an "old timer"! For shame! In the words of the old song—"Darling—you will *always* be young and beautiful to me!"

Cordially, Howard B. Gill

Edward R. Cass retired as secretary of ACA effective 1 January 1963. The Edward R. Cass Correctional Achievement Fund was established, and a committee was appointed that met in Portland, Oregon, 27 August 1963. The committee members were James V. Bennett, Richard A. McGee, Cass, Sanger B. Powers, James W. Curran, Joseph E. Ragen, Harold V. Langlois, Martha E. Wheeler, and E. Preston Sharp, chair. Those present at the meeting were Cass, Langlois, Powers, Wheeler, and Sharp. According to Janet York and Wheeler, when the Cass awards were established, Cass was still in control of ACA though he had just stepped down as secretary. Cass liked Wheeler, and he thought there should be a woman on the selection committee, so Wheeler was appointed. The selection was very informal. York and Wheeler talked about it before the meeting. One of the first recipients should be a woman, and it should be Mahan.

She was present in Portland to receive the award along with Richard A. McGee and G. Howland Shaw. Lucia Ballantine, who was at the awards banquet, recalled that "Edna's knees were shaking under the dinner table before the presentation."

The citation and certificate presented to her hung in her office with her honorary degree from Rutgers and the many pictures she had solicited over the years from her colleagues whom she referred to as "my delinquent friends." These awards by her professional colleagues attest to the high esteem they held her in. She was humbly proud of the recognition they bestowed on her.

Fiftieth Anniversary: "The Next Fifty Years Can Be as Productive of Good as Have Been the Past . . ."

According to the June 1913 minutes of the Board of Managers meeting, the formal opening of the institution was 26 May 1913. Plans for the fiftieth anniversary celebration of Clinton Farms began in the spring of 1963.

On 6 June 1963 the annual graduation exercises were held in the evening at Clinton Farms in conjunction with its fiftieth anniversary celebration. A buffet supper was served under a large tent to about 400 guests before the formal outdoor ceremonies. Nearly 800 people attended the graduation exercises, including state officials, corrections professionals from outside New Jersey, friends from near and far, many former inmates, and most of the current inmate population. Marian Anderson, the world-famed contralto, gave the commencement address.

The fiftieth anniversary program contains a short history of Clinton Farms written by Mahan and the Board of Managers:

> Fifty years ago the opening of Clinton Farms gave reality to the dream of a group of inspired, courageous women. Their belief was that society would best be served by a penal institution which rehabilitated offenders instead of just inflicting punishment on them.
>
> ...Good penology is a great cause in the world today. There are gifted and well-inspired penologists in every country and commendable institutions of different kinds. And yet we feel that Clinton Farms is unique, and visitors from far and wide have confirmed this proud impression.... As we look back, these are some of the milestones: the establishment of the honor system and a great measure of self-government almost from the start; the reliance upon psychological studies and classification of the girls for the guidance of the staff in discipline and character development; the transfer by the late William J. Ellis, then Commissioner, of all female prisoners from the Trenton Prison in 1929, so that Clinton became the sole correctional establishment for women in this state; successful integration throughout the institution; day parole, with its extension outside the institution of its principle of learning by apprenticeship.... Clinton Farms as a progressive institution, not moving too fast or going too far, has fortunately never had to beat a retreat. It is still essentially the open institution its founders dreamed of. The ideal dearest to them of a separate room for each woman has never been achieved, as our population has grown faster than new buildings were provided. In other respects, however, the reality has perhaps transcended their expectations with the establishment at Clinton Farms of certain innovations in penology not understood then and various perspectives just now opening to our more experienced view.
>
> Any consideration of Clinton's past constitutes a challenge as to the future. The next fifty years can be as productive of good as have been the past if we accept that challenge.

John K. Barnes, writing of the anniversary celebration in the 13 June 1963 Flemington *Democrat,* described it as emotion-packed. There were two unscheduled singing appearances by Anderson:

> Early in the program as the North Hunterdon Regional High School Band neared the end of the chorus of "The Star Spangled Banner," the guest speaker unexpectedly left her seat on the platform and walked forward to the microphone. As the applause died down—and the 70 members of the band struggled to maintain their composure—her big voice rang out effortlessly as she picked up in the key of B-flat and soared through the difficult vocal range of our national anthem. Forgetting preferred procedure, the audience broke into applause as she retired and Lloyd B. Wescott rose to introduce the honored guests seated on chairs on the lawn.
>
> But it was following Miss Anderson's short and simple commencement address that the ceremonies brought tears to the eyes of audience and inmates alike. The final musical offering was being sung by the Concert Choir of 22 inmates. It was the spiritual, "He's Got the Whole World in His Hands." As the full range of voices opened the first chorus...Marian Anderson again rose. She walked across to the far side of the stage as expectancy in the audience heightened.... To the audience it appeared that perhaps the famed singer would not herself sing. She stood silent in front of the choir through several choruses, then moved to the center microphone. Dropping an octave lower than usual, she picked up the next verse—"He's got a little bit of baby in His hands."
>
> In a voice so low as to appear impossible to sustain, and in a tone that was almost literally a cry, she proceeded through two more verses—"He's got the whole wide world . . ." and "He's got everybody here in his hands." In rapt silence the audience listened, many with wet eyes.

The fiftieth anniversary also served as a testimonial to Edna Mahan, who had been superintendent of Clinton Farms for thirty-five of its fifty years of existence. Elizabeth B. Schley, president of the Board of Managers, said that the major reason for Clinton Farms' success was "the fiery, forthright, and free" personality and the "glowing character" of Edna Mahan, which brought the audience to its feet.

The program contains the citations from her Doctor of Humane Letters and the Certificate of Merit from ACA as well as "Appreciations" from Geraldine Thompson, Austin MacCormick, Lloyd McCorkle, Sanford Bates, Lovell Bixby, and Lloyd Wescott.

Sanford Bates ended his appreciation, "This devoted, self-effacing and determined woman is truly a leader in the field of correction with women today, and has set an example for others to follow."

Before Anderson spoke, Eleanor Reppert introduced the graduates in various courses and McCorkle presented the certificates. Anderson's address was short, and she spoke directly to the inmates.

Following the address, Schley said:

I'm not even going to introduce the next speaker. The audience again rose to its feet as Miss Mahan came forward. She revealed that much of the preparations had been kept secret from her; particularly the tributes paid to her by state and national leaders in penology.

She noted messages from Governor Richard Hughes and three former governors and from many others. She then asked all the staff members present to rise so they could be recognized and then presented former inmates who had returned for the anniversary celebration. (Barnes 1963)

The audience dispersed quietly after the final spiritual. As the inmates walked back to their cottages, Bates, well aware of the recent discipline and runaway problems and the fact there were no walls and no correctional officers, "suggested to Mahan it was getting quite dark and was she not taking a bit of a risk. Her reply was characteristic. 'They might run away sometime but not tonight. They trust me because I trust them' " (Bates 1968).

Excerpts from some of the inmates' letters after the occasion give insight into their feelings.

[Elizabeth S.]: We had a big Fiftieth Anniversary celebration and Graduation on June 6th. It was held outdoors on the lawn. It was certainly a nice program. Lots of good speakers, two girls of the graduating class spoke and did beautifully. Miss Mahan spoke, several members of the Board of Managers spoke and our featured outstanding guest spoke and sang for us, it was Marian Anderson, she was marvelous. It was a lovely evening and a smashing success. The girls talked about nothing else for two days. We had a ten layer 200 lb. cake. All the girls milled about in the tent with the guests as free as could be and had cake and punch and ice cream. The local band was fine too. Wonder of wonders everybody behaved well and no one ran away despite all the freedom so you know it was a big success! When they were 100% absorbed, impressed and appreciative. Ordinarily that much freedom on a dark night is too great a temptation for someone.

[Alice B.]: We had quite a few celebrities and the illustrious Mrs. Marian Anderson she sang and spoke to all the women in other words an address. I shook hands with her and got her autograph which was a thrilling moment for me.... Mrs. Mahan, our superintendent has tried very hard to help some of us who were so unfortunate.... As each day come and go I realize how much time has been wasted but by the same token I may have a chance to prove my worth for a few remaining years.

[Thelma E.]: They had their 50th Anniversary Celebration. Marian Anderson was the guest speaker, spoke beautifully, our choir sang.... The superintendent here has done an awfully lot of good for an awfully lot of people.... God is good. It was also her anniversary, over 30 years of service, and a beautiful woman that certainly could find other interests if she so desired.

After the ceremonies Anderson and a group of Mahan's personal and professional friends went to Homestead to socialize in a more relaxed setting. When they had all departed, Mahan and Bode, who had come from Massachusetts and was staying with her, went to Morris's house, and they sat around and went over the whole event.

One of the highlights of the day for Mahan was "[Nancy] phoned from California!" She noted this in red in her diary and told the group animatedly that evening about the call.

Nancy was a long-term inmate from the thirties and forties whose offense was a tragic murder that generated a great deal of publicity. While she was at Clinton, Mahan worked with her closely to help her accept what had happened. Nancy was exceptionally bright, and Mahan fostered her intelligence and leadership qualities. Commissioner Ellis, Mahan, the Board of Managers, and professional staff strongly recommended her for a pardon from the governor, which was granted. They then worked hard to get her into military service when she left Clinton.

Lucy, who at age fourteen had been involved in a murder with her older brother and grew into womanhood at Clinton Farms, returned with her two young children to attend the anniversary celebration. They spent the night with Morris and the author. Lucy was devoted to Mahan and always called her "Mother." On 7 June Mahan notes in her diary: "[Lucy] and my grandchildren left after 1 pm."

The fiftieth anniversary celebration was the most outstanding of the many special events put on at Clinton Farms through its fifty-year history. MacCormick begins his "Appreciation" for Mahan: "The two greatest days in the history of Clinton Farms are its birthday fifty years ago, which marked the end of confining women in that ancient museum piece, Trenton Prison; and the arrival on campus thirty-five years ago of Edna Mahan as superintendent." That was the essence of the celebration.

Correctional institutions do not usually celebrate their foundings as colleges, universities, and other more decorous institutions do. Indeed, some people questioned and even criticized Mahan and the board. The board members of Clinton Farms throughout the years were as proud of the founding of it and of its founders as the alumnae and trustees of Mount Holyoke College are of its founding and its founder, Mary Lyon. Mount Holyoke in 1837 represented the first institution of higher education for women in the country. Clinton Farms represented the first separate institution for adult female offenders in New Jersey.

Clinton Farms' founders made it a "workshop for character building" as specified in the first annual report of its managers. For most of its fifty-year history it was blessed with capable and creative leaders who were not afraid to innovate new approaches to treatment and board members and commissioners who supported them. Mahan, because of her own abilities and personality, kept Clinton Farms unique into the 1960s. She wanted to show it off as an open institution where a student government and honor system still worked with most of the inmates. It was a reflection of her.

The anniversary party was a great success. Friends and colleagues called in the days following to tell Mahan how wonderful the evening was. One long-time friend described it as "spectacular." Anderson called to tell Mahan how much the evening meant to her. Many of the staff at Clinton Farms were involved in the planning, and most of them attended. This event enhanced the esprit de corps of the institution. "The lady was not discouraged enough to leave" Clinton Farms.

Friends

The remainder of June was reasonably quiet and routine at Clinton Farms. The swimming pool was open, and Mahan swam whenever she could. On Sunday, 16 June she wrote in her diary, "Did not go to office all day. Cleaned several closets—sunned and swam from 11:30 to 2." There are also notes in her diary indicating preparation for another trip abroad: 11 June, "To Flemington re passport," 24 June, "Second typhoid shot," 2 July, "Go to bank—get traveler's checks, 3rd typhoid shot." On 9 July Mahan flew to France to spend three weeks with Lucia Ballantine and her family.

Lucia and John Ballantine rented a villa in Provence, France, the summer of 1963 and invited Mahan to spend some time with them. It was a very quiet and restful time. Ballantine says she and Mahan took long walks each day. They talked about their lives, and it was at this time Mahan told Ballantine about her father and stepfather and the other men in her life—Frank Loveland, Richard Steinmetz, and Reading Gebhardt. Ballantine was contemplating separation from John Ballantine, and Mahan listened and helped her by recalling her own difficult decisions.

Though younger than Mahan, Ballantine had become an important personal friend through their common professional interests. Ballantine came to Clinton Farms as a volunteer with a strong commitment to work in corrections. Mahan recognized her abilities and commitment and fostered them. Ballantine also had a full life with family and social obligations, and Mahan often participated. They enjoyed professional and social activities together.

After her separation from Reading, Edna Mahan spent more time with personal friends. The Wescott sisters—Beulah Hagen and Beth James—were among those she saw a great deal of socially. Beulah and Edna bought a home together near Clinton Farms in 1960. It was an investment for both of them, but there was also some talk of it as a possible retirement home in the years to come. They rented it out for a couple of years and sold it in 1962.

Hagen, who worked at Harper Publishing in New York, introduced Mahan to Gertrude and Robert Hawley, who owned a home at Stonybrook, Long Island. Edna Mahan enjoyed Bob Hawley particularly. She spent weekends with them at Stonybrook. The Hawleys were also guests at St. Croix. Bob Hawley died unexpectedly of a heart attack on 21 February 1961 while Gertrude and he were visiting Edna in St. Croix.

Bob's unexpected death left Gertrude alone—they did not have children. Edna felt a responsibilty to Gertrude Hawley, and this continued until Mahan died. Gertrude Hawley went to work for Harper Publishing, but didn't have sufficient income to maintain her Fifth Avenue apartment in New York and the house at Stonybrook. Edna Mahan loved the Stonybrook house and its location close to the beach, so she bought it. She leased it a very low rate with the understanding she, Gertrude, and other friends could spend weekends and sometimes longer periods there.

Edan Mahan always had friends among the board members. Juliana Conover was the first of those. Over the years others included Anita Quarles, Mary Baird, Elizabeth Schley, and Sara Boutelle. They spent time together outside of Clinton Farms concerns. They and their families genuinely enjoyed Edna Mahan as she enjoyed them.

In her first two decades at Clinton Farms she did not develop personal friendships with other staff. Mary Cox, Elizabeth Connors, and Hildreth Cronshey were three she was very fond of and always kept in touch with after they left Clinton. However, outside of an occasional dinner, movie, or shopping trip together, they did little socializing outside of work. In her married life with Gebhardt, they had many married friends in the community with whom they socialized. As a couple they also spent social time with Commissioner Ellis and his family.

When Agnes Flack came to Clinton Farms as senior resident physician in 1953 and moved into the doctor's house, Mahan included her in social activities in the Clinton community. Flack was a little older than Mahan and had ended a successful obstetrical practice in her hometown of Wilkes Barre, Pennsylvania, a few years earlier. She was not ready to retire, and Clinton was closer to her home and aging father in Pennsylvania than Long Island where she went to work for a couple of years in a private mental hospital.

When Mahan began to go to St. Croix yearly in the 1950s, Flack often went with her. Flack remained at Clinton until 1962. After retiring from Clinton, she rented Mahan's house in St. Croix while she built her own. She spent several winters there.

Mahan was an excellent bridge player, and she loved the game. Flack played as did Josephine Hull, Morris, "Doc" Ackerman, Bee Black, the author, and several other staff who worked in the administration building. It was not unusual to have a foursome play a couple of hands after lunch either in Mahan's office or in the officer's lounge in the basement.

One of the major social activities of the Clinton Farms staff was playing cards, be it bridge, canasta, poker, or tripoli. Card evenings were hosted in homes on the grounds while those who lived in the community invited staff there.

Those who lived on the grounds played a lot of bridge together in the evenings at Flack's house, Morris's house, and at Homestead. After Hull and Flack left Clinton Farms and the author returned to work on her dissertation, Morris's house became the focal point for dinner and bridge.

Bee Black and Edna Mahan became friends. It was not unusual for Black to spend the night at Homestead, particularly in bad weather, as she lived in Morristown. Black shared a family home with her sister Ethel; their sister Verna and husband Bill Rogers lived nearby. The Black family was warm, full of fun, and open. They came to parties and functions at Clinton Farms, and Mahan spent time with the Blacks in Morristown. The Blacks became another of Mahan's families in the last years of her life. They all visited St. Croix. Bee and Ethel Black were with Edna Mahan in her last weeks in the Morristown hospital.

Of all the capable, younger staff who came to work at Clinton Farms with Edna Mahan, Lois Morris was the one Mahan knew had the greatest potential for working with inmates and staff. Morris came to Clinton Farms from Indiana in 1946 with the American Friends Service Committee's Institutional Unit. She had a lot of spunk and little money. With others from the unit, she hitchhiked into New York and spent the weekend, free, in one of Father Devine's Heavens in Harlem. Although Mahan reprimanded her and warned her it was not a safe thing to do, even in 1946, she admired her, for she herself had a lot of daring and desire to experience life. Morris went to Framingham to work in 1951, but was happy to return to Clinton in 1953 when Mahan called her and asked her to take over the new Guidance Center. Morris became head of cottage life in 1955 when Assistent Superintendent Cox left and Hull moved into that position. In 1960 Hull left and Morris became assistant superintendent.

The assistant superintendent and head of cottage life were the top administrative positions under the superintendent and were most responsible with Mahan for activities, programs, and staff directly concerned with the inmates. The assistant superintendent's office opened into Mahan's, and desks in the offices were placed so the two saw each other and talked directly when the door was open, as it usually was. The head of cottage life's office was close by. Mahan fostered open communication among all of the top administrative staff but relied most heavily on those two positions.

Morris was a dynamic person and administrator. Her administrative style was creative, open, and active. With cottage supervisors and officers she initiated changes in cottage routines, was direct but supportive in her work with both staff and inmates, and could usually sort out cottage situations before they developed into crises.

She admired Mahan and loved working *with* her. She never felt she was working *for* her. She disagreed with her at times and was critical and told her. Mahan admired Morris and depended on her in helping to run the institution. In Mahan's last years they developed a warm friendship. They were co-workers and good friends who really enjoyed each other whether it was working or socializing together.

Nomination for Federal Parole Board Vacancy: "She Has Seen the 'Seamy' Side and Yet Finds Her Faith Increasing"

By the mid-sixties Clinton Farms had been Edna Mahan's life and her family for thirty-five years, and after her first six months there, she was committed to staying. However, over the years, as might be expected, she was approached by a number of places asking if she would consider a job opening that was available. She never did. In 1964 she was nominated to fill a vacancy on the Federal Parole Board.

When Lyndon Johnson became president, Lady Bird Johnson asked for recommendations of qualified women to serve in his administration. On 7 April 1964 Bee Black, without consulting Mahan, wrote Johnson recommending Mahan. On 29 April Bess Abell, social secretary to Johnson, replied to thank Black for "drawing Mrs. Johnson's attention to the capabilities of Miss Edna Mahan. She is delighted to have your appraisal and asked me to forward your letter to the Bureau of Prisons, Department of Justice, for consideration."

There was at this time a vacancy on the Federal Parole Board that had been filled by a woman. Archibald Alexander, who was in Washington as assistant director of disarmament and arms control, wrote Attorney General Robert Kennedy on 16 June, "I should like to recommend strongly for your consideration [for the vacancy] Miss Edna Mahan...." On 17 June, Mary Baird wrote Frances Perkins asking her to write the attorney general on Mahan's behalf. Perkins wrote Kennedy on 17 July:

> My dear Mr. Attorney General:
>
> The most brillant, conscientious, and able person I have met in years in the correctional institutions of the states, or the United States, is Edna Mahan, the Superintendent of Clinton Farms, the Reformatory at Clinton, New Jersey. I have known Miss Mahan for a very long time—certainly since 1933—and I have seen the developments of her work at Clinton and have visited there myself and had great interest in the constructive and humane patterns which have developed in the former women's prison. Miss Mahan has a firm hand both as an administrator and as a designer and planner of many programs for the rehabilitation of women prisoners. She has that human quality of inspiring trust and confidence in other people without ever raising her voice or allowing excitement and nerves to creep into difficult situations. She has commanded the respect, the obedience, the gratitude and a high degree of human affection among the women of whom she has charge. I have been particularly impressed by the personal quality of their feeling for her. She is an expert administrator, knows the States' business

> intimately, cooperates with other government leaders, and can always be relied upon in general correctional circles throughout the country to indicate the clear line of moral responsibility of the community for these women whose mistakes in life are so obvious. She stands firmly without sentimentality for decent and humane treatment of those who come back as repeaters.
>
> I have been much impressed with Edna Mahan. She has an agreeable and attractive personality, a quiet and authoritative manner, some sense of humor—which makes her personal life in prison circles tolerable—and a large element of hopefulness and faith not only in the work she is doing but in many other good and practical programs for the development of a better life for the people of this Country. She has seen the "seamy" side and yet finds her faith increasing. Her standing in prison circles throughout the United States is very high. She is always listened to with respect and attention.
>
> I tell you all this about Edna Mahan because I have learned there is a vacancy on the U.S. Parole Board, and that the choosing of a new member will come to your attention shortly. I hope that you will give the appointment of Miss Mahan some serious consideration. Thank you very much for your attention.
>
> Sincerely yours, Frances Perkins

MacCormick wrote the attorney general and among other things assured him:

> Miss Mahan has more than the qualifications most women could offer in that she is not merely qualified to deal with the cases of women prisoners and parolees. She has thorough knowledge and understanding of male institutions and offenders also, and has the professional objectivity which women without her broad experience often lack.

Jim Bennett, director of the Federal Bureau of Prisons, wrote Mahan on 27 July:

> Dear Edna:
>
> Regardless of how our campaign for membership on our Parole Board turns out I should think you would be most happy and encouraged by the many letters that have been written on your behalf by your friends. They have all been most eloquent, heartwarming, and I should think satisfying to you.
>
> But the one that I should think you would treasure above all others was written by former Secretary of Labor Frances Perkins, and sent to me by Mary Baird. It really is a most eloquent and moving letter. I was particularly impressed by the second paragraph . . .
>
> The last line is a fitting badge of accomplishment and "well done though good and faithful servant"—"She has seen the seamy side and yet finds her faith increasing."
>
> I congratulate you.

> I wish you well. I have heard nothing further about what the Attorney General is going to do, if anything. Maybe he'll let the whole thing go over for the next Attorney General.
>
> With kind personal regards,
>
> Sincerely yours, James V. Bennett, Director

Baird wrote Perkins 30 September to thank her again for her "kindness in writing such a nice letter about Mahan to the Attorney General. There seems to be some uncertainty as to whether anything will be done before election."

Edna Mahan was relieved that the vacancy was not filled at that time, and she was not invited to fill it when that time came. She told Black she was very flattered, but she really wanted to remain at Clinton Farms always.

The Last Years

The major changes that were taking place at Clinton Farms in her last years presented challenges to Edna Mahan and made demands on her time. She was not able to take part in the Third United Nations Congress held in Stockholm in the fall of 1965. Edward Galway wrote her from Geneva, Switzerland, in June, "I have noted with great pleasure you are planning to attend the Congress...and on behalf of the Secretary General...I ask you to serve as a member of the small panel, *Measures to combat recidivism (with particular reference to adverse conditions of detention pending trial and inequality in the administration of justice).*" Mahan replied on 10 July thanking him for his letter and regretting that "Mary, Lucia, and I have decided against going to Stockholm. Too much is going on around here for us to be able to get away."

An article in the Trenton *Evening Times* 21 February 1966, "Crisis In Our Only Women's Prison, A New Breed of Girls At Clinton," details the problems:

> The teenage criminal and the drug addict are writing a script that is altering the role of one of the nation's leading penal instituitons....
>
> Miss Edna Mahan, veteran superintendent of Clinton, is struggling to preserve it as an "open" institution where inmates are permitted considerable freedom. But many feel she is fighting a losing battle in the face of the trouble stirred up by the new breed.
>
> Until a year or so ago you saw no high walls, guards or locks at Clinton Farms which resembles a college campus. Today, there is a new concrete block wall, about 12 feet high, skirting the maximum security building....
>
> In an era of rising juvenile delinquency, Clinton State Farms is not doing the job it should do, the officials concede. Clinton, rated as the most overcrowded of

> all state institutions, lacks adequate psychological help to cope with belligerent teenage girls who defy authority and resent help.... Many of the teenagers are dope addicts. Most of the addicts are heroin users....
>
> For years, inmates governed themselves under an honor system and student government. Today the system is undergoing a test of its effectiveness because of great changes in the characteristics of the prison population, admits Miss Mahan....
>
> Clinton Farms became famous throughout the world for its revolutionary rehabilitative procedures. "The privileges of an honor system are enjoyed here because the administration believes in the girls and insists that the girls believe in themselves," notes Miss Mahan, who has devoted her life to maintaining Clinton as an open institution.
>
> Friends who know her say Miss Mahan is not about to give it all up now, regardless of the new breed. Although some of her superiors feel Clinton must become less open, Edna Mahan hasn't seen enough to convince her that Clinton started off on the wrong track 53 years ago.

In these years, which were to be Mahan's last, she and the Board of Managers worked together to integrate the demands of greater security with a rehabilitative philosophy to keep the focus of Clinton Farms on the humane treatment of female offenders.

With the reopening in 1963 of the east wing of Center as a secure unit, separate from the rest of the institution with an enclosed exercise yard and male correctional officers around the clock, attention could be focused on the changes necessary to work more adequately with the younger, more volatile inmates and the increasing number of narcotic addicts. Besides crowding and the lack of psychological help, there was a lack of appropriate training programs. New buildings were on the drawing boards but an escalation in costs delayed the beginning of construction on most of them until after Mahan died. Two new programs off the grounds of Clinton Farms were opened in 1967 to ease the crowding: a unit at Vineland State School for the mentally retarded in South Jersey and a preparole unit in Carpenter House in the town of Clinton.

Vineland State School Unit and Carpenter House

Plans for the Vineland State School unit were first discussed in Trenton in July 1963. The Clinton Farms Board of Managers and classification committee worked on recommendations for the unit in the fall of 1963. Plans for a forty-bed cottage for Clinton inmates were submitted for bid in 1965, and the building was completed by early March 1967. In mid-April 1967 the first nineteen inmates were assigned there with cottage staff from Clinton Farms. C. W. Price wrote about the unit in the *Hunterdon County Democrat*, 1 June 1967:

> The girls are assigned to help state employees at the Vineland State School in South Jersey to look after mentally retarded girls there....
>
> The state has built a new building at Vineland to house Clinton inmates there with room for 40 girls. But Miss Edna Mahan, superintendent at Clinton Farms, is proceeding cautiously before assigning the additional 21 girls there. For one thing, she says, the new building is not quite finished. And she wants to gauge the performance of the first group assigned there.... So far, she says, it's working fine.
>
> Ten of the girls work in the food service department helping out cooking and serving food. Five gather dirty linen and pass out clean linen when it comes back from the laundry. Two assist in the clinic, and two more work in Vineland's Clinton unit as housekeepers.
>
> To be chosen for the honor of going to Vineland, Clinton Farms girls must first establish that they are both dependable workers and trustworthy. The girls regard it a real privilege.... They are allowed to wear their own clothes...and they are permitted—under supervision—to go downtown shopping, to the movies and to church....
>
> Miss Mahan plans to fill the quota of girls assigned to Vineland to the full 40 inmates within a year.

The Vineland State School unit lasted less than two years. Vineland is approximately 100 miles from Clinton, which made it difficult to supervise. Cottage staff from Clinton by and large were not anxious to go there, and often weaker staff were sent. The training program was a good one for the inmates, but in February 1968 Manpower Development Training Programs were approved for the Reformatory for Women, so new programs began to be developed there. The Vineland Unit was transferred back to Clinton in November 1968.

Carpenter House in the town of Clinton enjoyed a longer tenure. It was bought by the state in 1946 to house employees at Clinton Farms. Plans to convert Carpenter House were opposed by seventy-six residents of the town of Clinton in a petition filed with the town council in October 1966. An open meeting was held in Clinton 29 November to hear from town residents and Mahan and Albert Wagner for the Division of Correction and Parole. In an article from an unknown newspaper dated 30 November 1966 and headlined "Halfway House for Women? Clinton Residents Are Divided on Pre-parole Center Proposal," Mahan explained:

> Honor inmates 'carefully selected' by the reformatory board as they neared completion of their sentences would reside in the half-way house under supervision of a matron. They would be allowed to work the remaining three or four months in one of three areas of opportunity in surrounding communities.
>
> Wagner said these opportunities would include work under the present 'day parole' under which the honor inmates do housework once a week in homes of

> residents who request them, work in the State Sanatorium for Chest Diseases near Glen Gardner and at the Hunterdon Medical Center. The residents would receive nominal pay for their work.
>
> The house would accommodate eight inmates at a time. A matron would be on duty all day. The inmates would be unable to receive visitors at the house but could return to the reformatory to receive guests. He said this in response to expressions of concern about the possible influx in the town by persons with questionable motives.

Town residents who were against the opening of the house voiced their "concerns about the influence of the inmates of the house on their young children" and sought clarification of the "screening process to determine eligible residents." Day parole employees from the community "vouched for the inmates' work and behavior in their homes." Pastors from two of Clinton's largest churches who were among five ministers participating in the counseling ministry program for the women's reformatory "urged residents to overcome any fears or suspicions for the plan and realize the program's intended values." Mahan said, "All we ask is that the girls be allowed a chance to become decent, law-abiding, self-supporting citizens."

Clinton Farms had always been a good neighbor to the town of Clinton. There was no legal reason for not approving the halfway house, and there was as much sentiment in favor of it as opposed to it, so the council approved the plan. The Turrell Fund provided monies for renovations and additions to Carpenter House. On 3 June 1967 an open house was held to which the mayor, the town council, and all interested town residents were invited. The first residents from Clinton Farms were transferred there on 10 July 1967.

Carpenter House was the first halfway house for women in New Jersey. Although halfway houses had been in existence for some years, they did not begin to proliferate for offenders until the mid-sixties due to initiatives begun by Robert Kennedy when he was attorney general and followed up by Lyndon Johnson's administration. Mahan was always quick to pick up on programs that were innovative and rehabilitative and would help ease crowding. Carpenter House was vacant because the last staff family to live in it built their own home and most staff by this time did not expect or need housing provided.

The house continued to operate successfully for over five years. Although there were a few runaways and some of the inmates did not adjust and were sent back to the reformatory, the majority of the inmates completed the program and were successful in their return to their home communities. Edna Mahan lived only long enough to launch Carpenter House.

"The Woman Which Was Head of the Institution, Miss Mahan Died. It Was a Sorrowful Thing for She Was a Very Fair, Just Woman."

An inmate wrote the above to her aunt and uncle a few days after Edna Mahan died on 13 April 1968. She added in the letter, "Things will be a whole lot different now."

Mahan was not ill long. Her Christmas activities at Clinton Farms in December 1967 were as they had been for thirty-nine years—shopping, the Christmas pageant, writing the tags for each inmate's Christmas bag, and visiting each cottage on Christmas Eve. Christmas day was spent in Morristown with the Black family.

She had been experiencing intestinal discomfort off and on, and in January went to Morristown Memorial Hospital for tests. She was referred to a surgeon at the University of Pennsylvania Hospital, and before the end of January was operated on for colon cancer. Julia Duane talked with the surgeon, a friend, a few days afterward, and he was hopeful he had removed all the cancer. Mahan returned to Clinton Farms to recuperate during February. Morris and Black spent a great deal of time with her.

She had planned to spend March in St. Croix with Gertrude Hawley, and even though she was not recovered, she was determined to go. On 5 March they flew down. While she was there, on 13 March she wrote Morris:

> Dear Lois—
>
> Have just written Lucia and Mary B. Hope the writing hand will hold out for you....
>
> Pris phoned to invite us to Carlton for lunch with her brother & sister-in-law from Boston. I had to turn it down—don't feel up to such a long procedure....
>
> Dr. Patton's report reached Dr. Conrad Stevens yesterday. I'll feel more reassured after I see him (still problems with BM's, food, drainage, gas pains and sleep)....
>
> Gertrude is *continuing the fine standard of cooking which you began!* She made me a fine custard yesterday.
>
> Some day I hope to find words (or something) to let you know how grateful I am to you for all your attention during those dreary days after the return to Clinton. In the meantime keep your nose clean!
>
> Much love, EM

Dr. Stevens must have been concerned about her condition, for Mahan returned home on 13 March. Agnes Flack, who was at her home in St. Croix, flew back with her. By the time Mahan got to Homestead she was so weak, she was unable to walk up the stairs to her bedroom: she crawled. Morris watched, heartsick, and asked if she could spend the night at Homestead. Mahan was grateful, and Morris remained with her about two weeks until she was taken to Morristown Memorial Hospital. Bee and Ethel Black took over her day-to-day care then. Ethel recalled in her last days in the hospital Mahan said, "There is still so much to do." Mahan did not want people to see her in her condition, and she discouraged visitors. Most people did not know how ill she was.

When the author's mother called to say that Mahan was dead and there was to be a memorial service on 17 April, it was unbelievable, for she did not know anything about her condition. The author last saw her at her mother's on 14 October 1967. There was no indication then of any problems.

The service was held outside in front of the chapel, so all residents who wished could attend. It was a glorious warm April day. Before the service began, Anita Quarles said with tears running down her face, "I did not ever think I would be attending Edna Mahan's funeral." MacCormick's first words, breaking with sorrow, were, "I do not know if I shall be able to get through my eulogy for Edna Mahan."

New Jersey Corrections (1968) gave the following account of her death and memorial service:

> EDNA MAHAN SUCCUMBS: HEADED CLINTON 40 YEARS
>
> Edna Mahan, Superintendent of the Reformatory for Women at Clinton, died on Saturday, April 13th, following a brief illness....
>
> Her death brought to a close a career that attracted national recognition in the field of correctional administration. Miss Mahan's most valuable laurels were won as a person of compassion, one who always included understanding as a factor in seeking solutions to human problems. She loved Clinton Farms, "her girls" who were committed to its care and the staff who, under her direction, strove to develop those inner resources that generate hope from despair. Love and compassion were translated into daily activity. Because she felt one's own problems are never insignificant, Miss Mahan was ever ready to listen to troubled people and lend her energies in seeking positive resolutions. Her capacity to restore confidence in those who were beaten down by life's circumstances is best expressed by a former Reformatory ward, "I loved and respected her more than any other human being on earth. She gave me back my life when literally speaking it was over, just by having faith in me when I didn't have it in myself."
>
> Miss Mahan's liberal outlook that inspired this type of response is best illustrated in a statement that appeared in a Division publication, "we cannot demand respect; we get it only if we deserve it. Unless we ourselves are honest, truthful, sincere, industrious, and loyal, we could never develop these qualities in our inmates. By our example we are preparing them for decent living here and now for later in their own homes."
>
> Under Edna Mahan's enlightened leadership, the Reformatory for Women became known as a place for rehabilitation rather than punishment and earned the

reputation of being one of the country's outstanding "open" institutions. Her work took her on international trips in 1959 and 1960 to northern Europe where she visited penal and correctional institutions and to the Second United Nations Congress on the Prevention of Crime and the Treatment of Offenders in London.

On April 17th, a memorial service was conducted by Rev. Albert Van Deusen, Suffragan Bishop of the Episcopal Diocese of New Jersey; Rev. Edward Morris, Catholic Chaplain and Rev. Paul S. Goble, Jr., Protestant Chaplain, Reformatory for Women. Notables and resident women stood side by side to pay their last respects. Penologist Austin MacCormick eulogized Miss Mahan as a humanitarian who etched a living memorial in the lives of those she touched. A choir of Reformatory Women residents sang hymns. Honorary pallbearers included Edward R. Cass, Austin MacCormick, Dr. F. Lovell Bixby, Sanford Bates, Donald Goff, Dr. Joseph Furnas, and Frank Loveland. Pallbearers were Lloyd B. Wescott, Kenneth Holjes, Robert E. Personette, William J. Hoffman, John Ballantine, Jr., William Rogers, Daniel W. Carter, and Albert C. Wagner.

Clinton Farms was not only Edna Mahan's place of work, it was her home and her life. The resident women were, for her, an integral part of her family circle with all of the love and forgiveness, the willingness to sacrifice that the word family entails. The little cemetery on grounds adjacent to the chapel, became her place of final rest.

Telegrams and letters of condolence poured in from all over the world, from the governor of New Jersey to hundreds of inmates and former inmates. One former inmate wrote to Helen Philhower:

You will never know how grateful I am for your thoughtfulness in sending me the papers...no words can ever express what a grand and gracious lady she was.... All through the years, I have not, and will not, ever forget her, and just think that goes for thousands of girls, whom through misfortune had the wonderful honor of meeting her.

I received a card and note this Xmas from her. She didn't forget her girls.

A retired staff member wrote the Board of Managers:

I find it impossible to realize she will not come to meet me with her welcoming smile when I come to the Farms.

The world is a poorer place without her, but the effect of her vibrant personality will, like sound waves, go on far beyond those who knew her and loved her and were influenced by her.

It was a great privilege for me to have met her and worked with her. To me her outstanding quality was her belief in the essential goodness of human nature. It was incredible and inspiring in this day of doubt and despair.

Miriam Van Waters wrote Lois Morris:

> Anne Gladding has just told me of the death of our beloved Edna. I want you to know that I share your grief and sense of loss.
>
> Edna was both a great leader in the field of corrections and a great friend. I rejoice that I saw you both when you came to visit Mrs. Thompson in Brookdale. I think Mrs. Thompson brightened remarkably when she saw Edna. For she loved Edna and admired her so.
>
> Elizabeth [Bode] Van Waters says she will probably go to the services. Anne says they will be held out of doors in front of the chapel.
>
> This is an excellent creative idea of yours, for Edna loved the out-of-doors and now all the girls as well as her many friends can go.
>
> May God bless you in these trying times. I am sure Edna is blessing us all from Eternity.

Chapter 11

Edna Mahan's Legacy

Edna Mahan's career began in 1923 at the end of the Progressive era (1890–1920) and the fight for women's suffrage. In *Creating a Female Dominion in American Reform 1890–1935*, Robyn Muncy (1991) points out that many of the female reformers who "had inaugurated their careers during the Progressive era...continued to fight their reforming battles through the 1920's." These were middle-class white reformers "who were seeking channels to professionalism."

Muncy defines three types of "female experience...corresponding to the sort of profession a woman entered:" women in male-dominated professions, such as law and medicine; women in female-dominated professions, such as nursing and teaching; and women in between these two groups whose experience was in "new female professions created during the Progressive era." These professions included social work, public health nursing, and home economics.

Mahan's years at Berkeley (1918–22) raised her consciousness to feminist issues. A year after graduating she came under the tutelage of Miriam Van Waters. Born in 1887, Van Waters became enmeshed in the Progressive movement as she was growing up and beginning her career.

Mahan's career as a social worker with female offenders fell into all three of Muncy's categories of female professions. Prison work has always been a male-dominated profession. However, in the one hundred years between 1870 and 1970, women's sphere within penology, as demanded by early female reformers, was with female offenders. After graduating from Berkeley she joined "a large contingent of women [who clung] tenaciously to their reforming creed" (Muncy 1991). Her reform crusades lay in two arenas: (1) compensation, opportunities, and support for all women who work in corrections, including women's concerns within the American Prison/Correctional Association and (2) female correctional institutions and their clients, the offenders.

Reform on the Inside and Outside

Many of Mahan's concerns with compensation and opportunities for women in corrections were addressed in 1972 with the extension of Title VII of the Civil Rights Act of 1964 to include public employees. Correctional officers, male and female, are compensated on the same salary scale, and women are no longer restricted to working in women's institutions where there are limited opportunities for advancement. Mahan's efforts to attract qualified young women to work in the correctional field—summer seasonal assistants and student conferences—are supplanted today with academic programs in criminal justice and correctional concentrations in the professional schools of social work. However, corrections work remains a male domain and relatively few women seek it out as a preferred career.

As in all professions women find it hard to advance up the career ladder in corrections whether it be because of pressures from family responsibilities or the overt and covert barriers that discourage the advancement of women in the workplace. Today there are an increasing number of women who are top administrators of women's and men's institutions but only a handful of women as state commissioners or directors of corrections.

Within the American Correctional Association there has been an increase in the percentage of female members and in their active participation in the association. Since 1987 there appears to be an upward trend in women elected to the presidency—three. In 1990 women made up 48 percent of the Board of Governors as compared with 15 percent in 1980. In 1980, 20 percent of the Delegate Assembly were women; in 1990, 47 percent were. In 1992, 39 percent of ACA committee chairs were women. The Committee on Women in Corrections has more than two hundred participants.

Women in corrections have had to fight hard for the gains they have accomplished. They have organized themselves into women's committees within ACA and many state associations. Their sisters on the other side of the bars have not fared as well. They have no power base from which to operate. They still make up a very small percentage, approximately 6 percent to 7 percent, of the total incarcerated population and remain the "forgotten offenders."

A paramount issue in women's correctional institutions has always been inmate mothers and their babies. The fact that women's institutions must care for pregnant inmates as well as those who are the primary caretakers for their children in the community is a major difference between women's and men's correctional settings.

Mahan was always concerned with these issues at Clinton Farms and was not satisfied with their handling. In the 1950s she tried to find the money to study the children who had been born at Clinton Farms, but it was not forthcoming. In 1959 she advocated the need for a study "as to how these cases should best be handled for the benefit of mother, child and society." She also called for mothers to "be given full opportunity for training in caring for their children" and urged "the closest scrutiny must be made of foster homes. Many damaged personalities result from a series of unsuccessful foster home placements" (Mahan 1959).

Today most women's correctional settings, institutions or community, offer parenting training to some degree. Foster home placements are probably more uncertain today than they were forty years ago. Although there have always been excellent foster homes for children, in too many jurisdictions caseworkers are overworked and have large caseloads making it impossible to provide careful scrutiny of the homes and the foster parents as well as the follow-up work with children once they are placed.

Prison nurseries are as controversial today as they were in Mahan's time. Very few exist to provide for the bonding of mother and child known to be essential; the outstanding one is at Bedford Hills, New York. The ideal today is community residential settings where the women get pre- and postnatal care; parenting, substance abuse, and nutrition education; health care; and time for bonding. Legal and security issues make these difficult to attain. Society does not adequately meet the needs of nonoffending mothers and their children and is even less willing to provide for inmate mothers and children.

Society is conflicted today over pregnant substance-abusing women and those who are HIV-positive. Many citizens and legislators call for the criminalization of these women and separation of the child from the mother, who is deemed to be unfit. Mahan would have fought against this as much as she did against the child welfare workers who were reluctant to bring the Clinton inmates' children to visit them.

Programming for female offenders is an issue that was not adequately addressed in Mahan's time. In most states male prison administrators provided scant resources for the small numbers of women. In New Jersey, Mahan fought for programming at Clinton that was suited to the needs and interests of the inmates and realistic in terms of the occupational opportunities available for women. She stressed the difference between vocational education as training "which implies systematic instruction...theory and practice" (Mahan 1959) as opposed to routine maintenance work assignments. Society's attitudes on appropriate roles for women combined with the lack of financial resources made it difficult to develop more adequate training opportunities at Clinton.

Today great strides have been made throughout the correctional community in understanding what is involved in good programming for women and in efforts to provide it. Changes in society's attitudes toward appropriate work arenas for women have aided this. However, it has been difficult to realize adequate opportunities in women's institutions. This is in part due to the increasing numbers of women incarcerated today with subsequent crowding and financial constraints. It is also due to a lack of need felt by top administrators to provide parity in programming for women.

In her chapter on women's institutions, Mahan includes as "essential elements in a women's institution" medical, psychiatric, and psychological services; academic, social, and vocational education; library; leisure time; and religious activities. All of these are in the current edition (1990b) of *Standards for Adult Correctional Institutions.*

The student government honor system at Clinton Farms was its outstandingly unique component. Mahan expanded the system that was in place when she assumed superintendency. It was the core of the institution. Mahan's basic philosophy in working within it was to build restraints in people rather than in buildings. In the 1933–34 annual report of the reformatory she wrote about student government: "The women are given an opportunity to lead relatively normal lives without undue restraint.... They are encouraged to assume responsibility, to develop initiative, to adopt better standards and to become self-supporting."

Enlightened female offender programs throughout the country today spell out their goals to empower women to advocate for themselves to realize self-determination, take control of their lives, and become self-supporting. Most women's correctional institutions, however, reflect the security-driven needs of men's maximum security prisons. Using handcuffs and shackles to transport female inmates, sometimes even when they are in labor, is a routine, required administrative directive.

ACA's Task Force on Female Offenders survey found that the majority of female offenders commit nonviolent offenses and do not pose a great threat to the community. Within the institution they "are neither a threat to each other nor to staff, and they are less likely to damage property or to attempt escape" (ACA 1990a). In spite of this the task force found that many agencies had plans to build new institutions for women or build additions to existing facilities that would be "medium/maximum security institutions, with very few plans to build community centers" (ACA 1990a).

Mahan knew that oppression imposed inside institution walls fosters dependency and does not allow growth toward self-determination. She also knew there were times inmates needed to be confined in locked rooms. During her last decade the population at Clinton Farms included an increasing number of young, disturbed inmates many of whom were drug addicts. In her last years one of the cottages was transformed into a locked security unit. She never ceased to fight to keep Clinton Farms an open institution with a student government honor system, because she understood, as did the early female reformers, helping female offenders could not be accomplished in an institution fashioned in the male mold.

"She Has Helped Us to Resist 'Penological Automation' "

During the four decades of her distinguished career with female offenders, Mahan became a recognized leader of women in corrections. She challenged the correctional system, worked within it, and brought about change. Commissioner Ellis recognized her leadership potential when he interviewed her before she was appointed superintendent at the New Jersey Reformatory for Women. He helped her grow as a leader by giving her her rein and counseling and supporting her, whether it be with difficult board members or difficult inmates. His role in the successful launching of her career cannot be underestimated. She took risks that most commissioners would not have tolerated, and he admired her. He instilled the confidence in her she needed for the next forty years.

Mahan used her board skillfully to help her advance Clinton Farms to the forefront of women's reformatories in the country and to keep it from being put in the male mold of correctional institutions. She worked effectively and successfully with four commissioners. She challenged efforts to change programs or structure at Clinton Farms if the ideology would be threatened. Her challenges were sometimes subtle and sometimes direct using the full force of the board.

She was admired and respected by her peers in the Division of Correction and Parole. F. Lovell Bixby, director of the division under whom she worked most of her forty years, enjoyed working with her and lent her much strength. In the program of the fiftieth anniversary of Clinton Farms he wrote of her administrative courage:

> In the many years we have worked together Edna Mahan and I often debated this or that administrative detail. I always had to forfeit the debate because Edna was standing for the right of her girls to live and grow—and to make mistakes in the process. She has been willing to let the girls make mistakes that were embarrassing to her if it helped them to learn the better way of life. No other "method" can take the place of personal and administrative courage of that order. She has helped us to resist "penological automation." I am grateful to her.

Albert Wagner, who was director of the division when Mahan died, called her the "Dean of Superintendents." Charles Houston, a longtime member of the division who served as superintendent of the State Home for Boys, admired her and sought her advice because she encouraged him. She advised him to have the courage of what he believed. He said, "She was the kind of superintendent we all should be. She led the way. I always thought of her as the Statue of Liberty. She knew what she wanted, and she went ahead with it. Nothing stopped her."

Mahan's leadership roles in the American Prison/Correctional Association took place in two spheres. One was the women's committees. The other was the official administrative structure, such as officers, executive committee, and board of directors.

The women's committees of the American Prison Association in Mahan's time and earlier were composed of women who worked with female offenders, and the committees' agendas concerned female offender issues. These committees came and went from the time the first one was organized in 1912. Since there were so few women incarcerated as compared to men and so few female members of APA/ACA, they were not given much support by the parent association.

Mahan attended her first APA annual congress in 1929, the year a resolution was adopted to appoint a women's committee, which had not been active since 1917. She became a member and leader and worked hard to keep other female members involved and interested. In 1960 she was the prime mover in the resurrection of the committee after twelve years of inactivity.

She first served as a member of the APA Board of Directors in 1938. Commissioner Ellis had been president of APA in 1937 and was undoubtedly responsible for her appointment. She served in some official capacity for the rest of her life. She was admired and well liked by the men who were the reform leaders of the association, including secretary Edward R. Cass. Her two staunchest allies were Austin MacCormick and Sanford Bates. She was accepted as one of them and perhaps had more influence in the organization in this unofficial capacity than she did as a member of the Board of Directors or the Executive Committee. She was as relentless with them in pursuing what was right for the association and for issues concerning women as she was with the New Jersey corrections and government hierarchy.

In his essay "Correctional Leadership," John J. Larivee (1992) writes that leadership in corrections today has "retreated to the safety of the prison walls.... **No Escapes, No Riots, No Deaths;**...little innovation happens when success is gauged by this failure." We have become victims of "penological automation." Larivee goes on to state:

> As with most intractable problems, many in corrections cling to the belief that money is the scarcest resource. It is not. The scarcest resources are visions that connect corrections with the larger needs of society. They require leadership willing to examine...correctional paradigms, to reach out beyond the borders of corrections to other systems and professions, to listen to and learn from the community of its interests and needs. When this happens, the impressive personal energies of innovators in diverse settings will, finally, go beyond [penological automation].

We need leaders with the courage to accept innovative challenges and who are not afraid to take the risks. Edna Mahan was such a leader.

Bibliography

Books, Papers, and Periodicals

Ad Lib. 1961. Are we doing too much time? *Ad Lib* (June).

Ad Lib. 1964. A word to the wise. *Ad Lib* (May).

American Correctional Association. (aka National Prison Association, American Prison Association). 1870, 1883, 1885, 1890, 1895, 1900, 1910, 1912, 1915, 1920, 1925, 1929, 1930, 1950, 1951, 1959. *Proceedings of annual congresses*.

———. 1959. *Manual of correctional standards*. New York. Revised 1966.

———. 1960. Report on the Second United Nations Congress on the Prevention of Crime and the Treatment of Offenders. Paper presented at the 90th Congress of Correction. American Correctional Association, Denver, Colo.

———. 1963. Edward R. Cass Correctional Achievement Fund. *American Journal of Corrections* (September-October).

———. 1990a. *The female offender: What does the future hold?* Laurel, Md.: ACA.

———. 1990b. *Standards for adult correctional institutions*. Laurel, Md.: ACA.

American Prison Association. 1940. Introducing. *Prison World*. (November-December).

———. 1954. *Manual of correctional standards*. New York: APA.

Association on Programs for Female Offenders. 1989. A short history lesson: Where APFO came from. *Newsletter* (May).

Barnard, Chester I. 1940. *The functions of the executive*. Cambridge, Mass.: Harvard University Press.

Barnes, Harry E. 1918. *A history of the penal, reformatory and correctional institutions of the State of New Jersey, analytical and documentary*. Report of the Prison

Inquiry Commission, State of New Jersey 2. Trenton, N.J.: MacCrellish and Quigley.

Barnes, Harry E., and Negley K. Teeters. 1951. *New horizons in criminology.* Englewood Cliffs, N.J.: Prentice-Hall. Revised 1959.

Barnes, John K. 1963. Audience at Clinton Farms stirred by famous singer. *Flemington Democrat* (13 June).

Bates, Sanford. 1946. *Newark Sunday Call* (4 April).

———. 1968. Letter to the editor. *New York Times* (23 April).

Booth, Maud Ballington. 1912. Annual address of the president of the Association of Women Members. In *Proceedings of the annual congress of the American Prison Association.* Indianapolis: Wm. B. Burford.

Bowker, Lee H. 1982. *Corrections, the science and the art.* New York: Macmillan Publishing Co.

Close, Kathryn. 1949. Reform without locks. *Survey* (March).

Commission to Study the Dept. of Institutions and Agencies. 1959. *The state's organization for social welfare.* Trenton, N.J.: Commission to Study the Dept. of Institutions and Agencies.

Corcoran Journal. 31 May 1918.

———. Fall 1921.

Cox, William B., F. Lovell Bixby, William I. Root, eds. 1933. *Handbook of American prisons and reformatories.* New York: The Osborne Association.

Eaton, Joseph W. 1962. *Stone walls not a prison make.* Springfield, Ill.: Charles C. Thomas.

Ellis, William J. 1924. Experience in classifying defective delinquents and some results effected by transfer from correctional institutions to hospitals and institutions for feeble-minded. Presented at the American Association for the Study of Feeble-Minded, Washington, D.C., 2 June.

———. 1945. Public welfare in New Jersey, 1630-1944. In *The story of New Jersey,* ed. William Starr Myers. N. J.: Lewis Historical Publishing Co.

The Flemington Democrat. 1958. Edna Mahan gets honorary degree on "routine day." *The Flemington Democrat* (5 June).

———. 1990. Lloyd Wescott dies, civic leader was 83. *The Flemington Democrat.* 27 December.

Frankel, Emil, compiler. *Comparative statistics, 1913–1937.* Clinton, N.J.: N.J. Reformatory for Women.

Freedman, Estelle B. 1984. *Their sisters' keepers.* Ann Arbor, Mich.: University of Michigan Press.

Freeman, Lucy. 1950. Mental hospital has convict aides. *New York Times* (8 August).

Garrett, Paul W., and Austin B. MacCormick. 1929. *Handbook of American prisons and reformatories, 1929.* New York: National Society of Penal Information.

Henle, Werner. 1951. Address on the jaundice project. N.J. Reformatory for Women Commencement, Clinton, N.J., 27 June.

Hotchkiss, Bruce W. 1956. Babies being fed live polio virus. *Newark Evening News* (24 October).

Hunterdon Democrat. June 1950.

———. June 1953.

Hunterdon Republican. 21 December 1944.

———. 1 January 1945.

Jury, Florence, and Jacomena Maybeck. 1979. *The four year stretch.* Privately published.

Koprowski, Hilary, et al. 1956. Immunization of infants with living attenuated poliomyelitis virus. *Journal of the American Medical Association* 162 (December).

Lamendola, Linda. 1966. Crisis in our only women's prison. *The Trenton Evening Times* (21 February).

Larivee, John J. 1992. Correctional leadership. *Innovating* (Fall).

Lekkerkerker, Eugenia C. 1931. *Reformatories for women in the United States.* The Hague: J.B. Wolters.

Los Angeles Evening Express. 1923. Chance to help givers of aid. *Los Angeles Evening Express* (22 May).

Mahan, Edna. 1933. Correction through education. In *American Prison Association proceedings*. New York: APA.

———. 1944. Reflections on institutional discipline. *Prison World* 6 (March-April).

———. 1950. To what extent can open institutions take the place of the traditional prison? Presented at the Twelfth International Penal and Penitentiary Congress, The Hague.

———. 1960. Report on the Second United Nations Congress on the prevention of crime and the treatment of offenders. Presented at ACA's Nintieth Congress of Correction, Denver, Colo.

McCorkle, Lloyd W., Albert Elias, and F. Lovell Bixby. 1958. *The Highfields Story*. New York: Henry Holt and Co.

McGowan, Brenda G., and Karen L. Blumenthal. 1978. *Why punish the children? A study of children of women prisoners*. Hackensack, N.J.: National Council on Crime and Delinquency.

McGrath, Rosemary. 1963. Residential group center for delinquent girls. *The Welfare Reporter* 14 (July).

Moeller, H. G., ed. 1981. *The selected papers of Frank Loveland*. College Park, Md.: American Correctional Association.

Morris, Albert. 1934. *Criminology*. New York: Longmans, Green.

Morris County Daily Record. 1961. Smoldering battle on reformatories due for showdown. *Morris County Daily Record* (21 February).

Muncy, Robyn. 1991. *Creating a female dominion in American reform 1890–1935*. New York: Oxford University Press.

Myers, William Starr, ed. 1945. Public welfare in New Jersey, 1630–1944. In *The story of New Jersey*. N.J.: Lewis Historical Publishing Co.

National Advisory Commission on Criminal Justice Standards and Goals. 1973. *Corrections*. Washington, D.C.: U.S. Government Printing Office.

Newark Evening News. 1960. Board split on powers. *Newark Evening News* (19 February).

New Jersey Corrections. 1968. Edna Mahan succumbs. *New Jersey Corrections* (April).

N.J. Reformatory for Women. 1913, 1914, 1915, 1916, 1926, 1931, 1933–34, 1945–46, 1946–47, 1951–53, 1961–62, 1963–64. *Annual reports*. Clinton, N.J.: N.J. Reformatory for Women.

———. 1950. *About you and Clinton Farms*. Clinton, N.J.: N.J. Reformatory for Women. Revised 1961.

———. 1953. Program, 1913–1953, fortieth anniversary of the founding of Clinton Farms, the State Reformatory for Women at Clinton New Jersey. Clinton, N.J.: N.J. Reformatory for Women.

———. 1963. Program, 1913–1963, fiftieth anniversary of Clinton Farms, the State Reformatory for Women at Clinton, New Jersey. Clinton, N.J.: N.J. Reformatory for Women.

New York Times. 1950. Mental hospital has convict aides. *New York Times* (8 August).

———. 1990. Maternal bonds behind prison bars. *New York Times* (23 September).

Nicolai, Sandra. 1980. Synopsis and history of American Correctional Association Task Force on Women. Appended to Minutes/Midwinter Meeting ACA Women's Task Force. Las Vegas, Nev., 26 January 1982.

Philadelphia Evening Public Ledger. 1937. Mrs. Roosevelt visits son's ex-wife before addressing prison group here. *Philadelphia Evening Public Ledger* (13 September).

Potter, Ellen C. 1930. *Recommendations: Sub-committee on the care of infant children of the inmates of correctional institutions*. New York: National Committee on Prisons and Prison Labor.

Price, C. W. 1967. "Picked" girls at Clinton Farms now working at Vineland School. *Flemington Democrat* (1 June).

Prison Inquiry Commission of the State of New Jersey. 1917. *Report of the Prison Inquiry Commission 1*. Trenton, N.J.: Prison Inquiry Commission.

Procunier, R. K. 1959. Women's institutions. Draft of revised chapter for *Manual of Correctional Standards* (April).

Rafter, Nicole Hahn. 1990. *Partial justice: Women, prisons, and social control.* New Brunswick, N.J.: Transaction Publishers.

Roosevelt, Eleanor. 1956. My day. *Easton Express* (25 June).

Rowles, Burton J. 1962. *The lady at Box 99, the story of Miriam Van Waters.* Greenwich, Ct.: Seabury Press.

San Francisco Examiner. 1922. Girls exceed men at University of California's largest graduation. *San Francisco Examiner* (18 May).

Scott, Anne Firor. 1984. *Making the invisible woman visible.* Chicago: University of Illinois Press.

Simon, Rita James. 1975. *The contemporary woman and crime.* Rockville, Md.: National Institute of Mental Health.

Stroup, Herbert H. 1953. *Social work: An introduction to the field.* New York: American Book Company.

Sullivan, Larry E. 1990. *The prison reform movement.* Boston: Twayne Publishers.

Tannenbaum, Frank. 1930. The vision that came to Thomas Mott Osborne. *Survey* (October).

University of California, Berkeley. 1917–18, 1920–21, 1921–22. *Blue and gold: A record of the college years.* Berkeley, Calif.: University of California, Berkeley.

———. 1921 and 1922. *The Daily Californian.* Berkeley, Calif.: University of California.

Wagner, Albert C. 1965. Annual report—1964, Division of Correction and Parole. *Welfare Reporter* (April).

———. 1966. Annual report—1965, Division of Correction and Parole. *Welfare Reporter* (July).

Welfare Reporter. 1956. Mrs. Roosevelt tells Clinton graduates education is a "stepping stone of life." *Welfare Reporter* (June).

Wilson, Stephen H. 1969. Psychological and psychiatric services in institutions (other than jails) serving female offenders. Unpublished paper.

Wines, E. C., ed. 1871. *Transactions of the National Congress on Penitentiary and Reformatory Discipline.* Albany, N.Y.: Weed, Parsons and Co. Printers.

Yreka City Journal. 1900–1901.

Zalba, Serapio. 1964. *Women prisoners and their families.* Los Angeles: Delmar Publishing Co.

Correspondence

Abell, Bess, social secretary to Lady Bird Johnson. Letter to Beatrice Black, institutional parole officer, N.J. Reformatory for Women, 29 April 1964.

Alexander, Archibald, assistant director of Disarmament and Arms Control. Letter to Robert F. Kennedy, U.S. Attorney General, 29 April 1964.

Alloway, Joseph, director, N.J. State Board of Children's Guardians. Letter to Edna Mahan, superintendent, N.J. Reformatory for Women, 13 July 1938.

Baird, Mary Stevens, State Board of Control of Institutions and Agencies. Letter to Frances Perkins, secretary of Labor under Franklin D. Roosevelt, 17 June 1964.

Barton, Viola, cousin of Edna Mahan. Letter to Doris Whitney, 15 April 1968.

Bates, Sanford. Letter to Edward R. Cass, general secretary, American Prison Association, 18 October 1951.

———. Letter to Richard McGee, chairman, Committee to Revise 1954 *Manual of Correctional Standards*, 3 April 1959.

Bennett, James, director, Federal Bureau of Prisons. Letter to Edna Mahan, superintendent, N.J. Reformatory for Women, 27 July 1964.

Bixby, F. Lovell, director, Division of Correction and Parole, N.J. Dept. of Institutions and Agencies. Letter to M. Paul Conril, secretary general, Ministry of Justice, Belgium (n.d.).

Bode, Elizabeth. Letter to Miriam Van Waters, 15 September 1948. Schlesinger Library, Radcliffe College, Van Waters Papers, A-71, Box 5, File 197.

Cass, Edward R., general secretary, American Prison Association. Letter to Edna Mahan, superintendent, N.J. Reformatory for Women, 3 May 1937.

Cronshey, Hildreth, director of education, N.J. Reformatory for Women. Letter to Edna Mahan, superintendent, N.J. Reformatory for Women, June 1940.

Doll, Edgar A., psychologist. Letter to Edna Mahan, superintendent, N.J. Reformatory for Women, 20 July 1929.

Earle, E. P., president, N.J. State Board of Control of Institutions and Agencies. Letter to Janie Coggeshall, president, Board of Managers, N.J. Reformatory for Women, 1 February 1930.

Ellis, William J., commissioner, N.J. Dept. of Institutions and Agencies. Letter to Edna Mahan, superintendent, N.J. Reformatory for Women, 19 July 1929.

Gallup, Marian F., superintendent, Indiana Woman's Prison. Letter to Edna Mahan, superintendent, N.J. Reformatory for Women, 19 March 1945.

Galway, Edward, chief, Social Defense Section, United Nations. Letter to Edna Mahan, superintendent, N.J. Reformatory for Women, June 1965.

Gordon, Walter, chairman, Adult Authority, Dept. of Correction, Sacramento, Calif. Letter to Edna Mahan, superintendent, N.J. Reformatory for Women, 3 July 1947.

Hazard, Helen H., superintendent, Reformatory for Women, Dwight, Ill. Letter to Edna Mahan, superintendent, N.J. Reformatory for Women, 11 July 1937.

Jones, Lewis Webster, president, Rutgers University. Letter to Edna Mahan, superintendent, N.J. Reformatory for Women, 14 March 1958.

Kinsella, Nina, executive assistant to the director, Bureau of Prisons, Washington, D.C. Letter to Edna Mahan, superintendent, N.J. Reformatory for Women, 3 June 1938.

Kinsella, Nina, warden, Federal Reformatory for Women, Alderson, W.Va. Letter to Edna Mahan, superintendent, N.J. Reformatory for Women, 19 December 1949.

Lewis, Burdette, commissioner. Letter to Grace Robson, superintendent, N.J. Reformatory for Women, 20 July 1919.

MacCormick, Austin, executive director, Osborne Association, Inc. Letter to Robert F. Kennedy, U.S. Attorney General, 27 July 1964.

———. Letter to Edna Mahan, superintendent, N.J. Reformatory for Women, 27 May 1958.

———. Letter to Mary Quarles, 21 August 1962.

Mahan, Edna, superintendent, N.J. Reformatory for Women. Letter to Joseph Alloway, director, N.J. State Board of Children's Guardians, 30 June 1938.

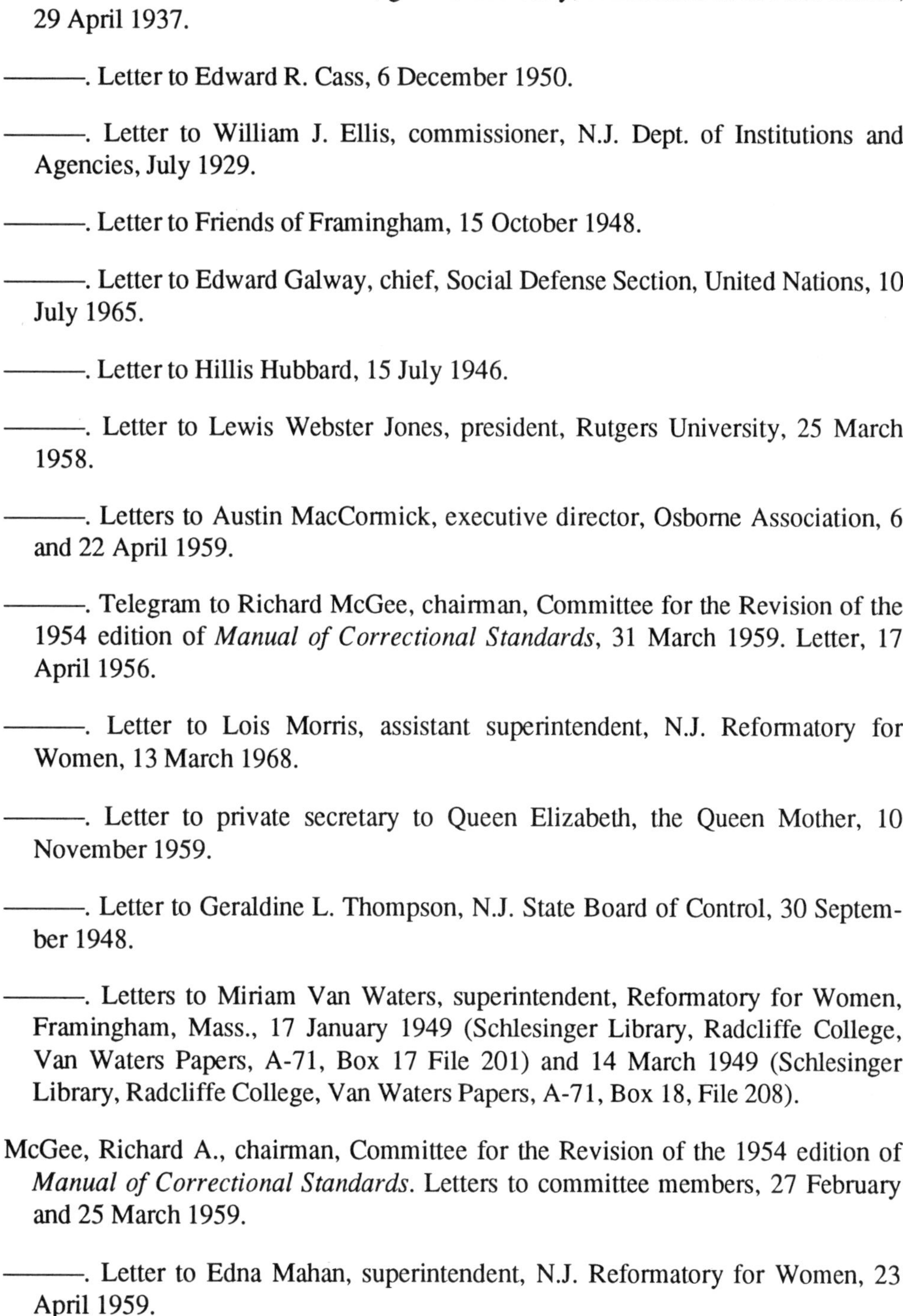

———. Letter to Edward R. Cass, general secretary, American Prison Association, 29 April 1937.

———. Letter to Edward R. Cass, 6 December 1950.

———. Letter to William J. Ellis, commissioner, N.J. Dept. of Institutions and Agencies, July 1929.

———. Letter to Friends of Framingham, 15 October 1948.

———. Letter to Edward Galway, chief, Social Defense Section, United Nations, 10 July 1965.

———. Letter to Hillis Hubbard, 15 July 1946.

———. Letter to Lewis Webster Jones, president, Rutgers University, 25 March 1958.

———. Letters to Austin MacCormick, executive director, Osborne Association, 6 and 22 April 1959.

———. Telegram to Richard McGee, chairman, Committee for the Revision of the 1954 edition of *Manual of Correctional Standards*, 31 March 1959. Letter, 17 April 1956.

———. Letter to Lois Morris, assistant superintendent, N.J. Reformatory for Women, 13 March 1968.

———. Letter to private secretary to Queen Elizabeth, the Queen Mother, 10 November 1959.

———. Letter to Geraldine L. Thompson, N.J. State Board of Control, 30 September 1948.

———. Letters to Miriam Van Waters, superintendent, Reformatory for Women, Framingham, Mass., 17 January 1949 (Schlesinger Library, Radcliffe College, Van Waters Papers, A-71, Box 17 File 201) and 14 March 1949 (Schlesinger Library, Radcliffe College, Van Waters Papers, A-71, Box 18, File 208).

McGee, Richard A., chairman, Committee for the Revision of the 1954 edition of *Manual of Correctional Standards*. Letters to committee members, 27 February and 25 March 1959.

———. Letter to Edna Mahan, superintendent, N.J. Reformatory for Women, 23 April 1959.

Older girls and student officers, N.J. Reformatory for Women. Letter to Edna Mahan, superintendent, N.J. Reformatory for Women, 14 August 1929.

Potter, Ellen C., acting superintendent, N.J. Reformatory for Women. Telegram to Edna Mahan, 4 June 1928.

———. Letters to Edna Mahan, 20 and 22 June 1928.

Private secretary to Queen Elizabeth, the Queen Mother. Letter to Edna Mahan, superintendent, N.J. Reformatory for Women, 29 May 1959.

Procunier, R. K., assistant editorial consultant for the Committee to Revise the 1954 *Manual*. Letter to Edna Mahan, superintendent, N.J. Reformatory for Women, 1 April 1959.

Robbins, Marsalette. Letter to Edna Mahan, superintendent, N.J. Reformatory for Women, 16 March 1953.

State Board of Charities, Albany, N.Y. Letter to May Caughey, superintendent, N.J. Reformatory for Women, 19 February 1915.

Van Waters, Miriam, referee, Los Angeles Juvenile Court. Letter to American Association of Social Workers, 10 December 1924.

———. Letters to Edna Mahan, 2 July 1926, 9 December 1927, 9 May 1928, 5 and 22 June 1928, 28 August 1928, 2 November 1928, 6 March 1929, 7 and 15 February 1931, 22 and 26 May 1931, 9 and 21 July 1931, 3 August 1931, 12 October 1931, 13 November 1931, 25 January 1932, 4 September 1933, and 3 July 1934. Telegram, 5 June 1928.

———. Letter to Lois Morris, 15 April 1968.

———. Letter to Maude and George Van Waters, 17 September 1931 (Schlesinger Library, Radcliffe College, Van Waters Collection, Box 6, File 62).

Wilde, Helen M., N.J. Parole Division. Letter to Edna Mahan, superintendent, N.J. Reformatory for Women, 21 January 1929.

Wilson, Franklin R., superintendent, State Industrial Home for Women, Muncy, Pa. Letter to Edna Mahan, superintendent, N.J. Reformatory for Women, 9 March 1945.

Wittpenn, Caroline B., founder and board member of N.J. Reformatory for Women and N.J. State Board of Control of Institutions and Agencies. Letter to Edna Mahan, 14 September 1932.

Interviews

Belmont, Leontine P., social worker, N.J. Reformatory for Women, 1947–50. Interview with author. Montclair, N.J., 11 June 1989.

Caughey, May, first superintendent of N.J. Reformatory for Women, and Eleanor Little, first psychologist. Interview with author. Guilford, Ct., 21 September 1963.

Connors, Elizabeth P., psychologist, N.J. Reformatory for Women 1930–55. Interview with author. Belmont, Mass., 19 February 1963.

DeGrazia, Lucia (Ballantine), Friendly Visitor at N.J. Reformatory for Women. Interview with author. Princeton, N.J., 29 September 1992.

DeGrouchy, Janet Ellis, daughter of Commissioner William J. Ellis and seasonal assistant at N.J. Reformatory for Women, summer 1943. Interview with author. Princeton, N.J., 28 September 1992.

Duane, Julia, pediatric consultant at N.J. Reformatory for Women. Interview with author. Pipersville, Pa., 6 September 1991.

Houston, Charles, retired superintendent, N.J. State Home for Boys. Interview with author. Pine Beach, N.J., 16 July 1991.

Kornitzky, Lillian, teacher and director of education, N.J. Reformatory for Women, 1933–55. Interview with author. Clinton, N.J., 7 June 1989.

Mahan, Edna, sixth superintendent, N.J. Reformatory for Women. Interviews with author. Clinton, N.J., 23 November 1963 and 19 July 1964.

Wescott, Lloyd B., board member, N.J. Reformatory for Women, and president, N.J. State Board of Control of Institutions and Agencies. Interview with author, Rosemont, N.J., 9 June 1989.

Wheeler, Martha E., president, American Correctional Association (1973), and superintendent, Reformatory for Women, Marysville, Ohio, and Janet York, superintendent, Connecticut Reformatory for Women. Interview with author. Niantic, Ct., 15 July 1989.

Zwarych, Marilyn Davenport, seventh superintendent of N.J. Reformatory for Women. Interview with author. Belvedere, N.J., 4 September 1990.

Other Sources

Board of Managers, N.J. Reformatory for Women. 1928–40, 1945–47, 1953–59. Minutes.

Committee for the Revision of Manual of Correctional Standards. New York City, 18 February 1959. Minutes.

Conditions under which Edna Mahan would work with the Turrell Project. n.d. Rough draft.

Mahan, Edna. 1918–22. Class notes and papers from University of California, Berkeley.

———. 1928, 1932–68. Diaries.

N.J. Reformatory for Women. 1930–31. Monthly statistical reports.

———. 1956–57. Budget request statements.

———. n.d. Transcript of staff orientation.

Philhower, Helen. 1944. Desk diary.

Superintendents of Correctional Institutions for Girls and Women. 1933, 1936, 1937, 1941–43, 1945, 1946. Minutes from annual conferences.

Index